CHILD ABUSE

BETRAYING A TRUST

ISSN 1534-1607

CHILD ABUSE
BETRAYING A TRUST

Mei Ling Rein

INFORMATION PLUS® REFERENCE SERIES
Formerly published by Information Plus, Wylie, Texas

GALE®

THOMSON

GALE

Detroit • New York • San Diego • San Francisco • Cleveland • New Haven, Conn. • Waterville, Maine • London • Munich

Child Abuse: Betraying a Trust
Mei Ling Rein

Project Editors
Kathleen J. Edgar and Ellice Engdahl

Editorial
Paula Cutcher-Jackson, Debra Kirby, Prindle
LaBarge, Charles B. Montney, Heather Price

Permissions
Debra Freitas

Product Design
Cynthia Baldwin

Composition and Electronic Prepress
Evi Seoud

Manufacturing
Keith Helmling

LIBRARY OF CONGRESS CATALOGING-IN-PUBLICATION DATA

ISBN 0-7876-5103-6 (set)
ISBN 0-7876-6069-8
ISSN 1534-1607

Printed in the United States of America
10 9 8 7 6 5 4 3 2 1

TABLE OF CONTENTS

This chapter describes historical opinions on children and abuse, especially the shift in attitudes that occurred around the beginning of the twentieth century, which led to current opinions on what constitutes abuse. Special attention is given to the history of child abuse protection legislation in the United States, and to international child labor, mutilation, and children's rights.

In order to identify and prevent child abuse, one must define it. However, it is difficult to draw a line between harsh discipline and outright abuse. Some general methods of determining if a child has been or is at risk of being abused are explored here.

This chapter examines the effectiveness of the child abuse reporting and investigation systems. Statistics on child abuse reporting and investigation are presented. The many controversies and criticisms surrounding these systems are also discussed.

The prevalence of child abuse in the United States is explored in this chapter. Statistics are provided on child abuse rates for people of different races, family structures, incomes, and other characteristics. The characteristics of abusers are also examined.

There is no definitive reason or reasons why people abuse children. The vast majority of adults never commit child abuse no matter what the circumstances. Similarly, the long-term consequences of being abused vary greatly from person to person. Patterns do exist, however, and some of the most pronounced are discussed here.

The sexual abuse of children is the most troubling of all forms of child abuse. It often has severe long-term consequences for the children who endure it. As described here, however, detecting, preventing, and treating child sexual abuse is unfortunately even more difficult than dealing with other forms of abuse.

Child abuse cases present many problems to the legal system, leading to a number of innovations and special procedures, which are outlined here. Also discussed are the legal issues surrounding false accusations of child abuse, laws against child pornography, and the registration of sex offenders.

Repressed memories of childhood abuse are an issue of great controversy. This chapter details the complex psychological and legal debates surrounding the reliability of repressed memories.

PREFACE

Child Abuse: Betraying a Trust is the latest volume in the ever-growing *Information Plus Reference Series*. Previously published by the Information Plus company of Wylie, Texas, the *Information Plus Reference Series* (and its companion set, the *Information Plus Compact Series*) became a Gale Group product when Gale and Information Plus merged in early 2000. Those of you familiar with the series as published by Information Plus will notice a few changes from the 1999 edition. Gale has adopted a new layout and style that we hope you will find easy to use. Other improvements include greatly expanded indexes in each book, and more descriptive tables of contents.

While some changes have been made to the design, the purpose of the *Information Plus Reference Series* remains the same. Each volume of the series presents the latest facts on a topic of pressing concern in modern American life. These topics include today's most controversial and most studied social issues: abortion, capital punishment, care for the elderly, child abuse, crime, health care, the environment, immigration, minorities, social welfare, women, youth, and many more. Although written especially for the high school and undergraduate student, this series is an excellent resource for anyone in need of factual information on current affairs.

By presenting the facts, it is Gale's intention to provide its readers with everything they need to reach an informed opinion on current issues. To that end, there is a particular emphasis in this series on the presentation of scientific studies, surveys, and statistics. These data are generally presented in the form of tables, charts, and other graphics placed within the text of each book. Every graphic is directly referred to and carefully explained in the text. The source of each graphic is presented within the graphic itself. The data used in these graphics are drawn from the most reputable and reliable sources, in particular from the various branches of the U.S. government and from major independent polling organizations.

Every effort was made to secure the most recent information available. The reader should bear in mind that many major studies take years to conduct, and that additional years often pass before the data from these studies are made available to the public. Therefore, in many cases the most recent information available in 2003 dated from 2000 or 2001. Older statistics are sometimes presented as well, if they are of particular interest and no more-recent information exists.

Although statistics are a major focus of the *Information Plus Reference Series* they are by no means its only content. Each book also presents the widely held positions and important ideas that shape how the book's subject is discussed in the United States. These positions are explained in detail and, where possible, in the words of those who support them. Some of the other material to be found in these books includes: historical background; descriptions of major events related to the subject; relevant laws and court cases; and examples of how these issues play out in American life. Some books also feature primary documents, or have pro and con debate sections giving the words and opinions of prominent Americans on both sides of a controversial topic. All material is presented in an even-handed and unbiased manner; the reader will never be encouraged to accept one view of an issue over another.

HOW TO USE THIS BOOK

The abuse of children is one of America's most tragic social problems. The effects of abuse on a child, be it verbal, physical, sexual, or neglect, can be considerable. Thousands of children die each year as a direct result of abuse, and countless others develop psychological and emotional problems that may well last a lifetime. The causes of abusive behavior in adults and their effects on children are therefore a matter of much scientific interest. The latest studies and theories on these issues are covered in this book. Dealing with child abuse also raises complicated and controversial legal questions, which this book presents and addresses.

Child Abuse: Betraying a Trust consists of eight chapters and three appendices. Each chapter is devoted to a particular aspect of the problem of child abuse in the United States. For a summary of the information covered in each chapter, please see the synopses provided in the Table of Contents at the front of the book. Chapters generally begin with an overview of the basic facts and background information on the chapter's topic, then proceed to examine sub-topics of particular interest. For example, Chapter 5: Causes and Effects of Child Abuse begins with a discussion of how the normal pressures of caring for children can sometimes overwhelm people and lead to abuse. It then examines the factors that have been linked to an increased likelihood of abuse, such as living in a single-parent family, young first-time parents, a history of drug abuse by the parents, and other characteristics. Later, the chapter addresses the effects of child abuse on a child's intelligence and behavior over the short and long term. Readers can find their way through a chapter by looking for the section and sub-section headings, which are clearly set off from the text. Or, they can refer to the book's extensive index, if they already know what they are looking for.

Statistical Information

The tables and figures featured throughout *Child Abuse: Betraying a Trust* will be of particular use to the reader in learning about this issue. These tables and figures represent an extensive collection of the most recent and important statistics on child abuse and related issues. For example, reports include statistics on child maltreatment, childhood victimization and later criminality, and the number of people in state sex offender registries in 1998 and 2001. Gale believes that making this information available to the reader is the most important way in which we fulfill the goal of this book: To help readers understand the issues and controversies surrounding child abuse in the United States and reach their own conclusions about them.

Each table or figure has a unique identifier appearing above it, for ease of identification and reference. Titles for the tables and figures explain their purpose. At the end of each table or figure, the original source of the data is provided.

In order to help readers understand these often complicated statistics, all tables and figures are explained in the text. References in the text direct the reader to the relevant statistics. Furthermore, the contents of all tables and figures are fully indexed. Please see the opening section of the index at the back of this volume for a description of how to find tables and figures within it.

In addition to the main body text and images, *Child Abuse: Betraying a Trust* has three appendices. The first is the Important Names and Addresses directory. Here the reader will find contact information for a number of organizations that study child abuse, fight child abuse, or that advocate influential opinions and policies on child abuse. The second appendix is the Resources section, which is provided to assist the reader in conducting his or her own research. In this section, the author and editors of *Child Abuse: Betraying a Trust* describe some of the sources that were most useful during the compilation of this book. The final appendix is this book's index. It has been greatly expanded from previous editions, and should make it even easier to find specific topics in this book.

ADVISORY BOARD CONTRIBUTIONS

The staff of Information Plus would like to extend their heartfelt appreciation to the Information Plus Advisory Board. This dedicated group of media professionals provides feedback on the series on an ongoing basis. Their comments allow the editorial staff who work on the project to make the series better and more user-friendly. Our top priorities are to produce the highest-quality and most useful books possible, and the Advisory Board's contributions to this process are invaluable.

The members of the Information Plus Advisory Board are:

- Kathleen R. Bonn, Librarian, Newbury Park High School, Newbury Park, California

- Madelyn Garner, Librarian, San Jacinto College— North Campus, Houston, Texas

- Anne Oxenrider, Media Specialist, Dundee High School, Dundee, Michigan

- Charles R. Rodgers, Director of Libraries, Pasco-Hernando Community College, Dade City, Florida

- James N. Zitzelsberger, Library Media Department Chairman, Oshkosh West High School, Oshkosh, Wisconsin

COMMENTS AND SUGGESTIONS

The editors of the *Information Plus Reference Series* welcome your feedback on *Child Abuse: Betraying a Trust*. Please direct all correspondence to:

Editors
Information Plus Reference Series
27500 Drake Rd.
Farmington Hills, MI, 48331-3535

ACKNOWLEDGMENTS

The editors wish to thank the copyright holders of material included in this volume and the permissions managers of many book and magazine publishing companies for assisting us in securing reproduction rights. We are also grateful to the staffs of the Detroit Public Library, the Library of Congress, the University of Detroit Mercy Library, Wayne State University Purdy/Kresge Library Complex, and the University of Michigan Libraries for making their resources available to us.

Following is a list of the copyright holders who have granted us permission to reproduce material in Child Abuse: Betraying a Trust. *Every effort has been made to trace copyright, but if omissions have been made, please let us know.*

For more detailed source citations, please see the sources listed under each individual table and figure.

Crimes Against Children Research Center, University of New Hampshire, and National Center for Missing & Exploited Children: Figure 6.6, Figure 6.7, Table 6.5.

David and Lucile Packard Foundation: Figure 3.2.

Family Research Laboratory, University of New Hampshire: Figure 5.7.

Institute of Medicine, Committee on the Training Needs of Health Professionals to Respond to Family Violence, National Academy Press: Table 3.1.

International Programme on the Elimination of Child Labour (IPEC), Statistical Information and Monitoring Programme on Child Labour (SIMPOC), International Labour Office. Reproduced by permission.: Table 1.3, Table 1.4.

Jon Morgenstern, Annette Riordan, Barbara S. McCrady, Kimberly Blanchard, Katherine H. McVeigh, and Thomas W. Irwin, *Barriers to Employability Among Women on TANF with a Substance Abuse Problem,* **Online: http://www.acf.dhhs. gov/programs/opre/barriers_employ/ barriers_employ/pdf. Reproduced by permission.:** Figure 3.4, Figure 3.5.

National Center on Child Abuse Prevention Research, Prevent Child Abuse America: Table 3.2, Table 5.1.

National Clearinghouse on Child Abuse and Neglect Information: Figure 5.3.

National Clearinghouse on Child Abuse and Neglect Information and National Center for Prosecution of Child Abuse. Reproduced by permission.: Table 1.1.

U.S. Department of Health and Human Services, Administration for Children and Families: Figure 3.1, Figure 3.3, Figure 4.1, Figure 4.2, Figure 4.3, Figure 4.4, Figure 4.5, Table 4.1, Table 4.2, Table 4.3, Table 4.4.

U.S. Department of Health and Human Services, National Center on Child Abuse and Neglect: Figure 1.1., Figure 4.6, Figure 4.7, Table 4.5, Table 4.6, Table 4.7, Table 4.8, Table 4.9, Table 4.10, Table 4.11, Table 4.12, Table 4.13, Table 4.14, Figure 5.1, Figure 5.2.

U.S. Department of Health and Human Services, Office of Applied Studies, Substance Abuse and Mental Health Services Administration: Figure 3.6.

U.S. Department of Justice, Bureau of Justice Statistics: Table 5.2, Table 5.8, Table 5.9, Table 6.2, Table 6.3, Table 6.4, Table 7.1.

U.S. Department of Justice, National Institute of Justice: Table 5.4, Table 5.5, Table 5.6, Table 5.7, Table 7.2.

U.S. Department of Justice, Office of Juvenile Justice and Delinquency Prevention: Table 2.1, Figure 4.8, Figure 5.4, Figure 5.5, Figure 5.6, Table 5.3, Figure 6.1, Figure 6.2, Figure 6.3, Figure 6.4, Figure 6.5, Table 6.1.

U.S. Department of State: Table 2.1.

CHAPTER 1

CHILD ABUSE—A HISTORY

OVERVIEW

The recognition of child abuse in its several forms (physical abuse, sexual abuse, emotional abuse, and neglect) came to the forefront in the twentieth century. Child abuse continues to be more likely recognized in economically developed countries than in developing countries. Children have been beaten and abandoned for many thousands of years, based primarily on the belief that children are the property of their parents.

Early civilizations regularly abandoned deformed or unwanted children, and the ritual sacrifice of children to appease the gods took place in the Egyptian, Carthaginian, Roman, Greek, and Aztec societies. In Roman society the father had complete control over the family, even to the extent that he could kill his children for disobedience. Sexual abuse of children was common in both Greek and Roman societies. Children were also sold as prostitutes. Women often participated in abuse. Petronius (c. 27–c. 66), a Roman writer, recorded the rape of a seven-year-old girl witnessed by a line of clapping women.

During the Middle Ages (c. 350–c.1450) in Europe, healthy but unwanted children were apprenticed to work or offered to convents and monasteries. Infanticide, or the murder of unwanted babies, was also common. The Roman Catholic Church contributed to infanticide when it declared that deformed infants were omens of evil and the product of relations between women and demons or animals. In another example of religious support for what would now be considered child abuse, the archbishop of Canterbury in the seventh century ruled that a man could sell his son into slavery until he reached the age of seven.

In thirteenth-century England the law read, "If one beats a child until it bleeds, it will remember, but if one beats it to death, the law applies." By the child's fourth year, harsh discipline played a major role in his or her socialization. Children and parents were taught that beatings were in the child's best interests. A mother taught her daughter to take a "smart rod" and beat her children until they cried for mercy: "Dear child by this lore/they will love thee ever more."

Children were beaten not only by their parents but also by their teachers. In a poem written around 1500, a schoolboy admitted that he would gladly become a clerk, but learning was such strange work because the birch twigs used for beating were so sharp. The children at an Oxford school must have felt justice was served when their schoolmaster, out early one morning to cut willow twigs for a switch to beat them, slipped, fell into the river, and drowned.

The late Middle Ages and the Renaissance (roughly the fourteenth through sixteenth centuries) saw changes in how society viewed children, but abuse was still common. Neil Postman, in *The Disappearance of Childhood* (Delacorte Press, New York, 1982), noted that the notion that children were small adults had started to change by that time. Among the upper classes children began to receive a long, formal education, increasingly separated from adults and kept with their peers. It was becoming apparent that children were not really that similar to adults after all, but rather like mounds of clay to be molded.

In sixteenth- and seventeenth-century Europe fathers commonly placed their children in apprenticeships to provide inexpensive labor. The apprentice system was the major job training method of pre-industrial Western society. The apprentice who trained with a master frequently worked under conditions that, by today's standards, would be considered severely abusive.

The practice of paternal control was brought to the American colonies, and the father ruled his wife and children. The mother, however, was also expected to discipline her children, inflicting corporal punishment as she saw fit. A child was little more than the property of the parents. At the same time, the child was an asset that could be used to perform work on the farm.

Parental discipline was typically severe, and parents, teachers, and ministers found support for stern discipline in the Bible. "Spare the rod and spoil the child" was cited as justification for beating children. It should be noted that the biblical "rod" referred to was a shepherd's rod used to guide the sheep in the right direction, not to beat the sheep. Church elders taught that children were born corrupted by original sin, and the only path to salvation was "to beat the Devil out of the child." (In Christian theology, original sin is humankind's inherent tendency to sin as a result of Adam's punishment for rebelling against God.) Some colonial legislatures even passed "stubborn children laws," giving parents the legal right to kill unruly children.

By their teens, many children were living with other families, bound out as indentured servants or apprentices. It was common for heads of households and masters to brutalize these children without fear of reprisal except in cases involving excessive beatings, massive injury, or death.

Holding a Child Abuser Accountable

The earliest recorded trial for child abuse involved a master and his apprentice. In 1639 in Salem, Massachusetts, Marmaduke Perry was charged in the death of his apprentice. The evidence showed the boy had been ill-treated and subjected to "unreasonable correction." Nevertheless, the boy's allegation that the master had been responsible for his fractured skull (which ultimately killed him) was called into question by testimony, which claimed that the boy had told someone else that the injury was a result of falling from a tree. Perry was acquitted.

In 1643 a master was executed for killing his servant boy. In 1655 in Plymouth, Massachusetts, a master found guilty of slaying a servant boy was punished by having his hand burned and all his property taken away. Other early records show brutal masters being warned for abusing young servants. In some cases, the children were freed because of the harsh treatment. Virginia passed laws protecting servants against mistreatment in 1700.

Most of the early recorded cases of child abuse were specifically related to offenses committed by masters against servants and did not involve protecting children from abusive parents. Society generally tolerated the abuse of family members as a personal matter while condemning abuse by strangers.

The few recorded cases involving family matters were limited to the removal of children from "unsuitable" home environments, which usually meant that parents were not giving their children a good religious upbringing or were refusing to instill the proper work ethic. In two Massachusetts cases, in 1675 and 1678, children were removed from such "unsuitable" homes. In the first case the children were taken from the home because the father refused to send them out to apprentice or work. In the second case

the same offense was compounded by the father's refusal to attend church services. Physical abuse was not an issue in either case.

ABUSE DURING THE INDUSTRIAL REVOLUTION

With the coming of industrialization in Europe and the United States, the implied right of abuse was transferred to the factory, where orphaned or abandoned children as young as five worked 16 hours a day. In many cases irons were riveted around their ankles to bind the children to the machines, while overseers with whips ensured productivity. In England the Factory Act of 1802 stopped this pauper-apprentice work system, but the law did not apply to children who had parents. Those youngsters worked in the mills for 12 hours a day at the mercy of often tyrannical supervisors.

Nonworking hours offered little relief to poor orphaned or abandoned children. Dependent children such as these were put into deplorable public poorhouses with adult beggars, thieves, and paupers. Not until the beginning of the nineteenth century did the public recognize the terrible abuses that occurred in these almshouses, and major efforts were begun to provide separate housing for children.

During the nineteenth century, middle-class families began to see their children as representative of the family's status. For many of these families, education for the child, rather than labor, became the goal. With this attitude, many of the labor abuses gradually came to an end. Eventually, child labor laws were passed in most industrialized countries to limit the kinds of jobs children could do and the number of hours they could work.

Private Organizations Take Action Against Abuse

It was during the nineteenth century that the American legal system began to change in favor of protecting children even against their own parents. In 1840 a Tennessee parent was prosecuted for excessive punishment of a child. According to the testimony, a mother had hit her daughter with her fists, pushed her head against the wall, whipped her, and tied her to a bedpost. A lower court convicted the abusive parent, but a higher court reversed the conviction.

The first case of child abuse that caught public attention in the United States occurred in 1874. Neighbors of Mary Ellen Connolly, a nine-year-old child in New York City, contacted a church social worker, Etta Angell Wheeler, when they heard disturbances from the little girl's apartment.

Upon investigating the child's home, the social worker found her suffering from malnutrition, serious physical abuse, and neglect. Mary Ellen was living with Mary and Francis Connolly. The girl, who was the illegitimate daughter of Mrs. Connolly's first husband, was apprenticed to the couple.

At that time there were laws protecting animals, but no local, state, or federal laws protected children. Consequently, Wheeler turned to the American Society for the Prevention of Cruelty to Animals (ASPCA) for help. The case was presented to the court on the theory that the child was a member of the animal kingdom and therefore entitled to the same protection from abuse that the law gave to animals. The court agreed, and the child, because she was considered an animal, was taken from her brutal foster mother.

In court Mary Ellen Connolly related how her foster mother beat her daily with a leather whip and cut her face with scissors. She was not allowed to play with other children and was locked in the bedroom whenever her "mamma" left the house. The court placed the child in an orphanage. She was later adopted by the social worker's family.

The court found Mary Connolly guilty of assault and battery for felonious assault with scissors and for beatings that took place during 1873 and 1874. She was sentenced to one year of hard labor in a penitentiary.

Mary Ellen Connolly's case led to the founding of the New York Society for the Prevention of Cruelty to Children. Similar societies were soon organized in other U.S. cities. By 1922, 57 societies for the prevention of cruelty to children and 307 other humane societies had been established to tend to the welfare of children. After the federal government began intervening in child welfare, the number of these societies declined.

The Beginnings of Federal Protection for Children

The first White House Conference on Children took place in 1909 under President Theodore Roosevelt (1858–1919). The conference recommended the creation of the Children's Bureau (under the U.S. Department of Health, Education, and Welfare) to research and provide information about children, a recommendation that President William Howard Taft (1857–1930) signed into law in 1912. The Children's Bureau promoted the passage of the Keating-Owen Act (39 Stat 675) in 1916, which limited the exploitation of children in factories and mines. The law, however, did not cover youngsters employed in agriculture, domestic work, and sweatshops (small manufacturing plants with long hours, low wages, and poor working conditions). The Bureau also advocated improved prenatal care, especially among the poor, and was a major supporter of the Sheppard-Towner Act of 1921 (42 Stat 224), which promoted prenatal care for mothers.

MODERN AMERICA

The federal government first provided child welfare services with the passage of the Social Security Act of 1935 (49 Stat 620). Under Title IV-B (Child Welfare Services) of the act, the Children's Bureau received funding for grants to states for "the protection and care of homeless, dependent, and neglected children and children in danger of becoming delinquent." Prior to 1961, Title IV-B was the only source of federal funding for child welfare services.

The 1962 Social Security Amendments (Public Law 87-543) required each state to make child welfare services available to all children. It further required states to provide coordination between child welfare services (under Title IV-B) and social services (under Title IV-A, or the Social Services program), which served families on welfare. The law also revised the definition of "child welfare services" to include the prevention and remedy of child abuse. In 1980 the U.S. Congress created a separate Foster Care program under Title IV-E.

Title IV-A became Title XX (Social Services Block Grant) in 1981, giving states more options regarding the types of social services to fund. Today child abuse prevention and treatment services have remained an eligible category of service.

State Programs That Help Children at Risk

Under Title IV-B Child Welfare Services (Subpart 1) and Promoting Safe and Stable Families (Subpart 2) programs, families in crisis receive preventive intervention so that children will not have to be removed from their homes. If this cannot be achieved, children are placed in foster care temporarily until they can be reunited with their families. If reunification is not possible, the children are put up for adoption.

States use the Foster Care (Title IV-E) program funds for the care of foster children and for the training of foster parents, program personnel, and private-agency staff. Title XX funds provide such services as child day care, child protective services, information and referral, counseling, and employment.

The Battered Child Syndrome and the Development of a Child Abuse Reporting Network

In 1961 Dr. C. Henry Kempe, a pediatric radiologist, and his associates proposed the term "battered child syndrome" at a symposium on the problem of child abuse held under the auspices of the American Academy of Pediatrics. The term refers to the collection of injuries sustained by a child as a result of repeated mistreatment or beatings. The following year *The Journal of the American Medical Association* published the landmark article, "The Battered Child Syndrome" (C. Henry Kempe et al., vol. 181, no. 17, July 7, 1962). The term "battered child syndrome" developed into "maltreatment," encompassing not only physical assault but other forms of abuse, such as malnourishment, failure to thrive, medical neglect, and sexual and emotional abuse.

Dr. Kempe had also proposed that physicians be required to report child abuse. By 1967, after Dr. Kempe's findings had gained general acceptance among health and welfare workers and the public, all 50 states had passed legislation that required the reporting of child abuse to official agencies. This was one of the most rapidly accepted pieces of legislation in American history. Initially only doctors were required to report and then only in cases of "serious physical injury" or "nonaccidental injury." Today all the states have laws that require most professionals who serve children to report all forms of suspected abuse and either require or permit any citizen to report child abuse.

One of the reasons for the lack of prosecution of early child abuse cases was the difficulty in determining whether a physical injury was a case of deliberate assault or an accident. In recent years, however, doctors of pediatric radiology have been able to determine the incidence of repeated child abuse through sophisticated developments in X-ray technology. These advances have allowed radiologists to see more clearly such things as subdural hematomas (blood clots around the brain resulting from blows to the head) and abnormal fractures. This brought about more recognition in the medical community of the widespread incidence of child abuse, along with growing public condemnation of abuse.

Federal Legislation against Child Abuse

In 1974 Congress passed the Child Abuse Prevention and Treatment Act (CAPTA; Public Law 93-247). The law stated:

> [Child abuse and neglect refer to] the physical or mental injury, negligent treatment, or maltreatment of a child under the age of 18, or the age specified by the child protection law of the state in question, by a person who is responsible for the child's welfare under circumstances which indicate that the child's health or welfare is harmed or threatened thereby as determined in accordance with regulations prescribed by the Secretary of Health, Education, and Welfare.

This law created the National Center on Child Abuse and Neglect (NCCAN), which developed standards for handling reports of child maltreatment. NCCAN also established a nationwide network of child protective services and served as a clearinghouse for information and research on child abuse and neglect.

Since 1974 CAPTA has been amended a number of times. (See Figure 1.1.) The Child Abuse Prevention, Adoption and Family Services Act of 1988 (Public Law 100-294) broadened the definition of abuse, adding a specific reference to sexual abuse and exploitation to the basic definition. The act also required the U.S. Department of Health and Human Services (HHS) to set up a national program to collect and analyze state data on child abuse and neglect. As a result of this provision, the HHS established the National Child Abuse and Neglect Data System (NCANDS), a voluntary reporting system.

The Children's Justice Act of 1986 (CJA; Public Law 99-401) offers grants to states to improve the investigation and prosecution of cases of child abuse and neglect, especially sexual abuse and exploitation. The program aims to reduce additional trauma to the child by training persons who are involved in child maltreatment cases, such as law enforcement, mental health personnel, prosecutors, and judges. CJA also supports legislation that would allow indirect testimony from children, shorten the time spent in court, and make their courtroom experience less intimidating.

Until 1995 none of the federal child abuse legislation dealt specifically with punishing sex offenders. In December of that year, with growing acknowledgment of and concern about sex crimes against minors, Congress passed the Sex Crimes against Children Prevention Act of 1995 (Public Law 104-71). The act increased penalties for those who sexually exploit children by engaging in illegal conduct, or for exploitation conducted via the Internet, as well as for those who transport children with the intent to engage in criminal sexual activity.

Three years later Congress enacted the Protection of Children from Sexual Predators Act of 1998 (Public Law 105-314) that, among other things, established the Morgan P. Hardiman Child Abduction and Serial Murder Investigative Resource Center (CASMIRC). The purpose of CASMIRC is "to provide investigative support through the coordination and provision of federal law enforcement resources, training, and application of other multidisciplinary expertise, to assist federal, state, and local authorities in matters involving child abductions, mysterious disappearances of children, child homicide, and serial murder across the country."

Pursuant to the CAPTA Amendments of 1996 (Public Law 104-235), NCCAN was abolished. Its functions have subsequently been consolidated within the Children's Bureau of the HHS.

On October 11, 2002, the U.S. House of Representatives passed H.R. 5601, the Keeping Children and Families Safe Act, reauthorizing CAPTA. As of October 17, 2002, however, the U.S. Senate had yet to act on the legislation.

THE INTERNATIONAL EXPLOITATION OF CHILDREN

Cleric Abuse

Allegations of child abuse have surfaced among several religious denominations. For example, since early 2002 dozens of Roman Catholic priests have been charged with child molestation. Some of the abuse had spanned several decades. It was revealed that church leaders who knew of the abuse as early as the 1950s chose to keep silent about it, instead paying millions of dollars to victims' families and moving the abusive priests from parish to parish. Nevertheless, the child sexual abuse

FIGURE 1.1

Child Abuse Prevention and Treatment Act

Legislative authority: Child Abuse Prevention and Treatment Act, as amended
U.S. Code citation: 42 USC 5101 et seq; 42 USC 5116 et seq
ACF regulations: 45 CFR 1340

Summary of legislative history:

The Child Abuse Prevention and Treatment Act (CAPTA) was originally enacted in PL 93-247. The law was completely rewritten in the Child Abuse Prevention, Adoption and Family Services Act of 1988 (PL 100-294, 4/25/88). It was further amended by the Child Abuse Prevention Challenge Grants Reauthorization Act of 1989 (PL 101-126, 10/25/89) and the Drug Free School Amendments of 1989 (PL 101-226, 12/12/89).

The Community-Based Child Abuse and Neglect Prevention Grants program was originally authorized by sections 402 through 409 of the Continuing Appropriations Act for FY 1985 (PL 98-473, 10/12/84). The Child Abuse Prevention Challenge Grants Reauthorization Act of 1989 (PL 101-126) transferred this program to the Child Abuse Prevention and Treatment Act, as amended.

A new title III, Certain Preventive Services Regarding Children of Homeless Families or Families at Risk of Homelessness, was added to the Child Abuse and Neglect Prevention and Treatment Act by the Stewart B. McKinney Homeless Assistance Act Amendments of 1990 (PL 101-645, 11/29/90).

The Child Abuse Prevention and Treatment Act was amended and reauthorized by the Child Abuse, Domestic Violence, Adoption, and Family Services Act of 1992 (PL 102-295, 5/28/92) and amended by the Juvenile Justice and Delinquency Prevention Act. Amendments of 1992 (PL 102-586, 11/4/92).

The Act was amended by the Older American Act Technical Amendments of 1993 (PL 103-171, 12/2/93) and the Human Services Amendments of 1994 (PL 103-252, 5/19/94).

CAPTA was further amended by the Child Abuse Prevention and Treatment Act Amendments of 1996 (PL 104-235, 10/3/96), which amended Title I, replaced the Title II Community-Based Family Resource Centers program with a new Community-Based Family Resource and Support Program and repealed Title III, Certain Preventive Services Regarding Children of Homeless Families or Families at Risk of Homelessness.

SOURCE: "Child Abuse Prevention and Treatment Act," as Amended, October 3, 1996, in *About the Federal Child Abuse Prevention and Treatment Act,* U.S. Department of Health and Human Services, National Center on Child Abuse and Neglect, Washington, DC [Online] http://www.calib.com/nccanch/pubs/factsheets/about.cfm [accessed November 13, 2002]

scandal is not confined to the Catholic Church in the United States. Allegations of sexual abuse by priests have also surfaced in Mexico, Ireland, Canada, Colombia, Venezuela, Italy, Australia, and Hong Kong. In March 2002 the Catholic Church in Ireland paid $110 million to victims of government-funded schools operated by 18 religious orders. Other Catholic religious orders in the United States and other parts of the world have issued letters of apologies to victims and their families and have paid tens of millions of dollars in settlements.

Other religious denominations have also been involved in sexual abuse allegations. Some members of the Jehovah's Witnesses are speaking out against their church's policy of handling reports of child sexual abuse. As of May 2002 two members had filed lawsuits, accusing church elders of failing to report molesters to authori-

ties. Church officials claim they do report suspected abuse if the state law requires it. In states with no mandatory reporting laws, the church, which has its own judicial system, conducts its own investigation. (As of December 31, 2000, just 18 states required the reporting of child abuse and neglect. Ten states required reporting by the clergy. (See Table 1.1)

Former Hare Krishna children have sued the International Society for Krishna Consciousness (Iskcon), a sect of Hinduism that became popular in the United States during the 1960s. The parents left the children in boarding schools while they went out to recruit new members and to solicit donations. The plaintiffs alleged physical, emotional, and sexual abuse, including being deprived of food and sleep, being severely beaten, being locked up in roach-infested rooms, and being offered in marriage to

TABLE 1.1

Mandatory reporters of child abuse and neglect

State	Professions that must report					Others who must report		Standard for reporting	Privileged communications
	Health care	Mental health	Social work	Education/ child care	Law enforcement	All persons	Other		
Alabama §§ 26-14-3(a) 26-14-10	✓	✓	✓	✓	✓		Any other person called upon to give aid or assistance to any child	Known or suspected	Attorney/client
Alaska §§ 47.17.020(a) 47.17.023 47.17.060	✓	✓	✓	✓	✓		Paid employees of domestic violence and sexual assault programs and drug and alcohol treatment facilities Members of a child fatality review team or multidisciplinary child protection team Commercial or private film or photograph processors	Have reasonable cause to suspect	
Arizona §§ 13-3620(A) 8-805(B)-(C)	✓	✓	✓	✓	✓		Parents Anyone responsible for care or treatment of children Clergy	Have reasonable grounds to believe	Clergy/penitent Attorney/client
Arkansas § 12-12-507(b)-(c)	✓	✓	✓	✓	✓		Prosecutors Judges Div. of Youth Services employees Domestic violence shelter employees and volunteers	Have reasonable cause to suspect Have observed conditions which would reasonably result	
California Penal Code §§ 11166(a), (c) 11165.7(a)	✓	✓	✓	✓	✓		Firefighters Animal control officers Commercial film and photographic print processors Clergy	Have knowledge of or observe Know or reasonably suspect	Clergy/penitent
Colorado §§ 19-3-304(1), (2) (2.5) 19-3-311	✓	✓	✓	✓	✓		Christian Science practitioners Veterinarians Firefighters Victim advocates Commercial film and photographic print processors	Have reasonable cause to know or suspect Have observed conditions which would reasonably result	
Connecticut §§ 17a-101(b) 17a-103(a)	✓	✓	✓	✓	✓		Substance abuse counselors Sexual assault counselors Battered women's counselors Clergy	Have reasonable cause to suspect or believe	
Delaware tit. 16, § 903 tit. 16, § 909	✓	✓	✓	✓		✓		Know or in good faith suspect	Attorney/client Clergy/penitent
District of Columbia §§ 2-1352(a), (b), (d) 2-1355	✓	✓	✓	✓	✓			Know or have reasonable cause to suspect	
Florida §§ 39.201(1) 39.204	✓	✓	✓	✓	✓	✓	Judges Religious healers	Know or have reasonable cause to suspect	Attorney/client
Georgia §§ 19-7-5(c)(1), (g) 16-12-100(c)	✓	✓	✓	✓	✓		Persons who produce visual or printed matter	Have reasonable cause to believe	
Hawaii §§ 350-1.1(a) 350-5	✓	✓	✓	✓	✓		Employees of recreational or sports activities	Have reason to believe	
Idaho §§ 16-1619(a), (c) 16-1620	✓		✓	✓	✓	✓		Have reason to believe Have observed conditions which would reasonably result	Clergy/penitent Attorney/client

TABLE 1.1

Mandatory reporters of child abuse and neglect [CONTINUED]

State	Professions that must report					Others who must report		Standard for reporting	Privileged communications
	Health care	Mental health	Social work	Education/ child care	Law enforcement	All persons	Other		
Illinois 325 ILCS 5/4 720 ILCS 5/11-20.2	✓	✓	✓	✓	✓		Homemakers, substance abuse treatment personnel Christian Science practitioners Funeral home directors Commercial film and photographic print processors	Have reasonable cause to believe	
Indiana §§ 31-33-5-1 31-33-5-2 31-32-11-1	✓	✓	✓	✓	✓	✓	Staff member of any public or private institution, school, facility, or agency	Have reason to believe	
Iowa §§ 232.69(1)(a)-(b) 728.14(1) 232.74	✓	✓	✓	✓	✓		Commercial film and photographic print processors Employees of substance abuse programs	Reasonably believe	
Kansas § 38-1522(a), (b)	✓	✓	✓	✓	✓		Firefighters Juvenile intake and assessment workers	Have reason to suspect	
Kentucky §§ 620.030(1), (2) 620.050(2)	✓	✓	✓	✓	✓	✓		Know or have reasonable cause to believe	Attorney/client Clergy/penitent
Louisiana Ch. Code art. 603(13) Ch. Code art. 609(A)(1) Ch. Code art. 610(F)	✓	✓	✓	✓	✓		Commercial film or photographic print processors Mediators	Have cause to believe	Clergy/penitent ChristianScience practitioner
Maine tit. 22, § 4011(1) tit. 22, § 4015	✓	✓	✓	✓	✓		Guardians *ad litem* and CASAs Fire inspectors Commercial film processors Homemakers	Know or have reasonable cause to suspect	Clergy/penitent
Maryland Family Law §§ 5-704(a) 5-705(a)	✓		✓	✓	✓	✓		Have reason to believe	Attorney/client Clergy/penitent
Massachusetts ch. 119, § 51A ch. 119, § 51B	✓	✓	✓	✓	✓		Drug and alcoholism counselors Probation and parole officers Clerks/magistrates of district courts Firefighters	Have reasonable cause to believe	
Michigan § 722.623 (1), (8) 722.631	✓	✓	✓	✓	✓			Have reasonable cause to suspect	Attorney/client
Minnesota §§ 626.556 Subd. 3(a), 8	✓	✓	✓	✓	✓			Know or have reason to believe	Clergy/penitent
Mississippi § 43-21-353(1)	✓	✓	✓	✓	✓	✓	Attorneys Ministers	Have reasonable cause to suspect	
Missouri §§ 210.115(1) 568.110 210.140	✓	✓	✓	✓	✓		Persons with responsibility for care of children Christian Science practitioners Probation/parole officers Commercial film processors	Have reasonable cause to suspect Have observed conditions which would reasonably result	Attorney/client
Montana § 41-3-201(1)-(2), (4)	✓	✓	✓	✓	✓		Guardians *ad litem* Clergy Religious healers Christian Science practitioners	Know or have reasonable cause to suspect	Clergy/penitent

TABLE 1.1

Mandatory reporters of child abuse and neglect [CONTINUED]

State	Professions that must report					Others who must report		Standard for reporting	Privileged communications
	Health care	Mental health	Social work	Education/ child care	Law enforcement	All persons	Other		
Nebraska §§ 28-711(1) 28-714	✓		✓	✓		✓		Have reasonable cause to believe Have observed conditions which would reasonably result	
Nevada §§ 432B.220(3), (5) 432B.250	✓	✓	✓	✓	✓		Clergy Religious healers Alcohol/drug abuse counselors Christian Science practitioners Probation officers Attorneys	Know or have reason to believe	Clergy/penitent Attorney/client
New Hampshire §§ 169-C:29 169-C:32	✓	✓	✓	✓	✓	✓	Christian Science practitioners Clergy	Have reason to suspect	Attorney/client
New Jersey § 9:6-8.10						✓		Have reasonable cause to believe	
New Mexico §§ 32A-4-3(A) 32A-4-5(A)	✓		✓	✓	✓	✓	Judges	Know or have reasonable suspicion	
New York Soc. Serv. Law § 413(1)	✓	✓	✓	✓	✓		Alcoholism/substance abuse counselors District Attorneys Christian Science practitioners	Have reasonable cause to suspect	
North Carolina §§ 7B-301 7B-310						✓	Any institution	Have cause to suspect	Attorney/client
North Dakota §§ 50-25.1-03 50-25.1-10	✓	✓	✓	✓	✓		Clergy Religious healers Addiction counselors	Have knowledge of or reasonable cause to suspect	Clergy/penitent Attorney/client
Ohio § 2151.421(A)(1), (A)(2), (G)(1)(b)	✓	✓	✓	✓			Attorneys Religious healers	Know or suspect	Attorney/client Physician/patient
Oklahoma tit. 10, § 7103(A)(1) tit. 10, § 7104 tit. 10, § 7113 tit. 21, § 1021.4	✓			✓		✓	Commercial film and photographic print processors	Have reason to believe	
Oregon §§ 419B.005(3) 419B.010(1)	✓	✓	✓	✓	✓		Attorneys Clergy Firefighters CASAs Funeral directors	Have reasonable cause to believe	Mental health/ patient Clergy/penitent Attorney/client
Pennsylvania § 23-6311(a),(b)	✓	✓	✓	✓	✓		Christian Science practitioners Clergy	Have reasonable cause to suspect	Clergy/penitent
Rhode Island §§ 40-11-3(a) 40-11-6(a) 40-11-11	✓					✓		Have reasonable cause to know or suspect	Attorney/client
South Carolina §§ 20-7-510(A) 20-7-550	✓	✓	✓	✓	✓		Judges Funeral home directors and employees Christian Science practitioners Film processors Religious healers Substance abuse treatment staff	Have reason to believe	Attorney/client Priest/penitent
South Dakota §§ 26-8A-3 26-8A-15	✓	✓	✓	✓	✓		Chemical dependency counselors Religious healers Parole or court services officers Employees of domestic abuse shelters	Have reasonable cause to suspect	

TABLE 1.1

Mandatory reporters of child abuse and neglect [CONTINUED]

State	Professions that must report					Others who must report		Standard for reporting	Privileged communications
	Health care	Mental health	Social work	Education/ child care	Law enforcement	All persons	Other		
Tennessee §§ 37-1-403(a) 37-1-605(a) 37-1-411	✓	✓	✓	✓	✓	✓	Judges Neighbors Relatives Friends Religious healers	Knowledge of/ reasonably know Have reasonable cause to suspect	
Texas Family Code §§ 261.101(a)-(c) 261.102	✓		✓			✓	Juvenile probation or detention officers Employees or clinics that provide reproductive services	Have cause to believe	
Utah §§ 62A-4a-403(1)-(3) 62A-4a-412(5)	✓					✓		Have reason to believe Have observed conditions which would reasonably result	Clergy/penitent
Vermont tit. 33, § 4913(a)	✓	✓	✓	✓	✓		Camp administrators and counselors Probation officers	Have reasonable cause to believe	
Virginia § 63.1-248.3(A) 63.1-248.11	✓	✓	✓	✓	✓		Mediators Christian Science practitioners Probation officers CASAs	Have reason to suspect	
Washington §§ 26.44.030 (1), (2) 26.44.060(3)	✓	✓	✓	✓	✓		Any adult with whom a child resides Responsible living skills program staff	Have reasonable cause to believe	
West Virginia §§ 49-6A-2 49-6A-7	✓	✓	✓	✓	✓		Clergy Religious healers Judges, family law masters or magistrates Christian Science practitioners	Reasonable cause to suspect When believe Have observed	Attorney/client
Wisconsin § 48.981(2), (2m)(c), (2m)(d)	✓	✓	✓	✓	✓		Alcohol or drug abuse counselors Mediators Financial and employment planners CASAs	Have reasonable cause to suspect Have reason to believe	
Wyoming §§ 14-3-205(a) 14-3-210						✓		Know or have reasonable cause to believe or suspect Have observed conditions which would reasonably result	Attorney/client Physician/patient Clergy/penitent
Totals, all states	**48**	**40**	**44**	**46**	**41**	**18**	**N/A**	**N/A**	**26**

SOURCE: *Statutes at-a-Glance: Mandatory Reporters of Child Abuse and Neglect,* National Clearinghouse on Child Abuse and Neglect Information, Washington, DC, and National Center for Prosecution of Child Abuse, Alexandria, VA, April 2001

older men who were patrons of Iskcon. Iskcon officials, while substantiating that the abuse had occurred, denied that hundreds of children were involved.

Child Soldiers

As more wars occur throughout the world, government armed forces and opposition groups have forced children to serve as soldiers. In the first-ever worldwide survey of child soldiers, the Coalition to Stop the Use of Child Soldiers found that more than 300,000 children under the age of 18 were involved in armed conflicts in more than 30 countries (*Child Soldiers Global Report,*

United Kingdom, May 2001). Hundreds of thousands of children in 85 countries had been recruited by the government and other armed groups. Many more were abducted and even branded as animals.

The coalition reported that most child soldiers were age 15 to 18, although its survey recorded children as young as seven years old. Children who are not engaged in combat lay and clear land mines, serve as human shields, or act as spies or messengers. Girls also fight on the frontlines. Many serve as sexual slaves to military officers. Many boys are also sexually exploited. According to the United Nations Children's Fund (UNICEF), in

TABLE 1.2

Definition of "severe forms of trafficking in persons"

The Act defines "severe form of trafficking in persons" as

(a) sex trafficking in which a commercial sex act is induced by force, fraud, or coercion, or in which the person induced to perform such act has not attained 18 years of age; or (b) the recruitment, harboring, transportation, provision, or obtaining of a person for labor or services, through the use of force, fraud or coercion for the purpose of subjection to involuntary servitude, peonage, debt bondage, or slavery.

Definition of Terms Used in the Term "Severe Forms of Trafficking in Persons":

"**Sex trafficking**" means the recruitment, harboring, transportation, provision, or obtaining of a person for the purpose of a commercial sex act.

"**Commercial sex act**" means any sex act on account of which anything of value is given to or received by any person.

"**Involuntary servitude**" includes a condition of servitude induced by means of (A) any scheme, plan, or pattern intended to cause a person to believe that, if the person did not enter into or continue in such condition that person or another person would suffer serious harm or physical restraint; or (B) the abuse or threatened abuse of the legal process.

"**Debt bondage**" means the status or condition of a debtor arising from a pledge by the debtor of his or her personal services or of those of a person under his or her control as a security for debt, if the value of those services as reasonably assessed is not applied toward the liquidation of the debt or the length and nature of those services are not respectively limited and defined.

"**Coercion**" means (A) threats of serious harm to or physical restraint against any person; (B) any scheme, plan or pattern intended to cause a person to believe that failure to perform an act would result in serious harm to or physical restraint against any person; or (C) the abuse or threatened abuse of the legal process.

SOURCE: "Definition of `Severe Forms of Trafficking in Persons,'" in *Victims of Trafficking and Violence Protection Act 2000: Trafficking in Persons Report*, U.S. Department of State, Washington, DC, June 2002

the 1990s more than 2 million children were killed in armed conflicts, and another 6 million children were injured or disabled. Not surprisingly, many of these children experienced psychological trauma.

Trafficking in Children

Trafficking in women and children is a worldwide problem. The U.S. Department of State reported in *Victims of Trafficking and Violence Protection Act 2000: Trafficking in Persons Report* (Washington, DC, June 2002) that between 700,000 and 2 million women and children are trafficked across national borders each year. This number does not include trafficking within countries. The total numbers are estimated to be between 1 to 4 million women and children.

The Trafficking Victims Protection Act (Division A of Public Law 106-386), enacted in 2000, defines "severe forms of trafficking in persons." (See Table 1.2.) In October 2001, as authorized by the act, the Department of State established the Office to Monitor and Combat Trafficking in Persons. The office works with other governments in prosecuting traffickers and in assisting victims domestically and globally.

Organized criminal groups in many countries work with one another in procuring or abducting young girls for the prostitution business, which makes millions of dollars. Very young children are forced into prostitution because clients mistakenly believe that a nine- or ten-year-old will not be infected with AIDS. In many Asian countries, in what is known as debt bondage, girls are traded for money to brothels by their parents or guardians. Many never leave prostitution because they cannot afford to pay for the additional debt added for food and rent. According to a UNICEF report, *Profiting from Abuse: An Investigation into the Sexual Exploitation of Our Children* (New York, NY, November 2001), in India alone an estimated 400,000 to 500,000 children worked as prostitutes. A survey of more than 6,000 sex workers in Phnom Penh, Cambodia, found that 31 percent of those interviewed were children younger than 18. Armed conflicts in many parts of the world have also resulted in increased trafficking of children. In refugee camps, criminals prey on minors who are separated from their families, kidnapping and selling them for adoption or prostitution.

Child Labor

In 1989 the United Nations General Assembly adopted the *Convention on the Rights of the Child* as an international human rights treaty. Article 32 of the *Convention* defines child labor as any economic exploitation or work that is likely to be hazardous or interferes with the child's education, or is harmful to the child's health or physical, mental, spiritual, moral, or social development.

The International Labour Office (ILO) estimated that, in 2000, about 351.7 million children ages 5 to 17 were engaged in economic activity, which included paid and unpaid work (*Every Child Counts: New Global Estimates on Child Labour,* International Programme on the Elimination of Child Labour, Statistical Information and Monitoring Programme on Child Labour, Geneva, Switzerland, June 2002). This means that almost one-fifth (17.6 percent) of all children in the world (1.5 trillion) were in the workplace. Overall, slightly more boys (52 percent) than girls (48 percent) worked. Among the youngest children ages 5 to 9, about 1 of 8 were economically active.

Among younger children ages 5 to 14, an estimated 211 million were economically active. Of this age group, the Asia and Pacific region had the largest numbers of

TABLE 1.3

Regional estimates of economically active children, ages 5-14, in 2000

Region	Number of children (in millions)	Work ratio (%)
Developed economies	2.5	2
Transition economies	2.4	4
Asia and the Pacific	127.3	19
Latin America & Caribbean	17.4	16
Sub-Saharan Africa	48.0	29
Middle East & North Africa	13.4	15
Total	**211**	**18**

SOURCE: "Table 2: Regional estimates of economically active children ages 5-14 in 2000," in *Every Child Counts: New Global Estimates on Child Labour,* International Programme on the Elimination of Child Labour (IPEC), Statistical Information and Monitoring Programme on Child Labour (SIMPOC), International Labour Office, Geneva, Switzerland, April 2002

TABLE 1.4

Estimated number of children in unconditional worst forms of child labor, 2000

Region*	Trafficked ('000s)	Forced & bonded labour ('000s)	Armed conflict ('000s)	Prostitution & pornography ('000s)	Illicit activities ('000s)
Asia/Pacific	250	5,500	120	590	220
Latin America & Caribbean	550	3	30	750	260
Africa	200	210	120	50	n/a
Transition economies	200	n/a	5	n/a	n/a
Developed industrialized economies	n/a	n/a	1	420	110
Total (rounded)	**1,200**	**5,700**	**300**	**1,800**	**600**

*Regions represent origin of trafficking flows. In some cases origin and destination region are identical.

SOURCE: "Table 10: Estimated number of children in unconditional worst forms of child labour, 2000," in *Every Child Counts: New Global Estimates on Child Labour,* International Programme on the Elimination of Child Labour (IPEC), Statistical Information and Monitoring Programme on Child Labour (SIMPOC), International Labour Office, Geneva, Switzerland, April 2002

child workers (127.3 million), followed by sub-Saharan Africa (48 million). Sub-Saharan Africa, however, had the largest proportion of child workers in the world. In this region one of every three children (29 percent) younger than 15 was working. (See Table 1.3.)

The ILO reported that, in sub-Saharan Africa, nearly one of four children (23.6 percent) who worked was younger than 10 years of age, compared to just 12.3 percent in the Asia-Pacific region. While some developing countries agree that children should not be forced to work, they argue that the parents are so destitute that they are forced to indenture their children. This way they have one less mouth to feed. In addition, they receive some income from their children.

Of the nearly 352 million children who were economically active in 2000, almost 7 out of 10 (69.8 percent), or 245.5 million, were involved in the worst forms of child labor. Overall, about half (48.5 percent), or 170.5 million, were performing hazardous labor, such as in mining, construction, and work that exposed the children to pesticides or heavy machinery. In addition, another 8.4 million were involved in the worst forms of child labor. These include 5.7 million children in forced and bonded labor, most of whom (5.5 million) were found in the Asia-Pacific areas, and 1.8 million in prostitution and pornography. (See Table 1.4.) Another 1.2 million children were trafficked within their countries or across borders, while the remaining 900,000 were involved in armed conflicts and other illicit activities, such as working in poppy farms and trafficking in drugs.

CHILDREN AS DOMESTIC WORKERS. In the 1990s public attention became focused on the problem of illegal child labor in such industries as the production of clothing. The largest group of child laborers in the world, however—domestic workers—has not received any attention

at all. UNICEF refers to these children as the "invisible workforce" because they usually work by themselves in private homes. The majority (approximately 90 percent) are girls ages 12–17, but they can be as young as 5 years old. These children receive very low or no salaries and put in long hours, sometimes seven days a week. In many cases the children's parents or other guardians collect the salaries. Most child domestic workers do not attend school. Those who live with their employers may not have contact with their families and peers.

The Central Intelligence Agency (CIA) has found that children as young as 10 are being smuggled into the United States to work as domestics (*International Trafficking in Women to the United States: A Contemporary Manifestation of Slavery and Organized Crime,* Amy O'Neill Richard, Washington, DC, November 1999). Parents actually pay the smugglers thousands of dollars to bring their children into the United States, in the hope that they will have a better life. The children may be moved from location to location. Due to language barriers, these children cannot even ask for help to save themselves.

Child Mutilation

Actions considered abusive in some cultures are often celebrated as rites of passage by others. According to the World Health Organization (WHO), female circumcision is practiced by followers of many religions, as well as by animists and nonbelievers. An estimated 100 million to 140 million women and girls have been circumcised worldwide. Each year about 2 million more girls are at risk of undergoing the procedure.

Female circumcision was first called female genital mutilation in the international document *Programme of Action,* from the International Conference on Population and Development in 1994 in Cairo, Egypt. Female circumcision may be performed as early as infancy, although the procedure is usually done between the ages of 4 and 12. It involves the partial or complete removal of the female genitalia. In its most severe form, called infibulation, after the major mutilation of the external genitalia and the joining of the scraped sides of the vulva across the vagina, a small opening "that may be as small as a matchstick" is kept for urination and menstruation. Because of the small vaginal opening, sexual intercourse is quite painful, and the infibulation scar may have to be recut to relieve penetration problems.

Female circumcision is practiced in many African countries, as well as in certain countries in Asia and the Middle East. People who migrate from these regions to the United States, Canada, and Europe bring the practice with them.

Some of the health implications of female circumcision include hemorrhage, shock, injuries to the surrounding tissues, and death. Infections may lead to sterility and chronic pelvic pain. If a woman has been infibulated, she may have to undergo a series of cutting and resewing procedures during her childbearing years. She may also develop cysts, abscesses, and incontinence as a result of damage to the urethra. The risk of being infected with the human immunodeficiency virus (HIV) that leads to acquired immunodeficiency virus (AIDS) is also possible because the circumciser typically uses the same knife for other procedures.

INTERNATIONAL EFFORTS TO STRENGTHEN CHILDREN'S RIGHTS

In May 2000 the United Nations General Assembly adopted two optional protocols to the *Convention on the Rights of the Child.* The first protocol bans the use of children in armed conflicts and raises the age at which children are allowed to participate in war from 15 to 18 . The second protocol bans the sale of children, child prostitution, and child pornography. The first protocol entered into force in January 2002 and the second in February 2002.

As a signatory to the first protocol, the United States agreed for the first time to establish 18 as the minimum age for deployment in armed conflicts. The United States, however, continues to allow 17-year-olds to enlist voluntarily in the armed forces with their parents' permission. The U.S. Department of Defense reported that fewer than 7,000 minors were in the armed forces, accounting for less than one-half of 1 percent of active U.S. soldiers. Each year, minors make up about 4 percent of new recruits.

CHAPTER 2
CHILD ABUSE—A PROBLEM OF DEFINITION

WHAT IS ABUSE?

Child abuse is often a secret. Since the 1960s, however, Americans have become increasingly aware of the problems of child abuse and neglect (together referred to as child maltreatment). In 1963 some 150,000 young victims of maltreatment were reported to authorities (*Juvenile Court Statistics,* Children's Bureau, U.S. Department of Health, Education, and Welfare, Washington, DC, 1966). In 2000 state child protective services (CPS) agencies received nearly 2.8 million reports of child maltreatment involving about 5 million children (*Child Maltreatment 2000,* U.S. Department of Health and Human Services, Administration for Children and Families, Washington, DC, 2002).

There is still no agreement on what constitutes child abuse. In August 2002 a mother in Brilliant, Ohio, was charged with three counts of felony child endangerment for allegedly allowing her three children to become seriously sunburned. A sheriff's deputy had arrested the woman after noticing that her three young children had sunburned faces while at the county fair under 95°F weather. The woman spent eight days in jail. Authorities later released the mother after determining that the children were not that badly burned. She was charged with a single count of misdemeanor child endangerment, which the prosecutor dismissed two months later.

In September 2002 a surveillance camera in a store in Mishawaka, Indiana, recorded a mother apparently beating and punching her four-year-old daughter inside her car. The videotape, which aired nationally, caused public outrage. The mother was charged with battery to a child, a felony that could bring her a maximum of three years in jail. The child was put in foster care while the case was under investigation. While extreme cases like this are easy to label, less severe cases, such as the sunburned children, are viewed differently by different people.

Federal Definition

Official definitions of child abuse and neglect differ among institutions, government bodies, and experts. According to the Child Abuse Prevention and Treatment Act (CAPTA) Amendments of 1996 (Public Law 104-235), which amended the 1974 CAPTA:

> The term "child abuse and neglect" means, at a minimum, any recent act or failure to act, on the part of a parent or caretaker [including any employee of a residential facility or any staff person providing out-of-home care who is responsible for the child's welfare], which results in death, serious physical or emotional harm, sexual abuse or exploitation, or an act or failure to act which presents an imminent risk of serious harm. [The term "child" means a person under the age of 18, unless the child protection law of the state in which the child resides specifies a younger age for cases not involving sexual abuse.]

It should be noted that this definition of child abuse and neglect specifies that only parents and caregivers can be considered perpetrators of child maltreatment. Abusive or negligent behavior by other persons—strangers or persons known to the child—is considered child assault. Nonetheless, both forms of abusive behavior are crimes against children.

Based on a concern that severely disabled newborns may be denied medical care, CAPTA also considers as child abuse and neglect the "withholding of medically indicated treatment," including appropriate nutrition, hydration, and medication, which in the treating physician's medical judgment would most likely help, improve, or correct an infant's life-threatening conditions. This definition, however, does not refer to situations where treatment of an infant, in the physician's medical judgment, would prolong dying, be ineffective in improving or correcting all the infant's life-threatening conditions, or would be futile in helping the infant to survive. In addition, this definition does not include circumstances where the infant is chronically or irreversibly comatose.

State Definitions

CAPTA provides a foundation for states by identifying a minimum set of acts or behaviors that characterize child abuse and neglect. Each state, based on CAPTA guidelines, has formulated its own definitions of the different types of child maltreatment. State definitions, however, such as of neglect, may be unclear. For example, states typically define neglect as the failure to provide adequate food, clothing, shelter, or medical care. About one-fifth of states do not have a separate definition for neglect. Moreover, most child protective services agencies consider recent incidence of neglect instead of patterns of behavior that may constitute chronic, or continuing, neglect.

States define child abuse and neglect in three areas in state statutes: reporting laws for child maltreatment, criminal codes, and juvenile court laws. Most state laws also include exceptions, such as religious exemptions, corporal punishment, cultural practices, and poverty.

CAPTA DEFINES FOUR MAIN TYPES OF CHILD MALTREATMENT

Physical Abuse

Physical abuse is the infliction of physical injury through punching, beating, kicking, biting, burning, shaking, or otherwise harming a child. Physical abuse is generally a willful act. There are cases, however, in which the parent or caretaker may not have intended to hurt the child. In such cases, the injury may have resulted from overdiscipline or corporal punishment. Nonetheless, if the child is injured, the act is considered abusive.

Sexual Abuse

Sexual abuse includes fondling a child's genitals, intercourse, incest, rape, sodomy, exhibitionism, and commercial exploitation through prostitution or the production of pornographic materials.

Emotional Abuse (Psychological Abuse, Verbal Abuse, or Mental Injury)

Emotional abuse includes acts or omissions by the parents or by other caregivers that have caused, or could cause, serious behavioral, cognitive, emotional, or mental disorders. In some cases of emotional abuse, the abuser's act alone, without any harm evident in the child's behavior or condition, is enough cause for intervention by CPS. For example, the parent/caregiver may use extreme or bizarre forms of punishment, such as locking a child in a dark room or closet.

Other forms of emotional abuse may involve more subtle acts, such as habitual scapegoating, belittling, or rejecting treatment. For CPS to intervene, demonstrable harm to the child is often required. Although any of the types of child maltreatment may be found separately, different types of abuse often occur in combination with one another. Nonetheless, emotional abuse is almost always present when other types are identified.

Child Neglect

Child neglect is an act of omission characterized by failure to provide for the child's basic needs. Neglect can be physical, educational, or emotional. Physical neglect includes failure to provide food, clothing, and shelter; refusal of or delay in seeking health care (medical neglect); abandonment; inadequate supervision; and expulsion from the home or refusal to allow a runaway to return home. Educational neglect includes permitting chronic truancy, failure to enroll a child of mandatory school age in school, and failure to take care of a child's special educational needs. Emotional neglect includes substantial inattention to the child's needs for affection, failure to provide needed psychological care, spousal abuse in the child's presence, and allowing drug or alcohol use by the child. It is very important to distinguish between willful neglect and a parent's or a caretaker's failure to provide the necessities of life because of poverty or cultural factors.

A DESCRIPTION OF MALTREATED CHILDREN

Perhaps better than a definition of child abuse is a description of the characteristics likely to be exhibited by abused and/or neglected children. The Department of Health and Human Services indicates that, in general, abused or neglected children are likely to have at least several of the following characteristics:

- They appear to be different from other children in physical or emotional makeup, or their parents inappropriately describe them as being "different" or "bad."

- They seem unduly afraid of their parents.

- They may often bear welts, bruises, untreated sores, or other skin injuries.

- Their injuries seem to be inadequately treated.

- They show evidence of overall poor care.

- They are given inappropriate food, drink, or medication.

- They exhibit behavioral extremes—for example, crying often or crying very little and showing no real expectation of being comforted; being excessively fearful or seemingly fearless of adult authority; being unusually aggressive and destructive or extremely passive and withdrawn.

- Some are wary of physical contact, especially when initiated by an adult. They become fearful when an adult approaches another child, particularly one who is crying. Others are inappropriately hungry for affection, yet may have difficulty relating to children and adults. Based on their past experiences, these children cannot risk getting too close to others.

- They may exhibit a sudden change in behavior—for example, displaying regressive behavior, such as pants wetting, thumb sucking, frequent whining, becoming disruptive, or becoming uncommonly shy and passive.

- They take over the role of the parent, being protective or otherwise attempting to take care of the parent's needs.

- They have learning problems that cannot be diagnosed. If a child's academic intelligence quotient (IQ) is average or better and medical tests indicate no abnormalities, but the child still cannot meet normal expectations, the answer may well be problems in the home—one of which may be abuse or neglect. Particular attention should be given to the child whose attention wanders and who easily becomes self-absorbed.

- They are habitually truant or late for school. Frequent or prolonged absences sometimes result when a parent keeps an injured child at home until the evidence of abuse disappears. In other cases, truancy indicates lack of parental concern or inability to regulate the child's schedule.

- In some cases, they arrive at school too early and remain after classes have ended, rather than go home.

- They are always tired and often sleep in class.

- They are inappropriately dressed for the weather. Children who never have coats or shoes in cold weather are receiving less than minimal care. Those who regularly wear long sleeves or high necklines on hot days, however, may be dressed to hide bruises, burns, or other marks of abuse.

Many of the psychological symptoms of abuse can be contradictory. One child may be excessively aggressive, while another may be too compliant. One child may be extremely independent, while another may exhibit a clinging behavior. A child may be overly mature, attending to the emotional needs of a parent who is incapable of meeting his or her own needs. These different behaviors are possible symptoms of abuse. No one behavior on the part of a child, however, is conclusive evidence of abuse.

Victims of Physical Abuse

Victims of physical abuse often display bruises, welts, contusions, cuts, burns, fractures, lacerations, strap marks, swellings, and/or lost teeth. While internal injuries are seldom detectable without a hospital examination, anyone in close contact with children should be alert to multiple injuries, a history of repeated injuries, new injuries added to old ones, and untreated injuries, especially in very young children. Older children may attribute an injury to an improbable cause, lying for fear of parental retaliation. Younger children, however, may be unaware that a severe beating is unacceptable and may admit to having been abused.

Physically abused children frequently have behavior problems. Especially among adolescents, chronic and unexplainable misbehavior should be investigated as possible evidence of abuse. Some children come to expect abusive behavior as the only kind of attention they can receive and so act in a way that invites abuse. Others break the law deliberately in order to come under the jurisdiction of the courts to obtain protection from their parents.

Parents who inflict physical abuse generally provide necessities, such as adequate food and clean clothes. Nevertheless, they get angry quickly, have unrealistic expectations of their children, and are overly critical and rejecting of their children. While many abusive parents have been mistreated as children themselves and are following a learned behavior, an increasing number who physically abuse their own children do so under the influence of alcohol and drugs.

Victims of Physical Neglect

Physically neglected children are often hungry. They may go without breakfast and have neither food nor money for lunch. Some take the lunch money or food of other children and hoard whatever they obtain. They show signs of malnutrition: paleness, low weight relative to height, lack of body tone, fatigue, inability to participate in physical activities, and lack of normal strength and endurance.

These children are usually irritable. They show evidence of inadequate home management and are unclean and unkempt. Their clothes are often torn and dirty. They may lack proper clothing for different weather conditions, and their school attendance may be irregular. In addition, these children may frequently be ill and may exhibit a generally repressed personality, inattentiveness, and withdrawal. They are in obvious need of medical attention for such correctable conditions as poor eyesight, poor dental care, and lack of immunizations.

A child who suffers physical neglect also generally lacks parental supervision at home. The child, for example, may frequently return from school to an empty house. While the need for adult supervision is, of course, relative to both the situation and the maturity of the child, it is generally held that a child younger than 12 should always be supervised by an adult or at least have immediate access to a concerned adult when necessary.

Parents of neglected children are either unable or unwilling to provide appropriate care. Some neglectful parents are mentally deficient. Most lack knowledge of parenting skills and tend to be discouraged, depressed, and frustrated with their role as parents. Alcohol or drug abuse may also be involved.

Physical neglect can be a result of poverty and/or ignorance and may not be intentional. According to the National Clearinghouse on Child Abuse and Neglect Information (*Acts of Omission: An Overview of Child Neglect,* April 2001), if poor parents fail to feed their children adequately, they would be charged with neglect only if they know of food assistance programs but have failed to use them.

Victims of Emotional Abuse and Neglect

Emotional abuse and neglect are as serious as physical abuse and neglect, although this condition is far more difficult to describe or identify. Emotional maltreatment often involves a parent's lack of love or failure to give direction and encourage the child's development. The parent may either demand far too much from the child in the area of academic, social, or athletic activity or withhold physical or verbal contact, indicating no concern for the child's successes and failures and giving no guidance or praise.

Parents who commit emotional abuse and neglect are often unable to accept their children as fallible human beings. The effects of such abuse can often be far more serious and lasting than those of physical abuse and neglect. Emotionally abused children are often extremely aggressive, disruptive, and demanding in an attempt to gain attention and love. They are rarely able to achieve the success in school that tests indicate they can achieve.

Emotional maltreatment can be hard to determine. Is the child's abnormal behavior the result of maltreatment on the part of the parents, or is it a result of inborn or internal factors? Stuart N. Hart, Marla R. Brassard, Nelson J. Binggeli, and Howard A. Davidson ("Psychological Maltreatment," *The APSAC Handbook on Child Maltreatment,* 2nd ed., Sage Publications, Inc., Thousand Oaks, CA, 2002) have listed problems associated with emotional abuse and neglect, including poor appetite, lying, stealing, enuresis (bed-wetting), encopresis (passing of feces in unacceptable places after bowel control has been achieved), low self-esteem, low emotional responsiveness, failure to thrive, inability to be independent, withdrawal, suicide, and homicide.

Victims of Medical Neglect and Abuse

Medical neglect refers to the parents' failure to provide medical treatment for their children, including immunizations, prescribed medications, recommended surgery, and other intervention in cases of serious disease or injury. Some situations involve a parent's inability to care for a child or lack of access to health care. Other situations involve a parent's refusal to seek professional medical care, particularly because of a belief in spiritual healing.

Thorny legal issues have been raised by cases in which parents' freedom of religion clashes with the recommendations of medical professionals. Medical abuse may also involve the Munchausen syndrome by proxy, in which psychologically disturbed parents create illnesses or injuries in children in order to gain sympathy for themselves.

RELIGIOUS BELIEFS. Religious beliefs sometimes prevent children from getting needed medical care. For example, Christian Scientists believe that God heals the sick and that prayer and perfect faith are the proper responses to illness. Other religions, most notably Jehovah's Witnesses, forbid blood transfusions. Religious exemption laws make it difficult to prosecute parents who do not seek treatment for a sick child because their religion forbids it, although courts generally order the emergency treatment of the children.

Rita Swan, a former Christian Scientist who lost her 16-month-old child to untreated meningitis, is the president of Children's Healthcare Is a Legal Duty, Inc. (CHILD, Inc.), an organization that seeks to protect children from abusive cultural and religious practices, especially religion-based medical neglect. CHILD, Inc., reported that as of November 2002, 39 states had religious exemptions from child abuse and neglect charges in the civil code, and 31 states had a religious defense to criminal charges. All states, except Mississippi and West Virginia, had religious exemptions from immunizations.

In "Child Fatalities from Religion-Motivated Medical Neglect" (*Pediatrics,* vol. 101, no. 4, April 1998), Swan and pediatrician Seth M. Asser reviewed the deaths of children in faith-healing religious sects in which the children were denied medical care. The authors found that in 140 of the 172 deaths, the likelihood of survival would have been at least 90 percent had the children received medical care. Another 18 deaths would have had survival rates of more than 50 percent.

According to CHILD, Inc., Sec. 113 (42 U.S.C. 5106i) of the CAPTA Amendments of 1996 allows parents to withhold medical care from their children based on religious beliefs. Section 113 states:

Nothing in this Act shall be construed:

1. as establishing a federal requirement that a parent or legal guardian provide a child medical service or treatment against the religious belief of the parent or legal guardian; and

2. to require that a state find, or to prohibit a state from finding, abuse or neglect in cases in which a parent or legal guardian relies solely or partially upon spiritual means rather than medical treatment, in accordance with the religious beliefs of the parent or legal guardian.

MUNCHAUSEN SYNDROME BY PROXY. Munchausen syndrome is a psychological disorder in which patients fake illness or make themselves sick in order to get medical attention. In cases of Munchausen syndrome by proxy (MSBP), parents or caregivers suffering from Munchausen syndrome call attention to themselves by hurting or inducing illnesses in their children. The perpetrator, usually the mother, may make up a child's medical history, alter a child's laboratory tests, or fabricate or cause an illness or injury. In some cases caregivers sexually abuse their children so that they can claim a crime has been committed. Table 2.1 illustrates some of the medical symptoms or illnesses exhibited by MSBP victims and the methods perpetrators use to cause these conditions.

In MSBP situations, children are usually subjected to endless and often painful diagnostic tests, medications, and even surgery. Some children have had as many as 300 clinic visits and repeated hospitalizations in their first 18 months of life. The abuse is most often perpetrated against infants and toddlers before they can talk. Some older children who have been abused in this way do not reveal the deception, however, because they fear they will be abandoned by their parents if they are no longer sick. Others come to believe that they must truly be ill. Experts claim that in about 10 percent of cases, MSBP has led to children's deaths.

Officially, MSBP represents fewer than 1,000 of the nearly 3 million alleged cases of abuse referred for investigation each year. This figure, however, is almost certainly underestimated because there are no conclusive tests to diagnose the disorder. Data that exist on MSBP reveal that mothers are the perpetrators in 98 percent of the cases. Although there are no specific numbers, experts believe that many of these mothers themselves have been abused as children. A mother with MSBP may think that by devoting her life to "helping" her sick child, she could be a nurturing parent, unlike her own abusive mother. She not only gets the attention that she craves but also the sympathy of those involved in her child's care.

In June 2000 David E. Hall et al. reported the diagnosis of MSBP in 23 out of 41 suspected cases at Children's Healthcare of Atlanta at Scottish Rite, Atlanta, Georgia ("Evaluation of Covert Video Surveillance in the Diagnosis of Munchausen Syndrome by Proxy: Lessons from 41 Cases," *Pediatrics,* vol. 105, no. 6). For four years the researchers, after notifying law enforcement, monitored the children through hidden video cameras to determine the reasons for their inexplicable illnesses. The video surveillance showed the mothers abusing their children, from suffocation to injection with chemicals. Critics charged that the families' right to privacy had been invaded, but the researchers argued that abused children cannot speak up for themselves and need others to protect them.

A FAMILY AT RISK FOR MALTREATMENT

While it is impossible to determine whether child maltreatment will occur, generally a family may be at risk if the

TABLE 2.1

Common presentations of Munchausen Syndrome by Proxy and the usual methods of deception

Presentation	Mechanism
Apnea (breathing stops)	Suffocation, drugs, poisoning, lying
Seizures	Lying, drugs, poisons, asphyxiation
Bleeding	Adding blood to urine, vomit, etc.; opening intravenous line
Fevers, blood infection	Injection of feces, saliva, contaminated water into the child
Vomiting	Poisoning with drugs that cause vomiting; lying
Diarrhea	Poisoning with laxatives, salt, mineral oil

SOURCE: "Common presentations of Munchausen Syndrome by Proxy and the usual methods of deception," in *Child Neglect and Munchausen Syndrome by Proxy,* U.S. Department of Justice, Office of Juvenile Justice and Delinquency Prevention, Washington, DC, 1997

parent is young, has little education, has had several children born within a few years, and is highly dependent on social welfare. A family may also be at risk if the parent:

• is a "loner"—feels isolated with no family to depend on, has no real friends, or does not get along well with the neighbors

• has no understanding of the stages of child development and does not know what to expect of a child at a given age

• has a poor self-image and feels worthless, with a pervading sense of failure

• feels unloved, unappreciated, and unwanted, with a great fear of rejection

• has severe personal problems, such as ill health, alcoholism, or drug dependency

• feels that violence can often be the solution to life's problems or has not learned to "blow off steam" in a socially acceptable manner

• is experiencing a time of severe stress—for example, sudden unemployment or painful divorce—without any coping mechanism

• was abused or neglected as a child

A family may also be at risk if the child:

• is "different"—smaller than average, more sickly, disabled, or considered unattractive or was premature

• resembles or reminds the parent of someone the parent hates, or if the child "takes after" a disappointing spouse or former loved one

• is more demanding or otherwise has more problems than do other children in the family

• is unwanted—seen as a "mistake" or burden, having "ruined things" for the parent

CHAPTER 3
REPORTING CHILD ABUSE

MANDATORY REPORTING

In 1974 Congress enacted the first Child Abuse Prevention and Treatment Act (CAPTA; Public Law 93-247) that set guidelines for the reporting, investigation, and treatment of child maltreatment. States had to meet these requirements in order to receive federal funding to assist child victims of abuse and neglect. Among its many provisions, CAPTA required the states to enact mandatory reporting laws and procedures so that child protective services (CPS) agencies can take action to protect children from further abuse. (The term "CPS" refers to the services provided by an agency authorized to act on behalf of a child when his or her parents are unable or unwilling to do so. CPS is also often used to refer to the agency itself.)

The earliest mandatory reporting laws were directed at medical professionals, particularly physicians, who were considered the most likely to see abused children. Currently each state designates mandatory reporters, including health care workers, mental health professionals, social workers, school personnel, child care providers, and law enforcement officers. Any individual, however, whether or not he or she is a mandatory reporter, may report incidents of abuse or neglect.

Some states also require maltreatment reporting from other individuals, such as firefighters, Christian Science practitioners, battered women's counselors, animal control officers, veterinarians, commercial/private film or photograph processors, and even lawyers. As of December 31, 2000, 18 states required all citizens to report suspected child maltreatment. Twenty-six states exempted from mandatory reporting the privileged communication between attorney and client, clergy and penitent, and physician and patient.

In 2000 more than half (56 percent) of all reports of alleged child maltreatment came from professional sources—educators (16.1 percent); legal, law enforcement, and criminal justice personnel (15.2 percent); social services and mental health personnel (14.4 percent); medical personnel (8.3 percent); and child day care and substitute care providers (2 percent). Friends, neighbors, parents, and other relatives comprised one-fifth (20.1 percent) of the reporters, while victims and self-identified perpetrators reported abuse in 1 percent of the cases. Another 22.8 percent of reports came from anonymous, unknown sources, or other sources. (See Figure 3.1.)

All states offer immunity to individuals who report incidents of child maltreatment "in good faith." Besides physical injury and neglect, most states include mental injury, sexual abuse, and the sexual exploitation of minors as cases to be reported.

FAILURE TO REPORT MALTREATMENT

Many states impose penalties, either a fine and/or imprisonment, for failure to report child maltreatment. A mandated reporter, such as a physician, may also be sued for negligence for failing to protect a child from harm. The landmark California case *Landeros v. Flood et al.* (17 Cal. 3d 399, 551 P.2d 389, 1976) illustrates such a case. Eleven-month-old Gita Landeros was brought by her mother to the San Jose Hospital in California for treatment of injuries. Besides a fractured lower leg, the girl had bruises on her back and abrasions on other parts of her body. She also appeared scared when anyone approached her. At the time Gita was also suffering from a fractured skull, but this was never diagnosed by the attending physician, A. J. Flood.

Gita returned home with her mother and subsequently suffered further serious abuse at the hands of her mother and the mother's boyfriend. Three months later Gita was brought to another hospital for medical treatment, where the doctor diagnosed "battered child syndrome" and reported the abuse to the proper authorities. After surgery the child

FIGURE 3.1

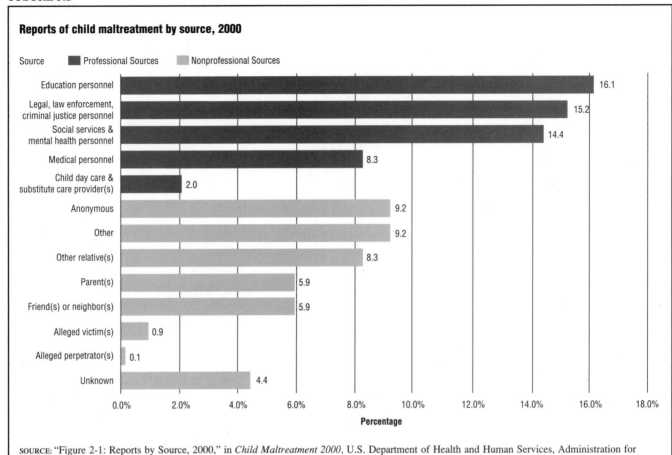

Reports of child maltreatment by source, 2000

Source ■ Professional Sources ▨ Nonprofessional Sources

Source	Percentage
Education personnel	16.1
Legal, law enforcement, criminal justice personnel	15.2
Social services & mental health personnel	14.4
Medical personnel	8.3
Child day care & substitute care provider(s)	2.0
Anonymous	9.2
Other	9.2
Other relative(s)	8.3
Parent(s)	5.9
Friend(s) or neighbor(s)	5.9
Alleged victim(s)	0.9
Alleged perpetrator(s)	0.1
Unknown	4.4

Percentage

SOURCE: "Figure 2-1: Reports by Source, 2000," in *Child Maltreatment 2000,* U.S. Department of Health and Human Services, Administration for Children and Families, Washington, DC, 2002

was placed with foster parents. The mother and boyfriend were eventually convicted of the crime of child abuse. The guardian *ad litem* (a court-appointed special advocate) for Gita Landeros filed a malpractice suit against Dr. Flood and the hospital, citing painful permanent physical injury to the plaintiff as a result of the defendants' negligence.

The trial court of Santa Clara County dismissed the Landeros complaint, and the case was appealed to the California Supreme Court. The California Supreme Court agreed that the "battered child syndrome" was a recognized medical condition that Dr. Flood should have been aware of and diagnosed. The court ruled that the doctor's failure to do so contributed to the child's continued suffering, and Dr. Flood and the hospital were liable for this. While this case applied specifically to a medical doctor, the principles reached by the court are applicable to other professionals. Most professionals are familiar with the court's decision in *Landeros.*

WHY MANDATED REPORTERS FAIL TO REPORT SUSPECTED MALTREATMENT

Gail L. Zellman and C. Christine Fair conducted a national survey to determine why mandated reporters may

not report suspected maltreatment ("Preventing and Reporting Abuse" *The APSAC Handbook on Child Maltreatment,* 2nd ed., Sage Publications, Inc., Thousand Oaks, CA, 2002). The researchers surveyed 1,196 general and family practitioners, pediatricians, child psychiatrists, clinical psychologists, social workers, public school principals, and heads of child care centers. Nearly 8 of 10 (77 percent) survey participants had made a child maltreatment report at some time during their professional career. More than 9 of 10 (92 percent) elementary school principals reported child maltreatment at some time, followed closely by child psychiatrists (90 percent) and pediatricians (89 percent). A lesser proportion of secondary school principals (84 percent), social workers (70 percent), and clinical psychologists (63 percent) reported child maltreatment at some time in their careers.

Nearly 40 percent of the mandated reporters, however, indicated that, at some time in their career, they had failed to report even though they had suspected child maltreatment. Almost 60 percent failed to report child maltreatment because they did not have enough evidence that the child had been maltreated. One-third of the mandated reporters thought the abuse was not serious enough to warrant reporting. An equal proportion of mandated reporters did not report suspected abuse because they felt they were in a better position to help the child (19.3 percent) or they did not want to end the treatment (19 percent) they were giving the child. Almost 16 percent failed to report because they did not think CPS would do a good job.

PEDIATRICIANS

Pediatricians, typically the first persons to come into contact with a maltreated child, may hesitate to report suspected abuse because they fear offending the parents who pay the bills and who may spread rumors about their competence, potentially damaging their practice. Some fear the time lost in reporting abuse, the possibility of being sued by an outraged parent, or having to testify in court. Most have not received proper training in handling and treating child abuse.

Addressing Child Sexual Abuse

A study of pediatricians and other pediatric practitioners revealed their lack of training in addressing child sexual abuse. Mary Ranee Leder et al., in "Addressing Sexual Abuse in the Primary Care Setting" (*Pediatrics,* vol. 104, no. 2, August 1999), interviewed six focus groups of 65 pediatric practitioners. The researchers found that these health care providers, while knowing the signs of sexual abuse, lacked training in identifying these signs in their patients. When they suspected possible sexual abuse, the practitioners did not know what questions to ask the patients and how to handle the cases. Two-thirds of the study participants indicated that, although they realized it was their responsibility to address the possible abuse, they did not feel comfortable in doing so.

Even as more physicians have become knowledgeable about the presentation (the manner in which the physical signs are exhibited) of child sexual abuse, experts have found that few differences can be found between the findings during genital examinations of children who had been sexually abused and those without history of sexual abuse. Abbey B. Berenson et al. ("A Case-Control Study of Anatomic Changes Resulting from Sexual Abuse," *American Journal of Obstetrics and Gynecology,* vol. 182, no. 4, April 2000) examined two groups of girls between the ages of three and eight. The genital examination of the 192 children who had been sexually abused and the 200 girls in the control group who had no history of past sexual abuse did not differ much. Sheela L. Lahoti et al. ("Evaluating the Child for Sexual Abuse," *American Family Physician,* vol. 63, no. 5, March 1, 2001) suggested that, since the physical presentation of sexual abuse may be inconclusive, the physician should interview the child thoroughly and document that interview. This medical interview may be allowed in court as reliable hearsay evidence.

Reporting Psychological Maltreatment of Children

According to the American Academy of Pediatrics (AAP), pediatricians play a major role in preventing, recognizing, and reporting psychological, or emotional, maltreatment (Steven W. Kairys, Charles F. Johnson, and the Committee on Child Abuse and Neglect, "The Psychological Maltreatment of Children—Technical Report," *Pediatrics,* vol. 109, no. 4, April 2002). Generally, pediatricians are the only professionals young children see before they attend school. Therefore, pediatricians are in a position to observe any abusive interaction between the child and the parent/caregiver. They should be able to identify parental characteristics, such as substance abuse and poor parenting skills that may predispose parents to abuse their children. Pediatricians should also be able to identify at-risk children, including those who are disabled or whose parents are undergoing a hostile divorce. The consequences of psychological maltreatment may take years to surface; hence, pediatricians are encouraged to report their suspicions, so that the child and the caregivers can get help right away.

SEXUAL ASSAULT NURSE EXAMINER

A sexual assault nurse examiner (SANE) is a registered nurse trained in forensic (using science to study evidence of a crime) examination of sexual assault victims. The SANE program emerged in the 1990s in response to the need for a more thorough collection of evidence, as well as compassionate care for the victim and better prosecution of the perpetrator. It has been recognized that, in the past, sexual assault victims have been retraumatized during forensic-evidence collection because the hospital personnel may lack training in dealing with such victims.

After the victim has received the proper medical care, the SANE gathers information about the patient and a history of the crime. The nurse evaluates the victim's mental state and performs a physical examination, collecting and preserving evidence. The nurse then documents the evidence obtained, as well as other findings. The SANE may also provide other care, including giving medication to counter sexually transmitted diseases and making referrals for other medical aid and psychological support. SANEs also testify in court as expert witnesses.

EDUCATORS

Felicia F. Romero, in "The Educator's Role in Reporting the Emotional Abuse of Children" (*Journal of Instructional Psychology,* vol. 27, no. 3, September 2000), pointed out that, whereas teachers attending in-service programs learn the behavioral indicators of neglect and physical and sexual abuse, they do not receive much information about emotional, or psychological, abuse. Victims of emotional abuse suffer "injuries" that are not visible, and educators may not realize that the consequences of such abuse is more severe than those from other forms of maltreatment.

TABLE 3.1

Accreditation requirements

Health care discipline	Accreditation institutions	Requirements related to family violence	Description
Medical schools	Liaison Commission on Medical Education (LCME)	S	"The curriculum should prepare students for their role in addressing the medical consequences of common societal problems, for example, providing instructions in the diagnosis, prevention, appropriate reporting and treatment of violence and abuse." Standards can be found on the LCME web site www.lcme.org.
	Accreditation Council for Graduate Medical Education (ACGME)	X	The institutional requirements of the ACGME are very practical in nature and do not outline any single curriculum requirements including any dealing with family violence.
	American Osteopathic Healthcare Association (AOHA)	NS	Institutions are required to include with the spectrum of "Emergency Procedures" some instruction regarding "abuse and neglect" of children. While these standards are not a requirement onto themselves, they do seem to be somewhat quantifiable.
Physician residencies	Residency Review Committees (RRC) of the ACGME	S	The residency review committees of the ACGME, which accredit programs rather than institutions, do have provisions for family violence in certain fields. Though the genetics area does not mention family violence, the areas of family practice and obstetrics indicate how to identify signs of family violence and the steps to take.
Dental schools	American Dental Association Commission on Dental Accreditation (ADA)	NS	There is no specific mention of family violence in the accreditation commission's standards. Such training is believed to fall under the purview of a provision for "ethical reasoning" and "professional responsibility."
Nursing schools	Commission on Collegiate Nursing Education Accreditation (CCNE)	X	CCNE guidelines are very generic and do not provide for any particular curriculum requirements. The guidelines allow schools to choose their own direction and philosophy and subsequently measures them against the standard they have chosen.
Nurse practitioners	National League for Nursing Accrediting Commission (NLNAC)	NS	"NLNAC does not include specific curriculum content areas within its standards and criteria. When specific curriculum content is designated it is usually from the State Boards of Nursing since NLNAC is voluntary." Standards can be accessed on the website at www.nlnac.org.
	National Association of Pediatric Nurse Associates & Practitioners, Inc. (NAPNAP)	NS	NAPNAP recognizes that there is "substantial scientific evidence that children who are abused physically, sexually, emotionally or who are neglected, are prevented from optimal development." NAPNAP has in place a thorough position statement on child abuse/neglect.
Psychology programs and internship sites	Committee on Accreditation of the American Psychological Association: accredits both school and internship sites (APA)	X	There is no mention of family violence in the APA accreditation guidelines. They take a broad stance on evaluating the goals that institutions set for themselves.
Social work programs	Council on Social Work Education (CSWE)	NS	CSWE has no specific requirements mandating that the issue of family violence be discussed on any level. There is an expectation that a program dealing with social work must at some point address the problem. Should an institution not do this, it would probably be cited.
Physician assistant	Commission on Accreditation of Allied Health Education (CAAHEP) Programs	X	There is no reference to family violence made in the CAAHEP standards or guidelines. Curriculum is the responsibility of the sponsoring institution with the exception of a few general study education requirements.
	Effective January 1, 2001, CAAHEP no longer will be the accreditor of physician assistant education programs. All current accreditations are being transferred from CAAHEP to the Accreditation Review Commission on Education of the Physician Assistant (ARC-PA) http://www.CAAHEP.org/caahep_pa.htm		

Note:
S = specific existing requirements.
NS = nonspecific requirements.
X = no identifiable requirements.

SOURCE: Felicia Cohn, Marla E. Salmon, and John D. Stobo, eds., *Confronting Chronic Neglect: The Education and Training of Health Professionals on Family Violence,* Institute of Medicine, Committee on the Training Needs of Health Professionals to Respond to Family Violence, National Academy Press, 2002

A NEED FOR FAMILY VIOLENCE EDUCATION

Although child abuse is a well-documented social and public health problem in the United States, few medical schools and residency training programs include child abuse education and other family violence education in their curricula. The Committee on the Training Needs of

Health Professionals to Respond to Family Violence of the Institute of Medicine examined the curricula on family violence for six groups of health professionals: physicians, physician assistants, nurses, psychologists, social workers, and dentists (*Confronting Chronic Neglect: The Education and Training of Health Professionals on Family Violence,* Felicia Cohn, Marla E. Salmon, and John D. Stobo, eds., National Academy Press, 2002).

The committee noted that as many as one out of four children and adults experience family violence during their lifetimes. Studies have shown that family violence is associated with many problems affecting health, including homelessness, alcohol and substance abuse, and delinquency. Although health professionals are usually the first people to interact with victims of family violence, their lack of education on family violence keeps them from identifying, treating, and helping their patients.

The committee found that most medical schools give instruction regarding at least one form of family violence. In most cases, education revolves around reporting requirements, patient interviewing skills, screening tools, health conditions related to violence, and service referrals for victims. The teaching sessions vary, ranging from a very brief discussion to several lectures or case discussions. Although about 95 percent of schools teach material related to child maltreatment, usually during pediatric rotation, the curricula is inadequate. Table 3.1 illustrates the minimal requirements for accreditation, a process that determines whether a medical school or program meets certain established standards. Accreditation is needed for eligibility to participate in federal student loan programs.

Medical residents specializing in fields in which they are most likely to interact with maltreatment victims are required to receive training in family violence. These include pediatricians, internists, obstetricians/gynecologists, geriatricians (specialists who treat the elderly), psychiatrists, and emergency-medicine doctors. The training consists of lectures and case discussions, and the training duration varies from program to program. As for continuing medical education on family violence, the committee found very little information, including some lectures offered every year, as well as programs on the Internet, for which health professionals can earn credits.

The committee also noted that not much is being done to evaluate the effects of family violence training. So far, evaluations that had been performed concerned short-term effects of the training, such as how the training had increased the health professionals' knowledge of family violence. The committee suggested that more in-depth evaluation of the training programs should measure the effects of training on health professionals' behavior and victims' health.

REPEATED FAILURE TO REPORT

The death of an eight-year-old boy in Washington, D.C., in the hands of his insane mother is an example of the failure of several adults to report the threat to his life. *Washington Post* investigative reporters, Scott Higham and Sari Horwitz ("Child Endangered, without a Lifeline," September 12, 2001) wrote of how police and hospital personnel failed to report the danger faced by the child in his mother's home. The mother was hearing voices telling her to kill the boy. When brought to the hospital psychiatric ward for evaluation, she was diagnosed with a psychotic disorder and yet allowed to leave the hospital. A neighbor reported the threat to the boy's life, but CPS failed to follow up because they did not consider the situation to be child neglect. In the end, the boy was stabbed so many times the coroner could not determine the number of wounds.

That was one of the many deaths investigated by the *Washington Post.* In September 2001 Horwitz, Higham, and Sarah Cohen wrote a series of four investigative articles, which ultimately won them the Pulitzer Prize. Their articles presented findings from their yearlong investigation of 229 children in Washington, D.C., who had died between 1993 and 2000, after their cases were brought to the attention of CPS. In 1995 the federal government had taken over control of the Washington, D.C., CPS because of widespread failures to protect the children under its care. This was the first time that a federal court had ever taken charge of a CPS agency.

Of the 180 cases for which the deaths were documented, 40 infants and toddlers died because CPS placed the children in unsafe homes or medical facilities or failed to take the proper steps to prevent the deaths. Examples of these cases include a 10-week-old infant who was left by CPS workers with the boyfriend of the infant's cocaine-addicted mother. CPS failed to provide help to the man, who was dying of cancer. The man died while the baby was in his care; the baby died of severe dehydration (Sari Horwitz, Scott Higham, and Sarah Cohen, "'Protected' Children Died as Government Did Little," September 9, 2001). Another case involved an eight-year-old severely mentally and physically disabled girl, who was sent to live in a Delaware nursing home. For the next six years, the girl languished in the facility, forgotten by the CPS and neglected by the nursing home staff. She died alone in the nursing home hallway, her body bent over in her wheelchair from scoliosis, a deformity characterized by curvature of the spine (Scott Higham and Sari Horwitz, "A Foster Girl Is Sent Away and Dies Alone," September 10, 2001).

CHILD PROTECTIVE SERVICES

Partly funded by the federal government, child protective services (CPS) agencies were first established in response to the 1974 Child Abuse Prevention and Treatment Act (CAPTA; Public Law 93-247), which mandated

FIGURE 3.2

Overview of steps followed by cases through the child protective services and child welfare systems

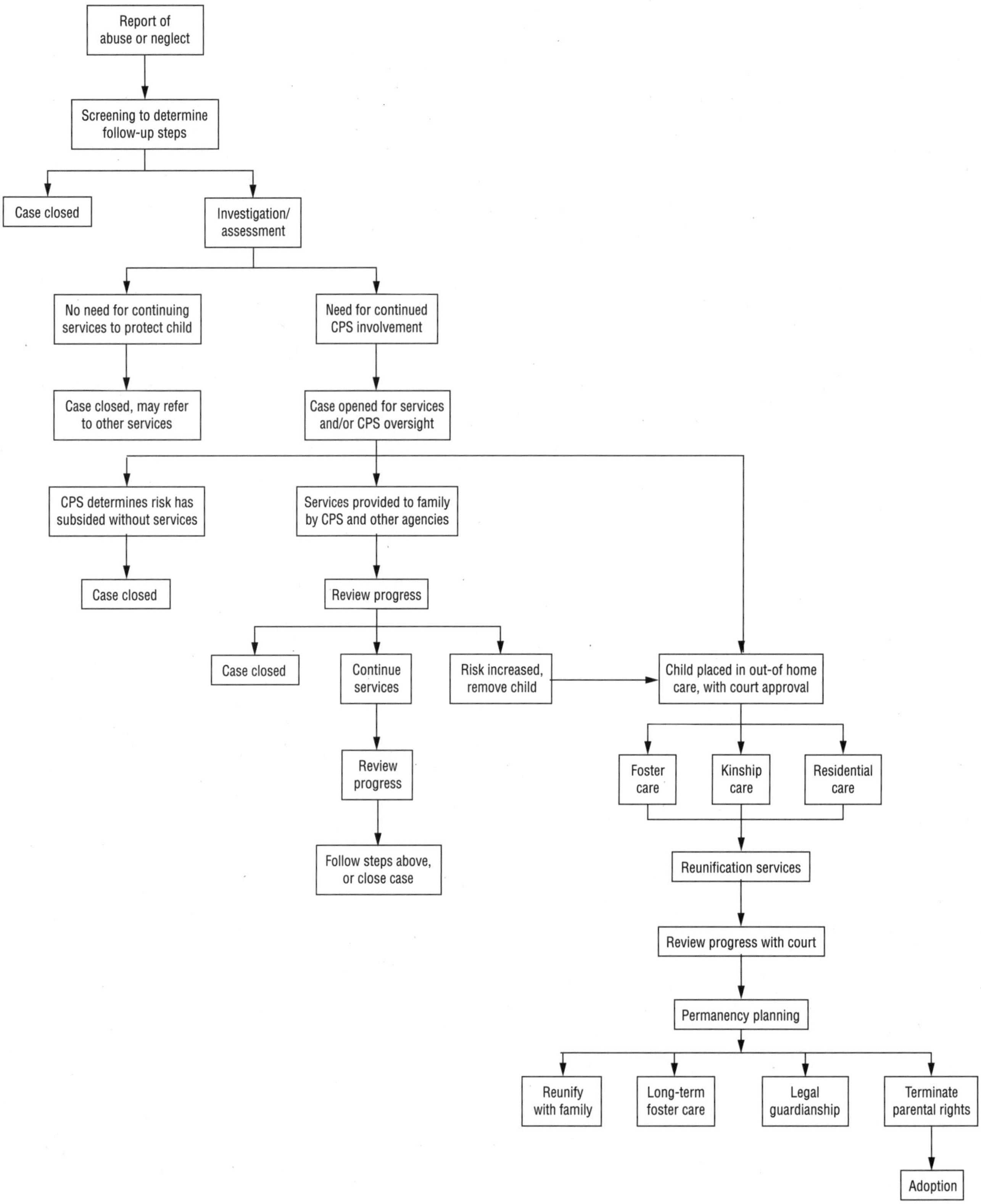

```
                    Report of
                 abuse or neglect
                        |
                        v
              Screening to determine
                 follow-up steps
                  |            |
                  v            v
            Case closed    Investigation/
                            assessment
                            |         |
                            v         v
              No need for continuing   Need for continued
              services to protect child   CPS involvement
                        |                     |
                        v                     v
              Case closed, may refer   Case opened for services
                to other services      and/or CPS oversight
                                        |         |              |
                                        v         v              |
                        CPS determines risk has   Services provided to family   |
                        subsided without services  by CPS and other agencies    |
                                |                     |                          |
                                v                     v                          |
                          Case closed          Review progress                  |
                                        |         |         |                    |
                                        v         v         v                    v
                                  Case closed  Continue   Risk increased,    Child placed in out-of home
                                               services    remove child  →   care, with court approval
                                                  |                            |         |         |
                                                  v                            v         v         v
                                               Review                     Foster    Kinship   Residential
                                               progress                    care      care       care
                                                  |                                    |
                                                  v                                    v
                                          Follow steps above,              Reunification services
                                            or close case                          |
                                                                                    v
                                                                          Review progress with court
                                                                                    |
                                                                                    v
                                                                          Permanency planning
                                                          |           |            |             |
                                                          v           v            v             v
                                                      Reunify     Long-term    Legal        Terminate
                                                     with family  foster care  guardianship  parental rights
                                                                                                  |
                                                                                                  v
                                                                                              Adoption
```

SOURCE: Patricia A. Schene, "Past, Present, and Future Roles of Child Protective Services," in *The Future of Children,* vol. 8, no. 1, spring 1998. Reprinted with permission of the David and Lucile Packard Foundation.

that all states establish procedures to investigate suspected incidents of child maltreatment. Upon receipt of a report of suspected child maltreatment, CPS screens the case to determine its proper jurisdiction. For example, if it is determined that the alleged perpetrator of sexual abuse is the victim's parent or caretaker, CPS conducts further investigation. If the alleged perpetrator is a stranger or someone who is not the parent or caregiver of the victim, however, the case is referred to the police because it does not fall within CPS jurisdiction as outlined under federal law. Cases of reported child abuse or neglect typically undergo a series of steps through CPS and child welfare systems. (See Figure 3.2.)

Court Involvement

The civil or juvenile court hears allegations of maltreatment and decides if a child has been abused and/or neglected. The court then determines what should be done to protect the child. The child may be left in the parents' home under the supervision of the CPS agency, or the child may be placed in foster care. If the child is removed from the home and it is later determined that the child should never be returned to the parents, the court can begin proceedings to terminate parental rights so that the child can be put up for adoption. The state may also prosecute the abusive parent or caretaker when a crime has allegedly been committed.

Family Preservation

The Adoption Assistance and Child Welfare Act of 1980 (Public Law 96-272) mandated: "In each case, reasonable efforts will be made (A) prior to the placement of a child in foster care, to prevent or eliminate the need for removal of the child from his home, and (B) to make it possible for the child to return to his home." Because the law, however, did not define the term "reasonable efforts," states and courts interpreted the term in different ways. In many cases, child welfare personnel took the "reasonable efforts" of providing family counseling, respite care, and substance abuse treatment, thus preventing the victim from being removed from abusive parents.

The law was a reaction to what was seen as zealousness in the 1960s and 1970s, when children, especially black children, were taken from their homes because their parents were poor. Today, however, many agree that circumstances have changed. They feel that problems of drug or substance abuse can mean that returning the child to the home is likely a guarantee of further abuse. In addition, some situations exist where a parent's live-in partner, who has no emotional attachment to the child, may also present risks to the child.

Dr. Richard J. Gelles, a prominent family violence expert, once a vocal advocate of family preservation, had a change of heart after studying the case of 15-month-old David Edwards, who was suffocated by his mother after the child welfare system failed to come to his rescue. Although David's parents had lost custody of their first child because of abuse, and despite reports of David's abuse, CPS made "reasonable efforts" to let the parents keep the child. In *The Book of David: How Preserving Families Can Cost Children's Lives* (BasicBooks, New York, NY, 1996), Dr. Gelles pointed out that CPS needs to abandon its blanket solution to child abuse in its attempt to use reasonable efforts to reunite the victims and their perpetrators.

Dr. Gelles finds that those parents who seriously abuse their children are incapable of changing their behaviors. On August 2, 2001, testifying before the U.S. House of Representatives during the reauthorization hearing on the CAPTA, Dr. Gelles reported:

> A major failing in child abuse and neglect assessments is the crude way behavioral change is conceptualized and measured. Behavioral change is thought to be a two-step process—one simply changes from one form of behavior to another. . . . [A]s yet, there is not empirical evidence to support the effectiveness of child welfare services in general or the newer, more innovative intensive family preservation services. The lack of empirical support for the effectiveness of intensive family preservation services was the finding of the National Academy of Sciences panel on Assessing Family Violence Prevention and Treatment Programs and the United States Department of Health and Human Services national evaluation of family preservation programs.

CPS SYSTEM UNDER SIEGE

Increased Caseloads

In 1997 the U.S. Government Accounting Office (GAO), the investigative arm of Congress, concluded that the CPS system was in crisis (*Child Protective Services: Complex Challenges Require New Strategies,* Washington, DC, July 1997). According to the GAO, reports of child maltreatment had continued to rise, resulting in heavier caseloads for CPS workers. The GAO noted that the increasing number of maltreatment reports was due in part to child abuse by drug-dependent parents and caretakers, the rising numbers of mandatory reporting by certain professionals, and the stresses of poverty among families. Since the GAO report, CPS caseloads have not eased up. Child welfare workers generally carry 40 to 60 cases, instead of the ideal 15 to 20 cases.

Weaknesses in the System

CPS agencies are continually plagued by weaknesses in the system. The work of protecting children from maltreatment can be quite complex. CPS agencies often have difficulty attracting and retaining experienced caseworkers. The low pay not only makes it difficult to attract qualified workers but also contributes to CPS employees leaving for better-paying jobs. In some jurisdictions, because of

FIGURE 3.3

Children age 0–17 living with one or more substance abusing parents by parent's primary problem, 1996

3.8 million children live with a parent who is alcoholic

2.1 million children live with a parent whose primary problem is with illicit drugs

2.4 million children live with a parent who abuses alcohol and illicit drugs in combination

8.3 million children live with at least one parent who is alcoholic or in need of substance abuse treatment

SOURCE: "Figure 4-1: Children age 0-17 living with one or more substance abusing parents by parent's primary problem, 1996," in *Blending Perspectives and Building Common Ground: A Report to Congress on Substance Abuse and Child Protection,* U.S. Department of Health and Human Services, Administration for Children and Families, Washington, DC, 1999

deficient hiring policies, employees have college degrees that may not necessarily be related to social work. In addition, limited funds preclude sufficient in-service training needed to help workers keep abreast of the changing environments in which child maltreatment occurs.

Dr. Gelles observed during the August 2001 CAPTA reauthorization hearing that during the 1970s, 1980s, and 1990s, "the field of child welfare has not been professionalized." Child welfare workers, who are sent to the field to investigate alleged child abuse and neglect, do not have the proper training and skills to assess the problem. Moreover, workers use risk assessment methods that are geared more to checking out such things as the cleanliness and neatness of the home. Finally, workers believe that parents are capable of changing their abusive behavior and that, if they are provided with the resources to do so, children could be kept in the home.

During the second hearing on the reauthorization of CAPTA on October 17, 2001, Sandra P. Alexander, executive director of the Georgia Council on Child Abuse, observed that, although child abuse is considered a crime, "well-meaning but poorly prepared" social workers are sent out alone to investigate suspected child maltreatment. And, since these workers believe they should try to preserve the family, many might end up causing more risk to children.

Slipping through the Cracks

CPS also has problems tracking families who move out of its jurisdiction without leaving a forwarding address. In June 2001 police in Hutchins, Texas, found an eight-year-old girl living in the lice-infested closet of a mobile home, where her mother, stepfather, and five sib-

lings lived. For about five years the girl had been living in her own squalor in the four-by-six-foot closet with very little food. When she was discovered, the child was just three feet tall, weighing 25 pounds. Five other siblings living in the same home had not suffered abuse.

CPS had investigated the family in 1995 and 1996, but lost track of it when the family moved. CPS officials claimed the case was eventually closed because they had other cases that required more attention. In January 2002 the mother received a sentence of life imprisonment without parole. On December 12, 2002, the child's stepfather was also sentenced to life imprisonment without parole.

In Florida the child welfare agency could not account for the disappearance of a five-year-old foster child, who had been missing for more than a year before the agency noticed her absence. As of July 2002 the agency had lost track of more than 530 children who, it claimed, had been kidnapped by parents or had run away from foster homes. In August 2002 the *South Florida Sun-Sentinel,* after examining 24 cases of missing foster children in three counties, reported it had located one-third of the children within a month. One boy, missing for eight years, was tracked down in the Dominican Republic after the *Sentinel* made three phone calls. That same month the child welfare agency in Michigan found that 302 children in its care were also missing. About 200 children were from Wayne County, which includes Detroit.

Problem of Substance Abuse

Child welfare workers are faced with the growing problem of substance abuse among families involved with the child welfare system. According to the U.S. Department of Health and Human Services (HHS), the latest *National Household Survey on Drug Abuse* that tracked children living with substance-abusing parents found that about 8.3 million children under age 18 in the United States, comprising 11 percent of all children in the nation, lived with such parents (*Blending Perspectives and Building Common Ground: A Report to Congress on Substance Abuse and Child Protection,* Washington, DC, 1999). Among these children, 3.8 million lived with an alcoholic parent, 2.1 million lived with a parent having an illicit drug problem, and another 2.4 million lived with parents who abused both alcohol and illicit drugs. (See Figure 3.3.)

The HHS noted that about one-third to two-thirds of substantiated child maltreatment reports (those having sufficient evidence to support the allegation of maltreatment) involved substance abuse. Younger children, especially infants, are more likely to be victimized by substance-abusing parents, and the maltreatment is more likely to consist of neglect than abuse. Many children experience neglect when a parent is under the influence of alcohol or is out of the home looking for drugs. Even when the parent is at home, he or she may be psychologically unavailable to the children.

FIGURE 3.4

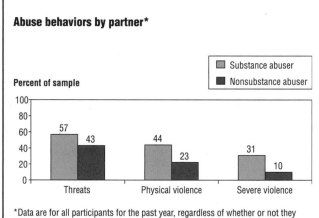

Abuse behaviors by partner*

Percent of sample

*Data are for all participants for the past year, regardless of whether or not they had a partner. Threats include physical violence; physical violence includes hitting or slapping partner; and severe violence includes beating up partner.

SOURCE: Jon Morgenstern, Annette Riordan, Barbara S. McCrady, Kimberly Blanchard, Katherine H. McVeigh, and Thomas W. Irwin, "Figure 10.B: Abuse Behaviors by Partner," in *Barriers to Employability Among Women on TANF With a Substance Abuse Problem,* [Online] http://www.acf.dhhs.gov/programs/opre/barriers_employ/barriers_employ.pdf [accessed October 13, 2002]

FIGURE 3.5

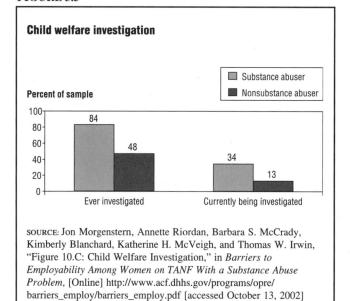

Child welfare investigation

Percent of sample

SOURCE: Jon Morgenstern, Annette Riordan, Barbara S. McCrady, Kimberly Blanchard, Katherine H. McVeigh, and Thomas W. Irwin, "Figure 10.C: Child Welfare Investigation," in *Barriers to Employability Among Women on TANF With a Substance Abuse Problem,* [Online] http://www.acf.dhhs.gov/programs/opre/barriers_employ/barriers_employ.pdf [accessed October 13, 2002]

A comprehensive study by the National Center on Addiction and Substance Abuse at Columbia University (CASA) found that substance abuse or addiction is responsible for 7 of 10 cases of child maltreatment (Jeanne Reid, Peggy Macchetto, and Susan Foster, *No Safe Haven: Children of Substance-Abusing Parents,* New York, NY, 1999). A Child Welfare League of America survey of state child welfare agencies (*Alcohol and Other Drug Survey of State Child Welfare Agencies,* Washington, DC, 1998) found that substance abuse and poverty were the top two main factors contributing to child maltreatment in 40 states.

SUBSTANCE ABUSE AMONG PARENTS ON WELFARE. The HHS has identified substance abuse as a barrier to employment among welfare recipients. While self-reports of substance abuse showed that 3 to 10 percent of women on welfare were substance abusers, these percentages were higher when the women were actually tested for drugs and alcohol—between 19 and 25 percent.

In 2002 a group of researchers from the National Center on Addiction and Substance Abuse at Columbia University, New Jersey Department of Human Services, Rutgers University, and the Mount Sinai School of Medicine conducted a study to examine the problems of substance-abusing women on welfare, also known as recipients of TANF (Temporary Aid to Needy Families) (Jon Morgenstern, Annette Riordan, Barbara S. McCrady, Kimberly Blanchard, Katherine H. McVeigh, and Thomas W. Irwin, *Barriers to Employability among Women on TANF with a Substance Abuse Problem,* October 3, 2002). The researchers found that, on average, the typical substance-

abusing woman had been on welfare for about 12 years since her 18th birthday. More than one-third (36 percent) received welfare for more than 15 years. About 40 percent reported having serious family problems in the month prior to the study. Twenty percent reported living with a partner who used drugs or drank alcohol. Compared to nonsubstance-abusing women receiving welfare benefits, substance abusers experienced higher rates of domestic violence. More than half (57 percent) had been threatened with physical violence by their partners, 44 percent had been physically abused (hit or slapped), and 31 percent had suffered severe violence (beaten up). (See Figure 3.4.)

The substance-abusing women typically had three to four children. At the time of the study, one-third (34 percent) were being investigated by CPS. More than 8 of 10 (84 percent) reported having been investigated by CPS at some time in the past. (See Figure 3.5.) Those who had ever been involved with CPS indicated having been investigated an average number of seven times.

SUBSTANCE ABUSE AMONG PREGNANT WOMEN. Illicit drug use among pregnant women continues to be a national problem. Each year the *National Household Survey on Drug Abuse* asks female respondents ages 15 to 44 about their pregnancy status and illicit drug use the month prior to the survey (*Results from the 2001 National Household Survey on Drug Abuse: Volume I. Summary of National Findings,* Substance Abuse and Mental Health Services Administration, Office of Applied Studies, Rockville, MD, 2002). In 2000 and 2001, 3.7 percent of respondents reported using illicit drugs during the past month. Females 15 to 17 years old had the highest illicit drug use (15.1 percent). (See Figure 3.6.) Although the overall rate for pregnant women was lower than that for nonpregnant

FIGURE 3.6

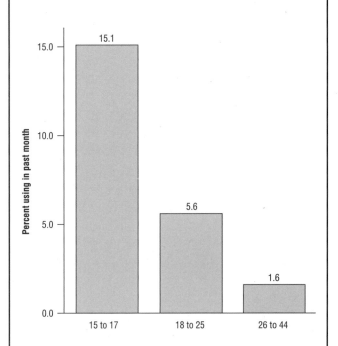

Illicit drug use during the past month among pregnant women, by age: 2000–2001 annual averages

SOURCE: "Figure 2.10. Past Month Illicit Drug Use among Pregnant Women, by Age: 2000-2001 Annual Averages," in *Results from the 2001 National Household Survey on Drug Abuse: Volume I. Summary of National Findings*, U.S. Department of Health and Human Services, Office of Applied Studies, Substance Abuse and Mental Health Services Administration, Rockville, MD, 2002

TABLE 3.2

Respondents observing an act of abuse and/or neglect, and their response to such observation

Observation	Yes	No	Total
Have you ever seen an adult neglect a child? (e.g. ignore a child's needs, failure to feed, withhold affection, etc.)	55%	42%	47%
Have you ever seen an adult physically abuse a child?	36%	30%	32%
Have you ever seen an adult emotionally abuse a child? (e.g. insult, taunt, harass, etc.)	71%	63%	66%
Total number of respondents	*449*	*799*	*1250*

Response to Observation	Yes	No	Total
Took action	62%	52%	56%
Failure to take action	36%	47%	43%
Total number of respondents	*354*	*574*	*930*

SOURCE: Deborah Daro, "Table 4: Respondents observing an act of abuse and/or neglect, and their response to such observation," in *Public Opinion and Behaviors Regarding Child Abuse Prevention: 1999 Survey*, National Center on Child Abuse Prevention Research, Prevent Child Abuse America, Chicago, IL, November 1999

women (8.3 percent), the rate of use for 15- to 17-year-olds was nearly equal that of their nonpregnant counterparts (14.1 percent).

Holding States Accountable

In February 2002 the HHS released the second in a series of annual reports on the states' performance in meeting the needs of at-risk children who have entered the child welfare system. The *Child Welfare Outcomes 1999: Annual Report* (HHS, Administration for Children and Families, Washington, DC) was required by the 1997 Adoption and Safe Families Act (ASFA; Public Law 105-89).

ASFA gives states more flexibility in interpreting the "reasonable efforts" required to reunify children with their birth families. When victims cannot safely return home, states can start proceedings to terminate parental rights for children who have been in foster care for 15 of the previous 22 months. Children can then be placed in permanent homes. The *Child Welfare Outcomes 1999: Annual Report* showed that in fiscal year 1999 (October 1, 1998, to September 30, 1999), 297,000 children entered foster care. About 251,000 exited foster care. Fifty-nine percent were reunited with their parents or caretakers, 10

percent went to live with relatives, 16 percent were adopted, and 7 percent were emancipated (recognized by the court as an adult). Three percent were transferred to another CPS agency and another 3 percent were put under guardianship. Two percent of foster children had run away. As of September 30, 2001, an estimated 565,000 children remained in foster care.

ASFA now requires that a set of outcome measures be developed to assess how states are meeting the needs of maltreated children, those in foster care, and those who are waiting for adoption. States will receive bonuses for increasing the number of adoptions and for shortening the time frames for permanent placement decisions for children. States that do not protect the children adequately, however, will be penalized.

Lives Saved

Although CPS agencies have had many problems and are often unable to perform as effectively as they should, many thousands of maltreated children have been identified, many lives have been saved, and many more have been taken out of dangerous environments. It is impossible to tally the number of child abuse cases that might have ended in death. These children have been saved by changes in the laws, by awareness and reporting, and by the efforts of the professionals who intervened on their behalf.

PUBLIC INVOLVEMENT IN PREVENTING CHILD MALTREATMENT

The latest survey by Prevent Child Abuse America (formerly the National Committee to Prevent Child Abuse) asked the American public if they had observed certain acts of abuse and/or neglect as adults (Deborah Daro, *Pub-*

lic Opinion and Behaviors Regarding Child Abuse Prevention: 1999 Survey, Chicago, IL, November 1999). More than half (55 percent) reported having seen a parent neglect a child, and 71 percent reported having seen a parent emotionally abuse a child. (See Table 3.2.) The survey found that respondents with children under age 18 were more likely to report having seen these behaviors.

Overall, 56 percent of all respondents who saw an abusive or neglectful behavior reported responding to this observation. Forty-three percent failed to take action. (See Table 3.2.) Those polled who responded to the situation reported using some combination of strategies, including calming or scolding the abusing parent, giving the abuser a disapproving look, distracting the child or removing him or her from the situation, or alerting an authority to what was happening. Approximately half of those who did not respond to the child maltreatment believed it was "none of their business" or were not sure how to respond.

REFORM OF THE REPORTING AND INVESTIGATING PROCESS

Over the years, child advocates and critics of CPS have called for the reform of child maltreatment reporting and investigation procedures. The Harvard Executive Session, a task force of child welfare administrators, practitioners, policy makers, and experts, suggested a new model for child protection.

The Harvard model of child protection called for a sharing of responsibilities between CPS and the community. CPS would respond to cases involving higher-risk cases of maltreatment, while other public or private agencies in the community would respond to lower-risk cases. These actions would ensure that the system acts aggressively to protect children at higher risk of maltreatment, while not intervening in a coercive manner with families at lower risk.

The Harvard model also stressed the importance of recruiting "informal helpers" to support at-risk families. The task force felt that, since abusive or neglectful parents may have been child maltreatment victims themselves, extended family members may not be ideal protectors for the children. In addition, there may be few social supports within poor neighborhoods for at-risk children. The model suggested that the larger community can provide the support and protection these children need ("Rethinking the Paradigm for Child Protection," The Future of Children: Protecting Children from Abuse and Neglect, vol. 8, no. 1, Spring 1998).

Preventing Inappropriate Reporting

Douglas J. Besharov, the first director of the U.S. National Center on Child Abuse and Neglect of the HHS, believes that abused and neglected children are dying,

both because neglect and abuse are not being reported to the authorities and because the authorities are being overwhelmed by the need to investigate inappropriate reports. In "Four Commentaries: How We Can Better Protect Children from Abuse and Neglect" (The Future of Children: Protecting Children from Abuse and Neglect, vol. 8, no. 1, Spring 1998), Besharov suggested various steps to overhaul the child protection system:

- Rewrite child maltreatment laws to clarify the reportable parental behaviors that put children at risk of abuse and neglect.

- Provide comprehensive continuing public education and training concerning conditions that warrant reporting as well as those that do not.

- Put in place policies and procedures for screening reports of maltreatment.

- Modify liability laws to address "good-faith" reporters as well as those who have failed to report what may later turn out to be actual child maltreatment.

- Let reporters know the outcome of their personal involvement, which in a later situation may help them assess the presence of maltreatment.

- Set up formal reporting policies for such public and private agencies as schools and child care centers.

IMPROPER ACCUSATION

Although people are outraged by stories about severely abused and/or neglected children missed by the authorities, there is also a backlash movement against the intrusiveness of CPS and wrongs committed when parents are unjustly accused of abuse. Some parents claim they keep their children home from school if they have a bruise for fear the teacher will report the parents and have them investigated for abuse.

In Wounded Innocents: The Real Victims of the War against Child Abuse (Prometheus Books, Buffalo, NY, 1990), Richard Wexler wrote that, because of the increasing number of accusations of alleged child molestation in the early 1980s, caregivers became afraid to show affection toward children. After a teacher in Waukeegan, Illinois, was charged with sexual abuse and sued by two parents, the Chicago Teachers' Union provided "self-defense" guidelines to its teachers. Educators were told to use public areas when holding conferences with students and to be discreet in their physical contacts when praising, rewarding, or comforting students.

Other critics of CPS point out that a large proportion of reports to CPS are unsubstantiated. For example, according to the HHS (Child Maltreatment 2000, Administration for Children and Families, Washington, DC,

2002), 58.4 percent of the reports of child maltreatment were unsubstantiated.

Hot lines for reporting abuse and neglect accept all calls, even when the reporter cannot give a reason why he or she thinks the child is being maltreated. In addition, CPS is now called upon to handle many cases that previously would have been handled by other agencies. Cutbacks in funding have pushed related problems of poverty, homelessness, truancy, and delinquency on CPS because it is known as a social agency that will at least investigate the reports.

Overreporting Needs to Be Controlled

Wexler, in *Wounded Innocents,* claimed that one reason the number of abuse reports is deceptive is that in the majority of reports, the children have not been maltreated at all. He explained that reports of child maltreatment are sometimes made when a parent is guilty of nothing more than poverty. For example, child abuse was reported in the following cases:

- A woman's home was in disrepair.

- A man could not pay his utility bill.

- A woman could not afford to buy a pair of eyeglasses for her child.

- A woman was evicted from two apartments because of "no children allowed" rules.

The Problem May Be Underreporting

David Finkelhor and Donileen Loseke, in "The Main Problem Is Still Underreporting, not Overreporting" (*Current Controversies on Family Violence,* Sage Publications, Inc., Thousand Oaks, CA, 1993), asserted that the problem is underreporting, not overreporting. One statistic they offered in support of their assertion is that, when adults are asked whether they were abused as children, the percentages are far higher than the number of children who are reported each year. If, for example, 15 percent of women and 5 percent of men were sexually abused in childhood (a low estimate according to some experts), this would translate to yearly rates of child abuse two to three times higher than the rates reported today.

Finkelhor and Loseke also rejected claims that many reports of abuse are "minor situations." They offered examples of cases that they said would be dismissed by critics but which they insisted are part of the crucial effort to discover an abusive situation before serious injury occurs. These include cases of emotional abuse, such as when a child is locked in a room or threatened with death; physical neglect, such as when a parent leaves young children alone, but the children do not come to any harm; or physical abuse, such as when a child is shot at but missed.

Diana E. H. Russell and Rebecca M. Bolen, experts in child sexual abuse research, also observed the underre-

porting of child maltreatment cases. In *The Epidemic of Rape and Child Sexual Abuse in the United States* (Sage Publications, Inc., Thousand Oaks, CA, 2000), the authors concluded from their studies of child sexual abuse, conducted since the 1980s, that just one-half of the cases of incestuous abuse known to professionals are reported. Incestuous abuse involves the use of a child for sexual satisfaction by family members.

Harassment

A small proportion of reports are false or ill-considered, either because the reporter has been mistaken or because the reporter has been deliberately lying to get the alleged abuser in trouble. Sexual abuse is the most common form of false accusation because it is such a heinous crime and does not require physical evidence.

False, vindictive reports are sometimes made anonymously to CPS to harass parents. Richard Wexler in *Wounded Innocents* reported how, in one case, social workers demanded entry to a woman's house more than five times in a two-year period. They ordered her to wake up her sleeping children and strip them naked while social workers examined them for signs of abuse. All of the reports turned out to be false, but the caller, whose anonymity was protected by the law, could start the process again with a simple phone call.

IS THERE BIAS IN REPORTING?

Some critics claim that reporting of child abuse and neglect is biased against parents and caretakers in the lower socioeconomic classes. Brett Drake and Susan Zuravin, in "Bias in Child Maltreatment Reporting: Revisiting the Myth of Classlessness" (*American Journal of Orthopsychiatry,* vol. 68, no. 2, April 1998), discussed four forms of potential bias that may be responsible for the overrepresentation of child maltreatment among the poor in CPS caseloads.

Visibility bias, also called "exposure bias," is the belief that poor families, who are more likely to use such public services as welfare agencies and public hospitals, tend to be noticed by potential reporters. The researchers claimed that, to date, no scientific studies have ever been done to investigate the visibility bias theory.

Drake and Zuravin surmised that if the visibility bias does exist, it will follow that mandated reporters who have more contact with the poor will file more reports of abuse among poor children. They studied six Missouri sites with the lowest percentage of families living below the poverty line. When they compared the mandated reports about child maltreatment among upper middle-class suburban families (44.4 percent) and among inner-city poor families (49.2 percent), they did not find a large overrepresentation of the poor.

The researchers also noted that mandated reporters (for example, law enforcement, medical, and social services personnel), who are more likely to come into contact with a larger proportion of poor families than nonpoor families, accounted for one-third of all referrals. This proportion could possibly be responsible for the overrepresentation of maltreatment reports of poor families.

Labeling bias refers to the predisposition to look for and find maltreatment among certain groups of individuals. Review of empirical studies showed no such bias existed among mandated reporters. Drake and Zuravin found, in one study, that Head Start personnel were not likely to look for signs of maltreatment among the children in their care just because these children belonged to a lower socioeconomic status.

Reporting bias implies a person's failure to report what he or she suspects to be child maltreatment among certain groups. In the late 1970s and early 1980s, studies found that professionals were very likely not to report child maltreatment among higher-income families. The authors found that mandated professionals were more likely to report maltreatment because of the legal ramifications associated with failure to comply with child maltreatment laws. Hence, the reporting bias theory does not hold true.

Substantiation bias describes any tendency on the part of CPS investigators to base substantiation conclusions on such factors as a family's socioeconomic status. Empirical studies show that this is not the case.

The researchers concluded that, although a large percentage of child abuse and neglect occurs among the poor, empirical studies have shown that this overrepresentation is not a result of reporting biases.

CHAPTER 4
HOW MANY CHILDREN ARE MALTREATED?

Statistics on child abuse are difficult to interpret and compare because there is very little consistency in how information is collected. The definitions of abuse vary from study to study, as do the methods of counting incidents of abuse. Some methods count only reported cases of abuse. Some statistics are based on estimates projected from a small study, while others are based on interviews. In addition, it is virtually impossible to know the extent of child maltreatment that occurs in the privacy of the home.

INCIDENCE AND PREVALENCE OF CHILD MALTREATMENT

Researchers use two terms—incidence and prevalence—to describe the estimates of the number of victims of child abuse and neglect. Andrea J. Sedlak and Diane D. Broadhurst (*Third National Incidence Study of Child Abuse and Neglect* [NIS-3], U.S. Department of Health and Human Services, National Center on Child Abuse and Neglect, Washington, DC, 1996) defined incidence as the number of new cases occurring in the population during a given period. The incidence of child maltreatment is measured in terms of incidence rate: the number of children per 1,000 children in the U.S. population who are maltreated annually. A major source of incidence data is surveys based on official reports by child protective services (CPS) agencies and community professionals. Private national organizations, such as Prevent Child Abuse America, also collect and analyze data regarding the incidence of child abuse and neglect.

Prevalence, as defined by NIS-3, refers to the total number of child maltreatment cases in the population at a given time. Some researchers use lifetime prevalence to denote the number of people who have had at least one experience of child maltreatment in their lives. To measure the prevalence of child maltreatment, researchers use self-reported surveys of parents and child victims. Examples of self-reported surveys are the landmark 1975 *National Family Violence Survey* and the 1985 *National Family Violence Resurvey* conducted by Murray A. Straus and Richard J. Gelles.

Official Reports

Studies based on official reports depend on a number of things happening before an incident of abuse can be recorded. The victim must be seen by people outside the home; these people must recognize that the child has been abused. Once they have recognized this fact, they must then decide whether to report the abuse and find out where to report it. Once CPS receives and screens the report for appropriateness, it can then take action.

In some cases the initial call to CPS is prompted by a problem that needs to be handled by a different agency. It may be a case of neglect due to poverty rather than abuse, although the initial report is still recorded as abuse.

For the data to become publicly available, CPS must keep records on its cases and then pass them on to a national group that collects those statistics. Consequently, final reported statistics are understated estimates—valuable as indicators but not definitive findings. It is very unlikely that accurate statistics on child abuse will ever be available.

COLLECTING CHILD MALTREATMENT DATA

The 1974 Child Abuse Prevention and Treatment Act (CAPTA; Public Law 93-247) created the National Center on Child Abuse and Neglect (NCCAN) to coordinate nationwide efforts to protect children from maltreatment. As part of the former U.S. Department of Health, Education, and Welfare, NCCAN commissioned the American Humane Association (AHA) to collect data from the states. The first time the AHA collected data, in 1976, it recorded an estimated 416,000 reports, affecting 669,000 children. Between 1980 and 1985 the AHA reported a 12 percent annual increase in maltreatment reports to CPS agencies. By 1990 reports of child maltreatment had risen to 1.7 million, affecting about 2.7 million children.

In 1985 the federal government stopped funding data collection on child maltreatment. In 1986 the National Committee to Prevent Child Abuse (NCPCA; now called Prevent Child Abuse America) picked up where the government left off. The NCPCA started collecting detailed information from the states on the number of children abused, the characteristics of child abuse, the number of child abuse deaths, and changes in the funding and extent of child welfare services.

In 1988 the Child Abuse Prevention, Adoption and Family Services Act (Public Law 100-294) replaced the 1974 CAPTA. The new law mandated that NCCAN, as part of the U.S. Department of Health and Human Services (HHS), establish a national data collection program on child maltreatment. In 1990 the National Child Abuse and Neglect Data System (NCANDS), designed to fulfill this mandate, began collecting and analyzing child maltreatment data from CPS agencies in the 50 states, the District of Columbia, the territories, and the armed services. The first three surveys were known as *Working Paper 1, Working Paper 2,* and *Child Maltreatment 1992.* NCANDS has since conducted the survey *Child Maltreatment 2000.*

As part of the 1974 CAPTA, Congress also mandated NCCAN to conduct a periodic *National Incidence Study of Child Abuse and Neglect* (NIS). Data on maltreated children were collected not only from CPS agencies but also from professionals in community agencies, such as law enforcement, public health, juvenile probation, mental health, and voluntary social services, as well as from hospitals, schools, and day care centers. The NIS is the single most comprehensive source of information about the incidence of child maltreatment in the United States, because it analyzes the characteristics of child abuse and neglect that are known to community-based professionals, including those characteristics not reported to CPS.

Pursuant to the CAPTA Amendments of 1996 (Public Law 104-235), NCCAN ceased operating as a separate agency. Since then all child maltreatment prevention functions have been consolidated within the Children's Bureau of the HHS.

CPS MALTREATMENT REPORTS

Collecting child maltreatment data from the states is difficult because each state has its own method of gathering and classifying the information. Most states collect data on an incident basis; that is, they count each time a child is reported for abuse or neglect. If the same child is reported several times in one year, each incident is counted. Consequently, the number of incidents of child maltreatment may be greater than the number of maltreated children.

In 2000 CPS agencies received 2,795,220 referrals, or reports, alleging the maltreatment of about 5 million children (*Child Maltreatment 2000,* HHS, Administration for Children and Families, Washington, DC, 2002). (This may include some children who were reported and counted more than once.) States may vary in the rates of child maltreatment reported. States differ not only in definitions of maltreatment but also in the methods of counting reports of abuse. Some states count reports based on the number of incidents or the number of families involved, rather than on the number of children allegedly abused. Other states count all reports to CPS, while others count only investigated reports.

In 2000, 34 states submitted child-level data for each report of alleged maltreatment. The data include, among other things, the demographics about the children and the perpetrators, types of maltreatment, and dispositions (findings after investigation or assessment of the case). The remaining 16 states and the District of Columbia submitted only summary statistics, such as the number of child victims of maltreatment. Nearly 62 percent of the reports (about 1.7 million) were screened in (accepted for further assessment or investigation). Overall, the rate of maltreatment ranged from 17 per 1,000 children (Indiana) to 86.1 per 1,000 children (Alaska) under age 18. (See Table 4.1.)

Dispositions of Investigated Reports

In previous years reports of alleged child maltreatment received one of three major findings after the report was investigated or assessed. Starting with 2000 data, two additional disposition categories were added by some states. Several states, including Louisiana, Minnesota, Missouri, New Jersey, Ohio, Oklahoma, and South Dakota, have established an alternative response program to the traditional investigative approach of responding to reports of alleged child maltreatment. If the child is at a serious and immediate risk of maltreatment, CPS responds with the traditional formal investigation, which may involve removing the child from the home. If it is determined, however, that the parent will not endanger the child, CPS workers use the alternative response to help the family. This involves a more informal approach. Instead of removing the child from the home environment, CPS steps in to assist the whole family by, for example, helping reduce stress that may lead to child abuse through provision of child care, adequate housing, and education in parenting skills. NCANDS used the following dispositions for its 2000 report:

- A disposition of "substantiated" means that sufficient evidence existed to support the allegation of maltreatment or risk of maltreatment.

- A disposition of "indicated or reason to suspect" means that the abuse and/or neglect could not be confirmed, but there was reason to suspect that the child was maltreated or was at risk of maltreatment.

TABLE 4.1

Referrals alleging child abuse, 2000

State	Child Population	Screened-Out Referrals	Screened-Out Rate	Screened-In Referrals	Screened-In Rate	Total Referrals	Total Rate
Alabama	1,123,422	16,600	14.8	22,368	19.9	38,968	34.7
Alaska	190,717	3,592	18.8	12,832	67.3	16,424	86.1
Arizona	1,366,947	217	0.2	32,321	23.6	32,538	23.8
Arkansas	680,369	11,200	16.5	16,822	24.7	28,022	41.2
California	9,249,829	136,900	14.8	243,312	26.3	380,212	41.1
Colorado	1,100,795	19,534	17.7	30,663	27.9	50,197	45.6
Connecticut	841,688	12,875	15.3	29,850	35.5	42,725	50.8
Delaware	194,587	2,900	14.8	5,566	28.6	8,466	43.5
District of Columbia	114,992	203	1.8	4,150	36.1	4,353	37.9
Florida	3,646,340	7,941	2.2	117,523	32.2	125,464	34.4
Georgia	2,169,234	20,647	9.5	52,176	24.1	72,823	33.6
Hawaii	295,767	16,000	54.1	3,298	11.2	19,298	65.2
Idaho	369,030	6,997	19.0	9,063	24.6	16,060	43.5
Illinois	3,245,451	48,000	14.8	60,547	18.7	108,547	33.4
Indiana	1,574,396	11,131	7.1	15,641	9.9	26,772	17.0
Iowa	733,638	11,917	16.2	21,276	29.0	33,193	45.2
Kansas	712,993	10,050	14.1	19,736	27.7	29,786	41.8
Kentucky	994,818	2,122	2.1	41,731	41.9	43,853	44.1
Louisiana	1,219,799	18,100	14.8	22,291	18.3	40,391	33.1
Maine	301,238	10,352	34.4	5,226	17.3	15,578	51.7
Maryland	1,356,172	20,100	14.8	30,985	22.8	51,085	37.7
Massachusetts	1,500,064	19,489	13.0	36,804	24.5	56,293	37.5
Michigan	2,595,767	47,430	18.3	64,794	25.0	112,224	43.2
Minnesota	1,286,894	10,162	7.9	16,565	12.9	26,727	20.8
Mississippi	775,187	11,500	14.8	18,041	23.3	29,541	38.1
Missouri	1,427,692	56,590	39.6	47,881	33.5	104,471	73.2
Montana	230,062	3,400	14.8	10,092	43.9	13,492	58.6
Nebraska	450,242	5,707	12.7	6,186	13.7	11,893	26.4
Nevada	511,799	7,600	14.8	12,797	25.0	20,397	39.9
New Hampshire	309,562	7,573	24.5	5,736	18.5	13,309	43.0
New Jersey	2,087,558	30,900	14.8	38,330	18.4	69,230	33.2
New Mexico	508,574	9,743	19.2	12,485	24.5	22,228	43.7
New York	4,690,107	141,028	30.1	140,446	29.9	281,474	60.0
North Carolina	1,964,047	29,100	14.8	61,167	31.1	90,267	46.0
North Dakota	160,849	2,400	14.8	4,054	25.2	6,454	40.1
Ohio	2,888,339	42,700	14.8	73,798	25.6	116,498	40.3
Oklahoma	892,360	18,364	20.6	34,791	39.0	53,155	59.6
Oregon	846,526	17,824	21.1	17,728	20.9	35,552	42.0
Pennsylvania	2,922,221	65,226	22.3	22,694	7.8	87,920	30.1
Rhode Island	247,822	4,799	19.4	7,573	30.6	12,372	49.9
South Carolina	1,009,641	5,693	5.6	19,084	18.9	24,777	24.5
South Dakota	202,649	3,000	14.8	4,843	23.9	7,843	38.7
Tennessee	1,398,521	13,028	9.3	35,805	25.6	48,833	34.9
Texas	5,886,759	29,769	5.1	119,013	20.2	148,782	25.3
Utah	718,698	9,398	13.1	15,680	21.8	25,078	34.9
Vermont	147,523	2,200	14.8	2,948	20.0	5,148	34.9
Virginia	1,738,262	16,180	9.3	22,511	13.0	38,691	22.3
Washington	1,513,843	42,746	28.2	24,406	16.1	67,152	44.4
West Virginia	402,393	6,175	15.3	16,525	41.1	22,700	56.4
Wisconsin	1,368,756	20,300	14.8	32,713	23.9	53,013	38.7
Wyoming	128,873	2,285	17.7	2,666	20.7	4,951	38.4
Total/Weighted Average	72,293,812	1,069,687	14.8	1,725,533	23.9	2,795,220	38.7
Number Reporting	51	35	35	49	49	35	35

Note: Screened-in referrals are those that are deemed appropriate for investigation or assessment.
Screened-out referrals are those that are not deemed appropriate for investigation or assessment.
The national screened-out rate, 14.8 screened-out referrals per 1,000 children in the population, was calculated from the screened-out referrals and child populations in the 35 states that reported screened-out data. Screened-out referrals in the 35 reporting states were compared to the total child populations in those states to get a rate of referrals per 1,000 children. The number of referrals in the other states were estimated by multiplying this rate by their child populations. Similar procedures were followed in developing the national estimated screen-in rate of 38.7.

SOURCE: "Table 2-1: Screened-In and Screened-Out Referrals, 2000," in *Child Maltreatment 2000*, U.S. Department of Health and Human Services, Administration for Children and Families, Washington, DC, 2002

• A disposition of "unsubstantiated" means that no maltreatment occurred or sufficient evidence did not exist to conclude that the child was maltreated or was at risk of being maltreated.

• A disposition of "alternative response—victim" means that, within the alternative response approach, the child was identified as a victim of maltreatment.

• A disposition of "alternative response—nonvictim" means that within the alternative response approach, the child was not identified as a victim of maltreatment.

FIGURE 4.1

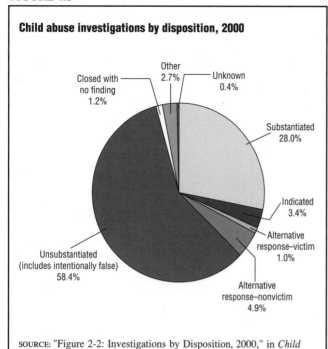

Child abuse investigations by disposition, 2000

SOURCE: "Figure 2-2: Investigations by Disposition, 2000," in *Child Maltreatment 2000*, U.S. Department of Health and Human Services, Administration for Children and Families, Washington, DC, 2002

FIGURE 4.2

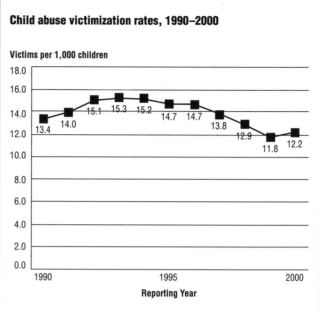

Child abuse victimization rates, 1990–2000

SOURCE: "Figure 3-2: Victimization Rates, 1990-2000," in *Child Maltreatment 2000*, U.S. Department of Health and Human Services, Administration for Children and Families, Washington, DC, 2002

Of the more than 1.7 million reports that were screened in or investigated, 58.4 percent were unsubstantiated. More than one-fourth (28 percent) were substantiated, and 3.4 percent were indicated. Of the two new disposition categories, 1 percent were determined alternative response—victim, and 4.9 percent were alternative response—nonvictim. Dispositions that were identified "closed with no finding" referred to cases in which the investigation could not be completed because the family moved out of the jurisdiction, the family could not be found, or the needed reports were not filed within the required time limit. Such dispositions accounted for 1.2 percent. (See Figure 4.1.)

VICTIMS OF MALTREATMENT

Rates of Victimization

In 2000 an estimated 879,000 children were victims of maltreatment in the United States. A total of 12.2 children for every 1,000 children in the population were victims of abuse or neglect. While this rate of victimization was higher than that for 1999 (11.8 per 1,000 children), it was lower than the rates for the previous years in the 1990s. The rate of maltreatment had peaked at 15.3 per 1,000 children in 1993. (See Figure 4.2.)

Types of Maltreatment

In 2000 more than three out of five maltreated children (62.8 percent) suffered neglect (including medical neglect). Nearly one-fifth (19.3 percent) were physically

abused, and 10.1 percent were sexually abused. An additional 7.7 percent were subjected to emotional, or psychological, maltreatment. Another 16.6 percent experienced other types of maltreatment, including abandonment, congenital drug addiction, and threats to harm a child. Some children were victims of more than one type of maltreatment.

RATES OF MALTREATMENT BY TYPE. Between 1996 and 2000 the rate of neglect (including medical neglect) declined from 8.1 to 7.8 per 1,000 children in the population. The rates for physical abuse and sexual abuse also declined, from 3.5 to 2.3 per 1,000 children for the former, and from 1.8 to 1.2 per 1,000 children for the latter. The rate for psychological abuse rose slightly from 0.9 to 1 per 1,000 children. (See Figure 4.3.)

Age of Victims

In 2000 younger children represented most of the maltreated victims. The older the child gets, the likelihood of abuse decreases. The victimization rate was 15.7 per 1,000 for infants and toddlers up through age 3, compared to 13.3 per 1,000 for children ages 4–7. The rate of victimization for children age 8–11 was 11.8 per 1,000 children, while teens age 16–17 experienced a rate of 5.8 per 1,000 children. (See Figure 4.4.)

The type of maltreatment is typically associated with the child's age. The number of children who suffered neglect decreased with age: 11.5 males and 11 females

FIGURE 4.3

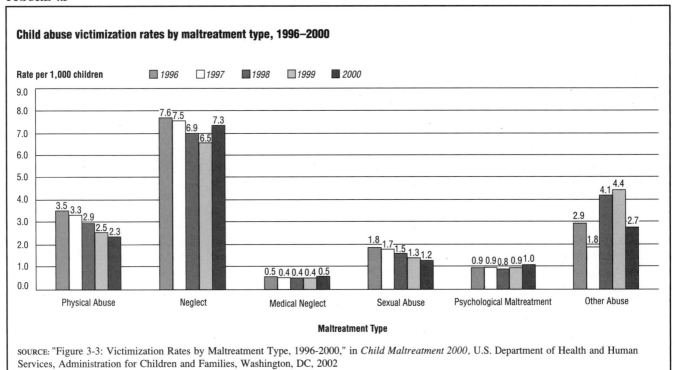

Child abuse victimization rates by maltreatment type, 1996–2000

SOURCE: "Figure 3-3: Victimization Rates by Maltreatment Type, 1996-2000," in *Child Maltreatment 2000,* U.S. Department of Health and Human Services, Administration for Children and Families, Washington, DC, 2002

FIGURE 4.4

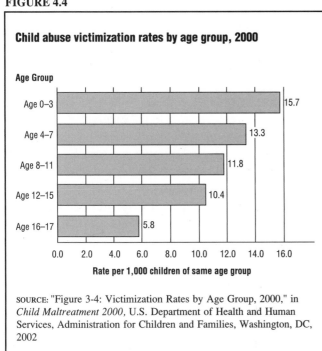

Child abuse victimization rates by age group, 2000

SOURCE: "Figure 3-4: Victimization Rates by Age Group, 2000," in *Child Maltreatment 2000,* U.S. Department of Health and Human Services, Administration for Children and Families, Washington, DC, 2002

TABLE 4.2

Child abuse victimization rates by age, sex, and maltreatment type, 2000

Age/Sex Group	Neglect	Physical Abuse	Sexual Abuse	Medical Neglect	Psychological/ Emotional Abuse
Male 0–3	11.5	2.2	0.2	0.6	1.2
Female 0–3	11.0	1.8	0.5	0.6	1.2
Male 4–7	8.6	2.7	0.7	0.3	1.1
Female 4–7	8.3	2.0	1.6	0.3	1.2
Male 8–11	7.1	1.9	0.5	0.2	0.7
Female 8–11	6.8	2.0	1.8	0.2	1.0
Male 12–15	4.9	2.2	0.4	0.2	0.2
Female 12–15	6.2	3.1	2.9	0.2	0.3
Male 16–17	2.3	1.0	0.3	0.1	0.1
Female 16–17	3.5	2.2	1.7	0.1	0.1
All Males	7.3	2.1	0.4	0.3	0.7
All Females	7.6	2.2	1.7	0.3	0.8
Median Age					
Male	6	8	8	5	7
Female	7	10	11	5	8

Based on data from 34 States: Arizona, Arkansas, California, Connecticut, Delaware, Florida, Hawaii, Illinois, Indiana, Iowa, Kansas, Kentucky, Louisiana, Maine, Massachusetts, Michigan, Minnesota, Missouri, Nebraska, New Hampshire, New Jersey, New Mexico, New York, North Carolina, Oklahoma, Pennsylvania, Rhode Island, Texas, Utah, Vermont, Virginia, Washington, West Virginia, and Wyoming.
N = 327,257 male and 346,981 female report-child victim pairs.
A report-child victim pair counts each child in each report in which he or she is found to be a victim, thus some children are counted more than once. Each child can be the victim of more than one type of maltreatment.
Rates were based on the number of victims of maltreatment for each age/sex group, divided by the same age/sex group in the population and multiplied by 1,000.

SOURCE: "Table 3-10: Victimization Rates by Age, Sex, and Maltreatment Type, 2000 (DCDC, Child File)," in *Child Maltreatment 2000,* U.S. Department of Health and Human Services, Administration for Children and Families, Washington, DC, 2002

per 1,000 for infants and toddlers up through age 3, compared with 2.3 males and 3.5 females per 1,000 for those 16–17 years old. In contrast, the victimization rate for children who were sexually abused is higher among 16- and 17-year-olds than it is with 0- through 3-year-olds. (See Table 4.2.)

TABLE 4.3

Child abuse victims to perpetrator relationship by maltreatment type, 2000

Perpetrators Relationship to Child Victims	Maltreatment Type					
	Neglect		Physical Abuse		Sexual Abuse	
	Number	Percent	Number	Percent	Number	Percent
Female Parent Acting Alone	131,166	46.9	28,130	32.1	1,659	3.9
Male Parent Acting Alone	33,866	12.1	24,718	28.2	9,057	21.5
Both Parents	61,200	21.9	11,826	13.5	3,409	8.1
Female Parent and Other	18,382	6.6	5,206	5.9	3,276	7.8
Male Parent and Other	4,831	1.7	1,547	1.8	1,690	4.0
Other Relative(s)	7,998	2.9	4,169	4.8	8,180	19.4
Child Day Care Provider(s)	2,302	0.8	794	0.9	1,141	2.7
Foster Parent(s)	1,765	0.6	937	1.1	424	1.0
Residential Facility Staff	497	0.2	225	0.3	175	0.4
Other	10,451	3.7	7,146	8.2	10,520	24.9
Unknown	7,484	2.7	2,909	3.3	2,667	6.3
Total	**279,942**	**100.1**	**87,607**	**100.1**	**42,198**	**100.0**

Based on data from 28 States: Arizona, Arkansas, Connecticut, Florida, Hawaii, Illinois, Indiana, Iowa, Kansas, Kentucky, Louisiana, Maine, Massachusetts, Michigan, Minnesota, Missouri, Nebraska, New Jersey, New Mexico, New York, Oklahoma, Pennsylvania, Rhode Island, Texas, Utah, Vermont, Washington, and Wyoming. Within the maltreatment types, a child victim is counted each time he or she is associated with a maltreatment and a perpetrator. A child may be counted in more than one type of maltreatment. Note that some of the percentage columns may not total 100 percent due to rounding of the category percentages.

SOURCE: "Table 4-4: Victims to Perpetrator Relationship by Maltreatment Type, 2000 (DCDC, Child File)," in *Child Maltreatment 2000*, U.S. Department of Health and Human Services, Administration for Children and Families, Washington, DC, 2002

Gender of Victims

Based on detailed information from 34 states in 2000, more female children (12.6 per 1,000) were maltreated than their male counterparts (10.8 per 1,000). Although victimization rates for both genders were about the same for physical abuse, neglect, medical neglect, and psychological abuse, more than four times as many females were sexually abused than males (1.7 versus 0.4 per 1,000). (See Table 4.2.)

Race and Ethnicity of Victims

In 2000 more than half (50.6 percent) of maltreatment victims were white, and one-quarter (24.7 percent) were black. Hispanics, who may be of any race, accounted for 14.2 percent of the victims. American Indians/Alaska Natives (1.6 percent) and Asians/Pacific Islanders (1.4 percent) made up the lowest proportions of victims.

PERPETRATORS OF CHILD MALTREATMENT

The law considers perpetrators to be those persons who abuse or neglect children under their care. They may be parents, foster parents, other relatives, or other caretakers. In 2000 more than 4 of 5 victims (83.7 percent) were maltreated by one or both parents. Relatives of the victims accounted for another 4.7 percent of perpetrators.

More than three-quarters (78.7 percent) of perpetrators were under age 40, with one-third between the ages of 20 and 29. Perpetrators were most likely to be female (59.9 percent).

Female parents acting alone were responsible for almost half of the cases of neglect (46.9 percent). Male parents, however, acting alone, perpetrated 21.5 percent of sexual abuse cases. Female parents acting alone (32.1 percent) were slightly more likely than male parents acting alone (28.2 percent) to inflict physical abuse on their children. (See Table 4.3.)

DEATHS FROM CHILD MALTREATMENT

Child fatality is the most severe result of abuse and neglect. In 2000 an estimated 1,200 deaths from child maltreatment were reported to CPS and other state agencies, including coroners' offices and fatality review boards. The national fatality rate was about 1.7 deaths per 100,000 children in the general population. Oklahoma reported the highest rate (5.04 per 100,000), followed by the District of Columbia (4.35 per 100,000) and Alaska (4.19 per 100,000). (See Table 4.4.)

Deaths occurred mostly among very young victims of abuse and neglect. Children age five and under accounted for a majority (85.1 percent) of deaths. Of these, infants younger than a year old comprised 43.7 percent of the fatalities. More male children (56.7 percent) died from maltreatment than did female children (43.3 percent).

Neglect alone was responsible for more than one-third (34.9 percent) of maltreatment deaths. About one-quarter (27.8 percent) of fatalities resulted from physical abuse. Another one-fifth (22.2 percent) were caused by a combination of physical abuse and neglect. (See Figure 4.5.) States also provided data on the victims' prior contact with CPS agencies. About 15 percent of the victims' families had received family preservation services during the five years before the deaths occurred.

TABLE 4.4

Child fatalities, 2000

State	Child Population	CPS Reported Child Fatalities	Child Fatalities Reported in Agency File	Total Child Fatalities	Fatalities Per 100,000 Children
Alabama	1,123,422	27		27	2.40
Alaska	190,717	8		8	4.19
Arizona	1,366,947	7	0	7	0.51
Arkansas	680,369	12		12	1.76
California	9,249,829	30	23	30	0.32
Colorado	1,100,795	31		31	2.82
Connecticut	841,688	4	4	8	0.95
Delaware					
District of Columbia	114,992	5		5	4.35
Florida	3,646,340	65		65	1.78
Georgia	2,169,234	45		45	2.07
Hawaii	295,767	3		3	1.01
Idaho	369,030	1		1	0.27
Illinois	3,245,451	61	15	76	2.34
Indiana	1,574,396	40	4	44	2.79
Iowa	733,638	10	3	13	1.77
Kansas	712,993	7		7	0.98
Kentucky	994,818	21	0	21	2.11
Louisiana	1,219,799	30	6	36	2.95
Maine	301,238	2	1	3	1.00
Maryland					
Massachusetts	1,500,064		4	4	0.27
Michigan	2,595,767		49	49	1.89
Minnesota	1,286,894	21		21	1.63
Mississippi	775,187	12		12	1.55
Missouri	1,427,692	48		48	3.36
Montana	230,062	2		2	0.87
Nebraska					
Nevada	511,799	3		3	0.59
New Hampshire	309,562		9	9	2.91
New Jersey	2,087,558	25	12	37	1.77
New Mexico	508,574		6	6	1.18
New York	4,690,107	79		79	1.68
North Carolina	1,964,047		47	47	2.39
North Dakota	160,849	0		0	0.00
Ohio	2,888,339	58		58	2.01
Oklahoma	892,360		45	45	5.04
Oregon	846,526	21		21	2.48
Pennsylvania	2,922,221	38		38	1.30
Rhode Island	247,822	3		3	1.21
South Carolina	1,009,641	20		20	1.98
South Dakota	202,649	6		6	2.96
Tennessee	1,398,521	3		3	0.21
Texas	5,886,759	177		177	3.01
Utah	718,698	12		12	1.67
Vermont	147,523	1	0	1	0.68
Virginia	1,738,262		29	29	1.67
Washington	1,513,843	7	7	14	0.92
West Virginia	402,393	4	0	4	0.99
Wisconsin	1,368,756	10		10	0.73
Wyoming	128,873	1	3	1	0.78
Total/Rate	**70,292,811**	**960**	**267**	**1,201**	**1.71**
Number Reporting	**48**	**41**	**21**	**48**	**48**

The rate of fatalities per 100,000 children, 1.71, is based on the child population of only those states that provided data. This rate was applied to the total U.S. population, resulting in a national estimate of 1,236. These deaths were reported to CPS agencies and, in some instances, might have included deaths identified by such other agencies as a coroner's office or a fatality review board.

SOURCE: "Table 5-2: Child Fatalities, 2000," in *Child Maltreatment 2000*, U.S. Department of Health and Human Services, Administration for Children and Families, Washington, DC, 2002

Perpetrators of Fatalities

In 2000 about four of five (79.1 percent) maltreatment deaths were inflicted by one or both parents of the victims. Compared with maltreatment perpetrators in gener-

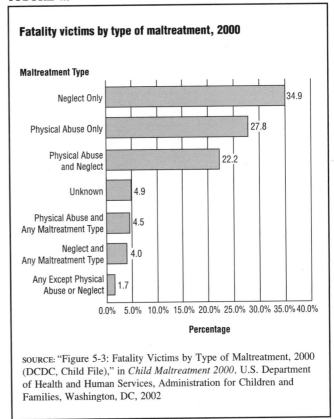

FIGURE 4.5

Fatality victims by type of maltreatment, 2000

Maltreatment Type

- Neglect Only — 34.9
- Physical Abuse Only — 27.8
- Physical Abuse and Neglect — 22.2
- Unknown — 4.9
- Physical Abuse and Any Maltreatment Type — 4.5
- Neglect and Any Maltreatment Type — 4.0
- Any Except Physical Abuse or Neglect — 1.7

0.0% 5.0% 10.0% 15.0% 20.0% 25.0% 30.0% 35.0% 40.0%

Percentage

SOURCE: "Figure 5-3: Fatality Victims by Type of Maltreatment, 2000 (DCDC, Child File)," in *Child Maltreatment 2000*, U.S. Department of Health and Human Services, Administration for Children and Families, Washington, DC, 2002

al, persons who commit fatal child abuse are often young adults in their mid-twenties. In the 1998 state reports to NCANDS, in which perpetrator ages were included, nearly two-thirds (62.3 percent) were under age 30. NCANDS researchers surmised that fatality victims, who are generally younger than other maltreatment victims, are more likely to have younger parents. In 1998 more females (60 percent) than males (39 percent) caused maltreatment deaths.

CHILD FATALITY REVIEW TEAMS

Historically, law enforcement, child protection agencies, and public health agencies worked separately in investigating child maltreatment deaths. In response to the increasing number of deaths, all states have created multidisciplinary child fatality review teams to investigate the deaths and develop solutions to support families in crisis. These teams consist of prosecutors, medical examiners, law enforcement personnel, CPS personnel, health care providers, and other professionals.

State teams are formed to work with local teams, which are responsible for the management of individual cases. The number of child deaths reviewed by a local team depends on the county size. A local team in a large county may review just cases referred by the medical examiner, while a team in a smaller county may review child deaths from all causes.

TABLE 4.5

National incidence of maltreatment under the Harm Standard in the NIS-3 (1993), and comparison with the NIS-2 (1986) and the NIS-1 (1980) Harm Standard estimates

Harm Standard Maltreatment Category	NIS-3 Estimates 1993		Comparisons With Earlier Studies					
			NIS-2: 1986			NIS-1: 1980		
	Total No. of Children	Rate per 1,000 Children	Total No. of Children	Rate per 1,000 Children		Total No. of Children	Rate per 1,000 Children	
All Maltreatment	1,553,800	23.1	931,000	14.8	*	625,100	9.8	*
Abuse:								
All Abuse	743,200	11.1	507,700	8.1	m	336,600	5.3	*
Physical Abuse	381,700	5.7	269,700	4.3	m	199,100	3.1	*
Sexual Abuse	217,700	3.2	119,200	1.9	*	42,900	0.7	*
Emotional Abuse	204,500	3.0	155,200	2.5	ns	132,700	2.1	m
Neglect:								
All Neglect	879,000	13.1	474,800	7.5	*	315,400	4.9	*
Physical Neglect	338,900	5.0	167,800	2.7	*	103,600	1.6	*
Emotional Neglect	212,800	3.2	49,200	0.8	*	56,900	0.9	*
Educational Neglect	397,300	5.9	284,800	4.5	ns	174,000	2.7	*

* The difference between this and the NIS-3 estimate is significant at or below the p < .05 level.
m The difference between this and the NIS-3 estimate is statistically marginal (i.e., .l0 > p > .05).
ns The difference between this and the NIS-3 estimate is neither significant nor marginal (p > .10).
Note: Estimated totals are rounded to the nearest 100.

SOURCE: Andrea J. Sedlak and Diane D. Broadhurst, "National incidence of maltreatment under the Harm Standard in the NIS-3 (1993), and comparison with the NIS-2 (1986) and the NIS-1 (1980) Harm Standard estimates," in *The Third National Incidence Study of Child Abuse and Neglect,* U.S. Department of Health and Human Services, National Center on Child Abuse and Neglect, Washington, DC, 1996

Are Child Maltreatment Fatalities Properly Reflected in Death Certificates?

Experts believe that there are likely more deaths each year due to child abuse and neglect than are reported to CPS and other agencies. The U.S. Advisory Board on Child Abuse and Neglect, in *A Nation's Shame: Fatal Child Abuse and Neglect in the United States* (HHS, Washington, DC, 1995), reported that an estimated 2,000 children (a rate of five children a day) die each year as a result of maltreatment. The National Center for Prosecution of Child Abuse, which provides aid and information to investigators, prosecutors, and professionals working for child maltreatment litigation, estimated the number of fatalities to be as high as 5,000.

According to Tessa L. Crume et al., although the federal government had concluded in 1993 that death certificates underreported child maltreatment fatalities, to date it has not done anything to remedy the problem. NCANDS, the only system that tracks child maltreatment deaths, may not provide complete information because most states report child fatalities only from cases that reach CPS. To determine whether child maltreatment is ascertained in death certificates, the researchers compared data collected by a child fatality review committee (CFRC) on child fatalities in Colorado between 1990 and 1998 with the death certificates issued for those fatalities ("Under-ascertainment of Child Maltreatment Fatalities by Death Certificates, 1990–1998," *Pediatrics,* vol. 110, no. 2, August 2002).

Crume and her colleagues found that only half of the maltreatment deaths were ascertained by death certificates. Of the 257 deaths confirmed by the CFRC to have resulted from maltreatment, just 147 were noted in the death certificates as such. Female children and non-Hispanic black children were more likely to be linked to higher ascertainment in the death certificates. Maltreatment was also more likely to be confirmed as the contributing factor when the death involved violence, such as bodily force, the use of firearms, or the use of sharp or blunt objects. A lower proportion of deaths (less than 20 percent) was attributed to less obvious child abuse, including neglect and abandonment.

NATIONAL INCIDENCE STUDY OF CHILD ABUSE AND NEGLECT

The *National Incidence Study of Child Abuse and Neglect* (NIS) was a congressionally mandated periodic survey of child maltreatment. The results of the first NIS were published in 1981, and those of the second NIS (NIS-2) in 1988. The most recent NIS, the *Third National Incidence Study of Child Abuse and Neglect,* (NIS-3)(HHS, National Center on Child Abuse and Neglect, Washington, DC), was published in 1996. NIS-3 differed from the annual *Child Maltreatment* reports because NIS-3 findings were based on a nationally representative sample of more than 5,600 professionals in 842 agencies serving 42 counties. NIS-3 included not only child victims investigated by CPS agencies, but also children seen by community institutions (such as day care centers, schools, and hospitals) and other investigating agencies (such as public health departments, police, and courts). In addition, victim counts were unduplicated, which means that each child was counted only once.

Definition Standards

NIS-3 used two standardized definitions of abuse and neglect:

- Harm Standard—required that an act or omission must have resulted in demonstrable harm in order to be considered as abuse or neglect

- Endangerment Standard—allowed children who had not yet been harmed by maltreatment to be counted in the estimates of maltreated children if a non-CPS professional considered them to be at risk of harm or if their maltreatment was substantiated or indicated in a CPS investigation

Incidence of Maltreatment

In 1993, under the Harm Standard, an estimated 1,553,800 children were victims of maltreatment, a 67 percent increase from the NIS-2 estimate (931,000 children) and a 149 percent increase from the first NIS estimate (625,100 children). Significant increases occurred for all types of abuse and neglect, as compared with the two earlier NIS surveys. The more than 1.5 million child victims of maltreatment in 1993 reflected a yearly incidence rate of 23.1 per 1,000 children under age 18, or 1 in 43 children. (See Table 4.5.)

In 1993, under the Endangerment Standard, an estimated 2,815,600 children experienced some type of maltreatment. This figure nearly doubled the NIS-2 estimate of 1,424,400. As with the Harm Standard, marked increases occurred for all types of abuse and neglect. The incidence rate was 41.9 per 1,000 children under age 18, or 1 in 24 children. (See Table 4.6.)

COMPARISON OF MALTREATMENT ESTIMATES UNDER THE TWO STANDARDS. In 1993 the Endangerment Standard included an additional 1,261,800 children under age 18 (an 81 percent increase) beyond those counted under the stricter Harm Standard. This means that children included under the Harm Standard represented 55 percent of those counted under the Endangerment Standard. Harm Standard children accounted for 61 percent of the Endangerment Standard total of all abused children, and 45 percent of the Endangerment Standard total of all neglected children.

Characteristics of Abused Children

GENDER. Under both the Harm and Endangerment Standards, more females were subjected to maltreatment than males. Females were sexually abused about three times more often than males. Males, however, were more

TABLE 4.6

National incidence of maltreatment under the Endangerment Standard in the NIS-3 (1993), and comparison with the NIS-2 (1986) Endangerment Standard estimates

Endangerment Standard Maltreatment Category	NIS-3 Estimates 1993		Comparison With NIS-2 1986		
	Total No. of Children	Rate per 1,000 Children	Total No. of Children	Rate per 1,000 Children	
All Maltreatment	2,815,600	41.9	1,424,400	22.6	*
Abuse:					
All Abuse	1,221,800	18.2	590,800	9.4	*
Physical Abuse	614,100	9.1	311,500	4.9	*
Sexual Abuse	300,200	4.5	133,600	2.1	*
Emotional Abuse	532,200	7.9	188,100	3.0	*
Neglect:					
All Neglect	1,961,300	29.2	917,200	14.6	*
Physical Neglect	1,335,100	19.9	507,700	8.1	*
Emotional Neglect	584,100	8.7	203,000	3.2	*
Educational Neglect	397,300	5.9	284,800	4.5	ns

*The difference between this estimate and the NIS-3 estimate is significant at or below the p < .05 level.
Note: Estimated totals are rounded to the nearest 100.

SOURCE: Andrea J. Sedlak and Diane D. Broadhurst, "National incidence of maltreatment under the Endangerment Standard in the NIS-3 (1993), and comparison with the NIS-2 (1986) Endangerment Standard estimates," in *The Third National Incidence Study of Child Abuse and Neglect,* U.S. Department of Health and Human Services, National Center on Child Abuse and Neglect, Washington, DC, 1996

likely to experience physical and emotional neglect under the Endangerment Standard. Under both standards, males suffered more physical and emotional neglect, while females suffered more educational neglect. Males were at a somewhat greater risk of serious injury and death than females. (See Table 4.7 and Table 4.8.)

AGE. NIS-3 found a lower incidence of maltreatment among younger children, particularly 0- to 5-year-olds. This may be due to the fact that, prior to reaching school age, children are less observable to community professionals, especially educators—the group most likely to report suspected maltreatment. In addition, NIS-3 noted a disproportionate increase in the incidence of maltreatment among children between the ages of 6 and 14. (See Figure 4.6 and Figure 4.7.) Sedlak and Broadhurst, the authors of NIS-3, noted a lower incidence of maltreatment among children older than 14 years. Older children are more likely to escape if the abuse becomes more prevalent or severe. They are also more able to defend themselves and/or fight back.

Under the Harm Standard, only 10 per 1,000 children in the 0–2 age group experienced overall maltreatment. The numbers were significantly higher for children ages 6–17. Under the Endangerment Standard, 26 per 1,000 children ages 0–2 were subjected to overall maltreatment. A slightly higher number of children (29.7 per 1,000

TABLE 4.7

Sex differences in incidence rates per 1,000 children for maltreatment under the Harm Standard in the NIS-3 (1993)

Harm Standard Maltreatment Category	Males	Females	Significance of Difference
All Maltreatment	21.7	24.5	m
Abuse:			
All Abuse	9.5	12.6	*
Physical Abuse	5.8	5.6	ns
Sexual Abuse	1.6	4.9	*
Emotional Abuse	2.9	3.1	ns
Neglect:			
All Neglect	13.3	12.9	ns
Physical Neglect	5.5	4.5	ns
Emotional Neglect	3.5	2.8	ns
Educational Neglect	5.5	6.4	ns
Severity of Injury:			
Fatal	0.04	0.01	ns
Serious	9.3	7.5	m
Moderate	11.3	13.3	ns
Inferred	1.1	3.8	*

* The difference is significant at or below the p < .05 level.
m The difference is statistically marginal (i.e., .10 > p > .05).
ns The difference is neither significant nor marginal (p > .10).

SOURCE: Andrea J. Sedlak and Diane D. Broadhurst, "Sex differences in incidence rates per 1,000 children for maltreatment under the Harm Standard in the NIS-3 (1993)," in *The Third National Incidence Study of Child Abuse and Neglect,* U.S. Department of Health and Human Services, National Center on Child Abuse and Neglect, Washington, DC, 1996

TABLE 4.8

Sex differences in incidence rates per 1,000 children for maltreatment under the Endangerment Standard in the NIS-3 (1993)

Endangerment Standard Maltreatment Category	Males	Females	Significance of Difference
All Maltreatment	40.0	42.3	ns
Abuse:			
All Abuse	16.1	20.2	*
Physical Abuse	9.3	9.0	ns
Sexual Abuse	2.3	6.8	*
Emotional Abuse	8.0	7.7	ns
Neglect:			
All Neglect	29.2	27.6	ns
Physical Neglect	19.7	18.6	ns
Emotional Neglect	9.2	7.8	*
Educational Neglect	5.5	6.4	ns
Severity of Injury:			
Fatal	0.04	0.01	ns
Serious	9.4	7.6	m
Moderate	14.1	15.3	ns
Inferred	2.1	4.6	*
Endangered	14.5	14.8	ns

* The difference is significant at or below the p>.05 level.
m The difference is statistically marginal (i.e., .l0>p>.05).
ns The difference is neither significant nor marginal (p>.10).

SOURCE: Andrea J. Sedlak and Diane D. Broadhurst, "Sex differences in incidence rates per 1,000 children for maltreatment under the Endangerment Standard in the NIS-3," in *The Third National Incidence Study of Child Abuse and Neglect,* U.S. Department of Health and Human Services, National Center on Child Abuse and Neglect, Washington, DC, 1996

children) in the oldest age group (15 to 17 years old) suffered maltreatment of some type. As with the Harm Standard, children between the ages of 6 and 14 had a higher incidence of maltreatment. (See Table 4.6.)

RACE. NIS-3 found no significant differences in race in the incidence of maltreatment. The authors noted that this finding may be somewhat surprising, considering the overrepresentation of black children in the child welfare population and in those served by public agencies. They attributed this lack of race-related difference in maltreatment incidence to the broader range of children identified by NIS-3, compared with the smaller number investigated by public agencies and the even smaller number receiving child protective and other welfare services. NIS-2 also had not found any disproportionate differences in race in relation to maltreatment incidence.

Family Characteristics

FAMILY STRUCTURE. Under the Harm Standard, among children living with single parents, an estimated 27.3 per 1,000 under age 18 suffered some type of maltreatment—almost twice the incidence rate for children living with both parents (15.5 per 1,000). The same rate held true for all types of abuse and neglect. Children living with single parents also had a greater risk of suffering serious injury (10.5 per 1,000) than did those living with both parents (5.8 per 1,000). (See Table 4.9.)

Under the Endangerment Standard, an estimated 52 per 1,000 children living with single parents suffered some type of maltreatment, compared with 26.9 per 1,000 living with both parents. Children in single-parent households were abused at a 45 percent higher rate than those in two-parent households (19.6 versus 13.5 per 1,000) and suffered more than twice as much neglect (38.9 versus 17.6 per 1,000). Children living with single parents (10.5 per 1,000) were also more likely to suffer serious injuries than those living with both parents (5.9 per 1,000). (See Table 4.10.)

FAMILY SIZE. The number of children in the family was related to the incidence of maltreatment. Additional children meant additional tasks and responsibilities for the parents; therefore, it followed that the rates of child maltreatment were higher in these families. Among children in families with four or more children, an estimated 34.5 per 1,000 under the Harm Standard and 68.1 per 1,000 under the Endangerment Standard suffered some type of maltreatment.

Surprisingly, households with only one child had a higher maltreatment incidence rate than did households with two to three children (22 versus 17.7 per 1,000 children under the Harm Standard, and 34.2 versus 34.1 per 1,000 children under the Endangerment Standard). The authors thought that an only child might have been in a situation where parental expectations were all focused on

FIGURE 4.6

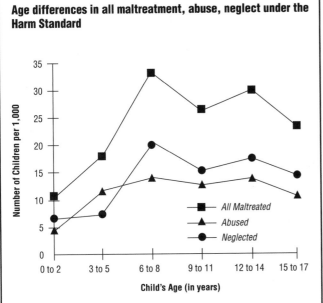

Age differences in all maltreatment, abuse, neglect under the Harm Standard

SOURCE: Andrea J. Sedlak and Diane D. Broadhurst, "Age difference in all maltreatment, abuse, neglect under the Harm Standard," in *The Third National Incidence Study of Child Abuse and Neglect,* U.S. Department of Health and Human Services, National Center on Child Abuse and Neglect, Washington, DC, 1996

FIGURE 4.7

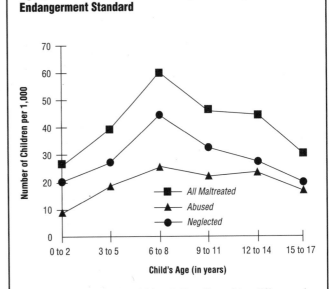

Age differences in all maltreatment, abuse, neglect under the Endangerment Standard

SOURCE: Andrea J. Sedlak and Diane D. Broadhurst, "Age differences in all maltreatment, abuse, neglect under the Endangerment Standard," in *The Third National Incidence Study of Child Abuse and Neglect,* U.S. Department of Health and Human Services, National Center on Child Abuse and Neglect, Washington, DC, 1996

TABLE 4.9

Incidence rates per 1,000 children for maltreatment under the Harm Standard in the NIS-3 (1993) for different family structures

Harm Standard Maltreatment Category	Both Parents	Single Parent — Either Mother or Father	Single Parent — Mother only	Single Parent — Father only	Neither Parent	Significance of Differences
All Maltreatment:	15.5	27.3	26.1	36.6	22.9	A, C, D
Abuse:						
All Abuse	8.4	11.4	10.5	17.7	13.7	D, e
Physical Abuse	3.9	6.9	6.4	10.5	7.0	a, D, e
Sexual Abuse	2.6	2.5	2.5	2.6	6.3	ns
Emotional Abuse	2.6	2.5	2.1	5.7	5.4	ns
Neglect:						
All Neglect	7.9	17.3	16.7	21.9	10.3	A, C, D
Physical Neglect	3.1	5.8	5.9	4.7	4.3	A, C
Emotional Neglect	2.3	4.0	3.4	8.8	3.1	a, G
Educational Neglect	3.0	9.6	9.5	10.8	3.1	A, B, f
Severity of Injury:						
Fatal	0.019	0.015	0.017	0.005	0.016	ns
Serious	5.8	10.5	10.0	14.0	8.0	A, C
Moderate	8.1	15.4	14.7	20.5	10.1	A
Inferred	1.6	1.4	1.3	2.1	4.8	ns

A Difference between "Both Parents" and "Either Mother or Father" is significant at or below the p<.05 level.
a Difference between "Both Parents" and "Either Mother or Father" is statistically marginal (i.e., .10>p>.05).
B Difference between "Either Mother or Father" and "Neither Parent" is significant at or below the p <.05 level.
C Difference between "Both Parents" and "Mother only" is significant at or below the p<.05 level.
D Difference between "Both Parents" and "Father only" is significant at or below the p<.05 level.
e Difference between "Mother only" and "Father only" is statistically marginal (i.e., .10>p>.05).
f Difference between "Mother only" and "Neither Parent" is statistically marginal (i.e., .10>p>.05).
G Difference between "Father only" and "Neither Parent" is significant at or below the p<.05 level.
ns No between-group difference is significant or marginal (all p's>.10).

SOURCE: Andrea J. Sedlak and Diane D. Broadhurst, "Incidence rates per 1,000 children for maltreatment under the Harm Standard in the NIS-3 (1993) for different family structures," in *The Third National Incidence Study of Child Abuse and Neglect,* U.S. Department of Health and Human Services, National Center on Child Abuse and Neglect, Washington, DC, 1996

TABLE 4.10

Incidence rates per 1,000 children for maltreatment under the Endangerment Standard in the NIS-3 (1993) for different family structures

| Endangerment Standard Maltreatment Category | Both Parents | Single Parent | | | Neither Parent | Significance of Differences |
		Either Mother or Father	Mother-only	Father-only		
All Maltreatment	26.9	52.0	50.1	65.6	39.3	A, C, D, G
Abuse:						
All Abuse	13.5	19.6	18.1	31.0	17.3	a
Physical Abuse	6.5	10.6	9.8	16.5	9.2	d
Sexual Abuse	3.2	4.2	4.3	3.1	6.6	ns
Emotional Abuse	6.2	8.6	7.7	14.6	7.1	ns
Neglect:						
All Neglect	17.6	38.9	37.6	47.9	24.1	A, C, D, G
Physical Neglect	10.8	28.6	27.5	36.4	17.1	A, c, D
Emotional Neglect	6.4	10.5	9.7	16.2	8.3	a
Educational Neglect	3.0	9.6	9.5	10.8	3.1	A, B,C, f
Severity of Injury:						
Fatal	0.020	0.015	0.017	0.005	0.016	ns
Serious	5.9	10.5	10.0	14.0	8.0	A, C
Moderate	9.6	18.5	17.7	24.8	11.5	A, b
Inferred	2.1	2.5	2.0	6.0	4.7	ns
Endangered	9.3	20.5	20.4	20.7	15.1	A, C

A Difference between "Both Parents" and "Either Mother or Father" is significant at or below the p < .05 level.
a Difference between "Both Parents" and "Either Mother or Father" is statistically marginal (i.e., .10 > p > .05).
B Difference between "Either Mother or Father" and "Neither Parent" is significant at or below the p < .05 level.
b Difference between "Either Mother or Father" and "Neither Parent" is statistically marginal (i.e., .10 > p > .05).
C Difference between "Both Parents" and "Mother only" is significant at or below the p < .05 level.
c Difference between "Both Parents" and "Mother only" is statistically marginal (i.e., .10 > p > .05).
D Difference between "Both Parents" and "Father only" is significant at or below the p < .05 level.
d Difference between "Both Parents" and "Father only" is statistically marginal (i.e., .l0 > p > .05)
f Difference between "Mother only" and "Neither Parent" is statistically marginal (i.e., .10 > p > .05).
G Difference between "Father only" and "Neither Parent" is significant at or below the p < .05 level.
ns No between-group difference is significant or marginal (all p's > .10).

SOURCE: Andrea J. Sedlak and Diane D. Broadhurst, "Incidence rates per 1,000 children for maltreatment under the Endangerment Standard in the NIS-3 (1993) for different family structures," in *The Third National Incidence Study of Child Abuse and Neglect,* U.S. Department of Health and Human Services, National Center on Child Abuse and Neglect, Washington, DC, 1996

that one child. Another explanation was that "only" children might have been in households where the parents were just starting a family and were relatively young and inexperienced.

FAMILY INCOME. Family income was significantly related to the incidence rates of child maltreatment. Under the Harm Standard, children in families with annual incomes less than $15,000 had the highest rate of maltreatment (47 per 1,000). The figure is almost twice as high (95.9 per 1,000) using the Endangerment Standard. Children in families earning less than $15,000 annually also sustained more serious injuries. (See Table 4.11 and Table 4.12.)

Characteristics of Perpetrators

RELATIONSHIP TO THE CHILD. Most child victims (78 percent) were maltreated by their birth parents. Parents accounted for 72 percent of physical abuse and 81 percent of emotional abuse. Almost half (46 percent) of sexually abused children, however, were violated by someone other than a parent or parent-substitute. More than a quarter (29 percent) were sexually abused by a birth parent, and 25 percent were sexually abused by a parent-

substitute, such as a stepparent or a mother's boyfriend. In addition, sexually abused children were more likely to sustain fatal or serious injuries or impairments when birth parents were the perpetrators. (See Table 4.13.)

PERPETRATORS' GENDERS. Overall, children were somewhat more likely to be maltreated by female perpetrators (65 percent) than by males (54 percent). Among children maltreated by their natural parents, most (75 percent) were maltreated by their mothers, and almost half (46 percent) were maltreated by their fathers. (Children who were maltreated by both parents were included in both "male" and "female" perpetrator counts.) Children who were maltreated by other parents and parent-substitutes were more likely to have been maltreated by a male (85 percent) than by a female (41 percent). Four of five children (80 percent) who were maltreated by other adults were maltreated by males, and only 14 percent were maltreated by other adults who were females. (See Table 4.14. Note that the numbers will not add to 100 percent because many children were maltreated by both parents.)

Neglected children differed from abused children with regard to the gender of the perpetrators. Because

TABLE 4.11

TABLE 4.12

Incidence rates per 1,000 children for maltreatment under the Harm Standard in the NIS-3 (1993) for different levels of family income

Harm Standard Maltreatment Category	<$15K/yr	$15-29K/yr	$30K+/yr	Significance of Differences
All Maltreatment	47.0	20.0	2.1	a
Abuse:				
All Abuse	22.2	9.7	1.6	a
Physical Abuse	11.0	5.0	0.7	a
Sexual Abuse	7.0	2.8	0.4	b
Emotional Abuse	6.5	2.5	0.5	b
Neglect:				
All Neglect	27.2	11.3	0.6	a
Physical Neglect	12.0	2.9	0.3	a
Emotional Neglect	5.9	4.3	0.2	ns
Educational Neglect	11.1	4.8	0.2	a
Severity of Injury:				
Fatal	0.060	0.002	0.001	ns
Serious	17.9	7.8	0.8	a
Moderate	23.3	10.5	1.3	a
Inferred	5.7	1.6	0.1	b

a All between-group differences are significant at or below the p < .05 level.
b The highest income group ($30,000 or more) differs significantly from the others (p's < .05), but the difference between the <$15,000 group and the $15,000 to $29,999 group is statistically marginal (i.e., .10 > p > .05).
ns No between-group difference is significant or marginal (all p's > .10).

SOURCE: Andrea J. Sedlak and Diane D. Broadhurst, "Incidence rates per 1,000 children for maltreatment under the Harm Standard in the NIS-3 (1993) for different levels of family income," in *The Third National Incidence Study of Child Abuse and Neglect*, U.S. Department of Health and Human Services, National Center on Child Abuse and Neglect, Washington, DC, 1996

Incidence rates per 1,000 children for maltreatment under the Endangerment Standard in the NIS-3 (1993) for different levels of family income

Endangerment Standard Maltreatment Category	<$15K/yr	$15-29K/yr	$30K+/yr	Significance of Differences
All Maltreatment	95.9	33.1	3.8	*
Abuse:				
All Abuse	37.4	17.5	2.5	*
Physical Abuse	17.6	8.5	1.5	*
Sexual Abuse	9.2	4.2	0.5	*
Emotional Abuse	18.3	8.1	1.0	*
Neglect:				
All Neglect	72.3	21.6	1.6	*
Physical Neglect	54.3	12.5	1.1	*
Emotional Neglect	19.0	8.2	0.7	*
Educational Neglect	11.1	4.8	0.2	*
Severity of Injury:				
Fatal	0.060	0.002	0.003	ns
Serious	17.9	7.9	0.8	*
Moderate	29.6	12.1	1.5	*
Inferred	7.8	2.7	0.2	*
Endangered	40.5	10.3	1.3	*

*All between-group differences are significant at or below the p < .05 level.
ns No between-group difference is significant or marginal (all p's > .10).

SOURCE: Andrea J. Sedlak and Diane D. Broadhurst, "Incidence rates per 1,000 children for maltreatment under the Endangerment Standard in the NIS-3 (1993) for different levels of family income," in *The Third National Incidence Study of Child Abuse and Neglect*, U.S. Department of Health and Human Services, National Center on Child Abuse and Neglect, Washington, DC, 1996

mothers or other females tend to be the primary caretakers, children were more likely to suffer all forms of neglect by female perpetrators (87 percent versus 43 percent by male perpetrators). In contrast, children were more often abused by males (67 percent) than by females (40 percent). (See Table 4.14.)

CHILD MALTREATMENT DATA FROM THE CRIMINAL JUSTICE SYSTEM

In the past, child abuse data were compiled solely by child welfare agencies. Although child assault had long been recognized as not just a child welfare concern but also a crime, law enforcement data had been lacking. A new initiative by the Federal Bureau of Investigation, the National Incident-Based Reporting System (NIBRS), compiles more detailed information about police experience with child maltreatment. An analysis of NIBRS data from 12 states showed that parents and caretakers accounted for one of five (19 percent) of all violent crimes and nonforcible sex offenses against children under age 18. Caretakers included stepparents, grandparents, babysitters, other adult family members, and parents' boyfriends or girlfriends (David Finkelhor and Richard Ormrod, *Child Abuse Reported to the Police,* U.S. Department of Justice, Office of Juvenile

Justice and Delinquency Prevention, Washington, DC, May 2001).

In addition, while strangers accounted for just 10 percent of crimes against children, noncaretaker acquaintances (both juveniles and adults) were responsible for nearly two-thirds (63 percent) of crimes against children. Noncaretaker family members (mostly juveniles) comprised another 8 percent of persons who committed offenses against children.

The authors found that more than one-fourth (26 percent) of sexual assaults and nearly half (49 percent) of child kidnappings were committed by parents and other caretakers. These two groups also accounted for 18 percent of simple assault and 16 percent of aggravated assault of children. (See Figure 4.8.) Assault refers to a crime in which one person attacks another with the intent to harm. In simple assault, no dangerous or deadly weapon is used. In aggravated assault, the attack is especially brutal and a dangerous or deadly weapon is used.

Overall, more girls (58 percent) than boys (42 percent) were victimized by parents and other caretakers, with 80 percent of these girls experiencing sexual assault. Child maltreatment made up more than half of the crimes against children two years old or younger reported to law

TABLE 4.13

Distribution of perpetrator's relationship to child and severity of harm by the type of maltreatment

Category	Percent Children in Maltreatment Category	Total Maltreated Children	Percent of Children in Row with Injury/Impairment. . .		
			Fatal or Serious	Moderate	Inferred
Abuse:	100%	743,200	21%	63%	16%
Natural Parents	62%	461,800	22%	73%	4%
Other Parents and Parent/substitutes	19%	144,900	12%	62%	27%
Others	18%	136,600	24%	30%	46%
Physical Abuse	100%	381,700	13%	87%	+
Natural Parents	72%	273,200	13%	87%	+
Other Parents and Parent/substitutes	21%	78,700	13%	87%	+
Others	8%	29,700	*	82%	+
Sexual Abuse	100%	217,700	34%	12%	53%
Natural Parents	29%	63,300	61%	10%	28%
Other Parents and Parent/substitutes	25%	53,800	19%	18%	63%
Others	46%	100,500	26%	11%	63%
Emotional Abuse	100%	204,500	26%	68%	6%
Natural Parents	81%	166,500	27%	70%	2%
Other Parents and Parent/substitutes	13%	27,400	*	57%	24%
Others	5%	10,600	*	*	*
Neglect:	100%	879,000	50%	44%	6%
Natural Parents	91%	800,600	51%	43%	6%
Other Parents and Parent/substitutes	9%	78,400	35%	59%	*
Others	^	^	^	^	^
Physical Neglect	100%	338,900	64%	15%	21%
Natural Parents	95%	320,400	64%	16%	20%
Other Parents and Parent/substitutes	5%	18,400	*	*	*
Others	^	^	^	^	^
Emotional Neglect	100%	212,800	97%	3%	+
Natural Parents	91%	194,600	99%	*	+
Other Parents and Parent/substitutes	9%	*	*	*	+
Others	^	^	^	^	+
Educational Neglect	100%	397,300	7%	93%	+
Natural Parents	89%	354,300	8%	92%	+
Other Parents and Parent/substitutes	11%	43,000	*	99%	+
Others	^	^	^	^	+
All Maltreatment	100%	1,553,800	36%	53%	11%
Natural Parents	78%	1,208,100	41%	54%	5%
Other Parents and Parent/substitutes	14%	211,200	20%	61%	19%
Others	9%	134,500	24%	30%	46%

+This severity level not applicable for this form of maltreatment.
*Fewer than 20 cases with which to calculate estimate; estimate too unreliable to be given.
^These perpetrators were not allowed by countability requirements for cases of neglect.

SOURCE: Andrea J. Sedlak and Diane D. Broadhurst, "Distribution of perpetrator's relationship to child and severity of harm by the type of maltreatment," in *The Third National Incidence Study of Child Abuse and Neglect,* U.S. Department of Health and Human Services, National Center on Child Abuse and Neglect, Washington, DC, 1996

enforcement. The police also found that, where more than one child was being abused in a household, the children were more likely to be under age 12. About 70 percent of children in multiple-victim abuse were younger than 12.

TABLE 4.14

Distribution of perpetrator's gender by type of maltreatment and perpetrator's relationship to child

Category	Percent Children in Maltreatment Category	Total Maltreated Children	Percent of Children in Row with Perpetrator Whose Gender was . . .		
			Male	Female	Unknown
Abuse:	100%	743,200	67%	40%	*
Natural Parents	62%	461,800	56%	55%	*
Other Parents and Parent/substitutes	19%	144,900	90%	15%	*
Others	18%	136,600	80%	14%	*
Physical Abuse	100%	381,700	58%	50%	*
Natural Parents	72%	273,200	48%	60%	*
Other Parents and Parent/substitutes	21%	78,700	90%	19%	*
Others	8%	29,700	57%	39%	*
Sexual Abuse	100%	217,700	89%	12%	*
Natural Parents	29%	63,300	87%	28%	*
Other Parents and Parent/substitutes	25%	53,800	97%	*	*
Others	46%	100,500	86%	8%	*
Emotional Abuse	100%	204,500	63%	50%	*
Natural Parents	81%	166,500	60%	55%	*
Other Parents and Parent/substitutes	13%	27,400	74%	*	*
Others	5%	10,600	*	*	*
All neglect:	100%	879,000	43%	87%	*
Natural Parents	91%	800,600	40%	87%	*
Other Parents and Parent/substitutes	9%	78,400	76%	88%	*
Others	^	^	^	^	^
Physical Neglect	100%	338,900	35%	93%	*
Natural Parents	95%	320,400	34%	93%	*
Other Parents and Parent/substitutes	5%	18,400	*	90%	*
Others	^	^	^	^	^
Emotional Neglect	100%	212,800	47%	77%	*
Natural Parents	91%	194,600	44%	78%	*
Other Parents and Parent/substitutes	9%	18,200	*	*	*
Others	^	^	^	^	^
Educational Neglect	100%	397,300	47%	88%	*
Natural Parents	89%	354,300	43%	86%	*
Other Parents and Parent/substitutes	11%	43,000	82%	100%	*
Others	^	^	^	^	^
All Maltreatment	100%	1,553,800	54%	65%	1%
Natural Parents	78%	1,208,100	46%	75%	*
Other Parents and Parent/substitutes	14%	211,200	85%	41%	*
Others	9%	134,500	80%	14%	7%

*Fewer than 20 cases with which to calculate, estimate too unreliable to be given
^These perpetrators were not allowed by countability requirements for cases of neglect.

SOURCE: Andrea J. Sedlak and Diane D. Broadhurst, "Distribution of perpetrator's gender by type of maltreatment and perpetrator's relationship to child," in *The Third National Incidence Study of Child Abuse and Neglect,* U.S. Department of Health and Human Services, National Center on Child Abuse and Neglect, Washington, DC, 1996

FIGURE 4.8

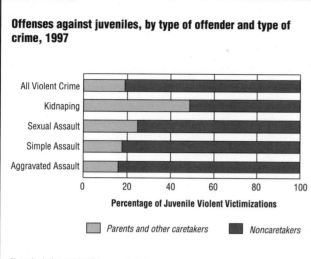

Offenses against juveniles, by type of offender and type of crime, 1997

Percentage of Juvenile Violent Victimizations

☐ Parents and other caretakers   ■ Noncaretakers

Note: Includes nonforcible sex offenses.

SOURCE: David Finkelhor and Richard Ormrod, "Figure 2: Offenses Against Juveniles, by Type of Offender and Type of Crime," in *Child Abuse Reported to the Police*, U.S. Department of Justice, Office of Juvenile Justice and Delinquency Prevention, Washington, DC, May 2001

CHAPTER 5

CAUSES AND EFFECTS OF CHILD ABUSE

Raising a child is not easy. Everyday stresses, strains, and sporadic upheavals in family life, coupled with the normal burdens of child care, cause most parents to feel angry at times. People who would not dream of hitting a colleague or an acquaintance when they are angry may think nothing of hitting their children. Some feel remorse after hitting a loved one; nevertheless, when they are angry, they still resort to violence. The deeper intimacy and greater commitment in a family make emotionally charged disagreements more frequent and more intense.

Murray A. Straus and Richard J. Gelles, experts in child abuse research, believe that cultural standards permit violence in the family. The family, which is the center of love and security in most children's lives, is also the place where the child is punished, often physically.

The 1975 *National Family Violence Survey* and the 1985 *National Family Violence Resurvey,* conducted by Straus and Gelles, are the most complete studies of spousal and parent–child abuse yet prepared in the United States. The major difference between these two surveys and most other surveys discussed in Chapter 4 is that the data from these surveys came from detailed interviews with the general population, not from cases that came to the attention of official agencies and professionals. Straus and Gelles had a more intimate knowledge of the families and an awareness of incidences of child abuse that were not reported to the authorities. (Straus and Gelles incorporated research from the two surveys and additional chapters into the book *Physical Violence in American Families: Risk Factors and Adaptations to Violence in 8,145 Families,* Transaction Publishers, New Brunswick, NJ, 1990.)

CONTRIBUTING FACTORS TO CHILD ABUSE

The factors contributing to child maltreatment are complex. The *Third National Incidence Study of Child Abuse and Neglect* (NIS-3; Andrea J. Sedlak and Diane D.

Broadhurst, U.S. Department of Health and Human Services [HHS], National Center on Child Abuse and Neglect, Washington, DC, 1996), the most comprehensive federal source of information about the incidence of child maltreatment in the United States, found that family structure and size, poverty, alcohol and substance abuse, domestic violence, and community violence are contributing factors to child abuse and neglect.

For example, under the Harm Standard of NIS-3, children in single-parent households were at a higher risk of physical abuse and all types of neglect than were children in other family structures. Children living with only their fathers were more likely to suffer the highest incidence rates of physical abuse and emotional and educational neglect. (See Figure 5.1.) Under the Endangerment Standard, higher incidence rates of physical and emotional neglect occurred among children living with only their fathers than among those living in other family structures. (See Figure 5.2.)

Sedlak and Broadhurst noted that the increase in illicit drug use since the second *National Incidence Study of Child Abuse and Neglect* (NIS-2), in 1986, may have contributed to the increased child maltreatment incidence reported in NIS-3. Children whose parents are alcohol and substance abusers are at very high risk of abuse and neglect because of the physiological, psychological, and sociological nature of the addiction.

While several factors increase the likelihood of child maltreatment, they do not necessarily lead to abuse. It is important to understand that the causes of child abuse and the characteristics of families in which child abuse occurs are only indicators. The vast majority of parents, even in the most stressful and demanding situations, and even with a personal history that might predispose them to be more violent than parents without such a history, do not abuse their children.

FIGURE 5.1

FIGURE 5.2

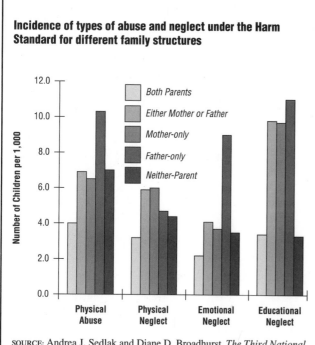

Incidence of types of abuse and neglect under the Harm Standard for different family structures

SOURCE: Andrea J. Sedlak and Diane D. Broadhurst, *The Third National Incidence Study of Child Abuse and Neglect*, U.S. Department of Health and Human Services, National Center on Child Abuse and Neglect, Washington, D.C., 1996

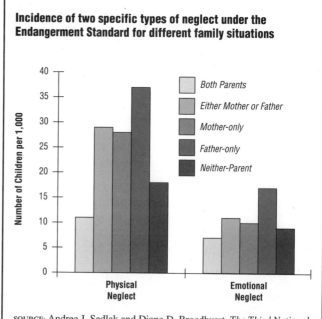

Incidence of two specific types of neglect under the Endangerment Standard for different family situations

SOURCE: Andrea J. Sedlak and Diane D. Broadhurst, *The Third National Incidence Study of Child Abuse and Neglect*, U.S. Department of Health and Human Services, Washington, D.C., 1996

Straus and Christine Smith noted, in "Family Patterns and Child Abuse" (*Physical Violence in American Families: Risk Factors and Adaptations to Violence in 8,145 Families,* Transaction Publishers, New Brunswick, NJ, 1990), that one cannot simply single out an individual factor as the cause of abuse. The authors found that a combination of several factors is more likely to result in child abuse than is a single factor by itself. Also, the sum of the effects of individual factors taken together does not necessarily add up to what Straus and Smith called the "explosive combinations" of several factors interacting with one another. Nonetheless, even "explosive combinations" do not necessarily lead to child abuse.

Socioeconomic Status

WHICH COMES FIRST—POVERTY OR ABUSE? Although the most comprehensive U.S. government report on the incidence of child maltreatment, NIS-3, found a correlation between family income and child abuse and neglect, most experts agree that the connection between poverty and maltreatment is not easily explained. According to Diana J. English, the stress that comes with poverty may predispose the parents to use corporal punishment that may lead to physical abuse ("The Extent and Consequences of Child Maltreatment," *The Future of Children: Protecting Children from Abuse and Neglect,* vol. 8, no. 1, Spring 1998).

English noted that most poor parents do not maltreat their children. Rather, the effects of poverty, such as

stress, may influence other risk factors, including depression, substance abuse, and domestic violence. These risk factors, in turn, may predispose the parents to violent behavior toward their children.

UNEMPLOYMENT. The 1975 *National Family Violence Survey* found rates of child abuse that were considerably higher among families suffering from unemployment than among those in which the husband was working full time. Families in which the husband was not working had a significantly higher rate of child abuse than other families (22.5 versus 13.9 per 100 children). This finding did not recur, however, in the 1985 survey, although wives of unemployed husbands did have a higher rate of abuse than wives of husbands working full time (16.2 versus 11 per 100 children). Straus and Smith ("Family Patterns and Child Abuse") thought that this higher rate for wives might have been caused by added family stress because the father was unemployed. Generally, workers in the lower economic class face greater stress because they often have less control over their employment situation, are more likely to find themselves unemployed, and have fewer resources to help ease their stress.

The rate of abuse in the 1985 *National Family Violence Resurvey* was considerably higher in families in which the husband was a blue-collar worker. Blue-collar fathers committed abuse at a rate of 11.9 per 100 children, compared with 8.9 per 100 children among white-collar workers. The abuse rate for the wives of blue-collar workers was even greater: 13.9 per 100 children versus 8.1 per 100 children among wives of white-collar workers.

Stress

There are no "vacations" from being a parent, and parenting stress has been associated with abusive behavior. When a parent who may be predisposed toward maltreating a child must deal with a particularly stressful situation, it is possible that little time, energy, or self-control is left for the children. In times of stress, the slightest action by the child can be "the last straw" that leads to violent abuse.

Often, when striking out at a child, the parent may be venting anger at his or her own situation rather than reacting to some misbehavior on the part of the child. Abused children have indicated that they never knew when their parents' anger would explode and that they were severely beaten for the most minor infractions. The child may also be hostile and aggressive, contributing to the stress.

Caring for Children with Disabilities

According to the National Clearinghouse on Child Abuse and Neglect Information, in *The Risk and Prevention of Maltreatment of Children with Disabilities* (HHS, Washington, DC, February 2001), children with disabilities were 1.7 times more likely to suffer maltreatment than children with no disabilities. The National Center on Child Abuse and Neglect of the HHS found that, of the different types of maltreatment, children with disabilities were 2.8 times as likely to experience emotional abuse than children with no disabilities.

Children with disabilities are potentially at risk for maltreatment because society generally treats them as different and less valuable, thus tolerating violence against them. These children require a lot of special care and attention, and parents may not have the social support to help ease stressful situations. A lack of financial resources further exacerbates the situation.

Some parents may feel disappointment at not having a "normal" child. Others may expect too much and feel frustrated if the child does not live up to their expectations. Children under the care of nonfamily members are at risk for maltreatment, not only from those caregivers who abuse their power or who feel no bond with them, but also from other children, especially in an institutional setting.

According to the Committee on Child Abuse and Neglect and the Committee on Children with Disabilities, both of the American Academy of Pediatrics (AAP; "Assessment of Maltreatment of Children with Disabilities," *Pediatrics,* vol. 108, no. 2, August 2001), children with disabilities may also be vulnerable to sexual abuse. Dependent on caregivers for their physical needs, these children may not be able to distinguish between appropriate and inappropriate touching of their bodies. The opportunities for sexual abuse may also be increased if the child depends on several caregivers for his or her needs.

The AAP also noted that children with disabilities may not be intellectually capable of understanding that they are being abused. They may not have the communication skills to reveal the abuse. In addition, children who experience some pain when undergoing therapy may not be able to distinguish between inflicted pain from therapy pain.

Toilet Training

Toilet training can be one of the most frustrating events in the lives of parents and children. Researchers are now linking it to many of the more serious, even deadly, cases of abuse in children between the ages of one and four. Some parents have unrealistic expectations, and when their children are unable to live up to these demands, the parents explode in rage. Parental stress and inability to control emotions play a role in child abuse, but they require a trigger to set off the explosion. Soiled clothes and accidents frequently serve as this trigger.

When children are brought to the emergency room with deep, symmetrical scald burns on their bottoms, health care personnel conclude that they were deliberately immersed and held in hot water. This form of abuse is nearly always committed as the result of a toilet accident. Even a one-second contact with 147°F water can cause third-degree burns. Some parents think that immersing a child in hot water will make the child go to the bathroom.

Toileting accidents can be especially dangerous for children because the parent has to place his or her hands on the child to clean up the mess, making it easy for the parent's rage to be taken out on the child's body. This abuse is more common among less-educated, low-income mothers who mistakenly believe that children should be trained by 12 to 16 months of age. Better-educated parents are more likely to be aware that successful training for girls happens at around two years of age and sometimes not until age three or later for boys.

THE VIOLENT FAMILY

Spousal Conflicts

Child abuse is sometimes a reflection of other forms of severe family conflict. Violence in one aspect of family life often flows into other aspects. According to Straus and Smith ("Family Patterns and Child Abuse"), the 1985 *National Family Violence Resurvey* found that parents who were in constant conflict were also more likely to abuse their children. The researchers measured the level of husband–wife conflict over such issues as money, sex, social activities, housekeeping, and children. The child abuse rate for fathers involved in high marital conflict was 13 per 100 children, compared with 7.4 per 100 children for other men. Mothers in high-conflict relationships reported an even higher child abuse rate: 13.6 per 100 children versus 8 per 100 children among mothers in lower-conflict homes.

Spousal Verbal Aggression and Child Abuse

Husbands and wives sometimes use verbal aggression to deal with their conflicts. The 1985 *National Family Violence Resurvey* found that spouses who verbally attacked each other were also more likely to abuse their children. Among verbally aggressive husbands, the child abuse rate was 11.2 per 100 children, compared with 4.9 per 100 children for other husbands. Verbally aggressive wives had a child abuse rate of 12.3 per 100 children, compared with 5.3 per 100 children for other wives. Straus and Smith believed that verbal attacks between spouses, rather than clearing the air, tended to mask the reason for the dispute. The resulting additional tension made it even harder to resolve the original source of the conflict.

Spousal Physical Aggression and Child Abuse

In "Family Patterns and Child Abuse," Straus and Smith reported that one of the most distinct findings of the 1985 *National Family Violence Resurvey* was that violence in one family relationship is frequently associated with violence in other family relationships. In families in which the husband struck his wife, the child abuse rate was much higher (22.3 per 100 children) than in other families (8 per 100 children). Similarly, in families in which the wife hit the husband, the child abuse rate was also considerably higher (22.9 per 100 children) than in families in which the wife did not hit the husband (9.2 per 100 children).

In "Risk of Physical Abuse to Children of Spouse Abusing Parents" (*Child Abuse and Neglect,* vol. 20, no. 7, January 1996), Susan Ross, who did further research based on the 1985 *National Family Violence Resurvey,* reported that marital violence was a statistically significant predictor of physical child abuse. Ross noted that the probability of child abuse by a violent husband increased from 5 percent with one act of marital violence to near certainty with 50 or more acts of spousal abuse. The percentages were similar for violent wives.

Ross found that, of those husbands who had been violent with their wives, 22.8 percent had engaged in violence toward their children. Similarly, 23.9 percent of violent wives had engaged in at least one act of physical child abuse. These rates of child abuse were much higher than those of parents who were not violent toward each other (8.5 percent for fathers and 9.8 percent for mothers). In other words, the more frequent the spousal violence, the higher the probability of child abuse.

Verbal Abuse of Children

Parents who verbally abuse their children are also more likely to physically abuse their children. Respondents to the 1975 *National Family Violence Survey* who verbally abused their children reported a child abuse rate six times that of other parents (21 versus 3.6 per 100 children). The 1985 survey found that verbally abusive mothers physically abused their children about nine times more than other mothers (16.3 versus 1.8 per 100 children). Fathers who were verbally aggressive toward their children physically abused the children more than three times as much as other fathers (14.3 versus 4.2 per 100 children).

TRENDS IN THE USE OF VERBAL ABUSE. Prevent Child Abuse America (PCA America) surveyed American parents regarding their use of verbal abuse (Deborah Daro, *Public Opinion and Behaviors Regarding Child Abuse Prevention: 1999 Survey,* Chicago, IL, November 1999). The proportion of parents who reported having verbally abused (insulted or sworn at) their children in the last year had declined, from 53 percent in 1988 to 38 percent in 1999. Since 1997 PCA America has asked parents about their failure to meet their children's emotional needs in the past year. The percentage of parents (about half of the respondents) who reported doing so has remained the same.

ATTITUDES TOWARD THE USE OF VERBAL ABUSE. Through the years 1987–99, the majority (71–79 percent) of the respondents to PCA America's survey believed that repeated yelling and swearing lead to long-term emotional problems for the child. In 1999 nearly three-quarters (74 percent) of the American public believed that repeated yelling and swearing very often or often emotionally harms a child, while just 5 percent thought such parental behavior is rarely or never harmful to a child's emotional well-being. (See Table 5.1.)

WOMAN BATTERING AND CHILD MALTREATMENT

Some experts believe that a link exists between woman battering and child maltreatment. According to the National Clearinghouse on Child Abuse and Neglect Information (*In Harm's Way: Domestic Violence and Child Maltreatment,* HHS, Washington, DC, undated), published studies have shown that there is a 30–60 percent overlap between violence against children and violence against women in the same families. (See Figure 5.3.)

Although researchers and policy makers have studied the plight of battered women since the 1970s, no national data about children living in violent homes have ever been collected. A November 2000 report by Patricia Tjaden and Nancy Thoennes showed that annually about 1.3 million women were physically assaulted by an intimate partner (*Full Report of the Prevalence, Incidence, and Consequences of Violence against Women: Findings from the National Violence against Women Survey,* U.S. Department of Justice, National Institute of Justice [NIJ], Washington, DC, and the Centers for Disease Control and Prevention, Atlanta, GA). *Child Maltreatment 2000* (HHS, Administration for Children and Families, Washington, DC, 2002) reported that an estimated 879,000 children were victims of child maltreatment in 2002.

TABLE 5.1

Public attitudes toward parent behavior (in percentage), 1987–1999

	1999	1998	1997	1996	1995	1994	1993	1992	1991	1990	1989	1988	1987
Question: How often do you think physical punishment of a child leads to injury to the child?													
Very often/often	34%	30%	32%	33%	32%	38%	38%	36%	31%	35%	35%	33%	40%
Occasionally	33	35	36	37	36	34	35	38	44	37	35	38	31
Hardly ever/never	18	19	18	23	22	22	20	20	18	19	21	23	24
Not sure	9	9	7	7	10	6	7	6	7	9	8	6	5
Question: How often do you think repeated yelling and swearing leads to long-term emotional problems for the child?													
Very often/often	74%	75%	76%	78%	75%	74%	79%	74%	75%	76%	73%	71%	73%
Occasionally	15	14	15	14	16	17	14	17	18	15	18	18	17
Hardly ever/never	5	5	4	7	6	7	5	7	5	6	6	8	7
Not sure	3	3	2	2	3	2	2	2	2	3	2	2	2
Number of respondents	1250	1250	1253	1274	1263	1250	1250	1250	1250	1250	1250	1250	1250

SOURCE: Deborah Daro, "Table 1: Public attitudes toward parent behavior (in percentage)," in *Public Opinion and Behaviors Regarding Child Abuse Prevention: 1999 Survey,* Prevent Child Abuse America, National Center on Child Abuse Prevention Research, Chicago, IL, November 1999

FIGURE 5.3

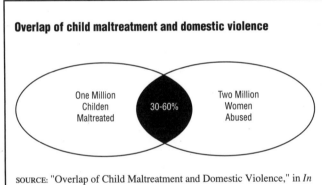

Overlap of child maltreatment and domestic violence

One Million Children Maltreated | 30-60% | Two Million Women Abused

SOURCE: "Overlap of Child Maltreatment and Domestic Violence," in *In Harm's Way: Domestic Violence and Child Maltreatment,* U.S. Department of Health and Human Services, National Clearinghouse on Child Abuse and Neglect Information, Washington, DC, not dated

TABLE 5.2

Number of violent offenders in state prisons for crimes against inmates who were residing with their children prior to entering prison

The prisoners who were convicted of intimate violence and who had children under age 18 had an average of 2.2 young children.

	Percent of State prisoners convicted of crimes against intimates
No children under age 18	36%
Children under age 18	64
Living with offender before prison	40%
Not living with offender	25

Note: About 4 in 10 violent offenders in state prisons for crimes against intimates were residing with their children (natural, adopted, or step-children) under age 18 prior to entering prison.

SOURCE: Lawrence A. Greenfeld et al., "About 4 in 10 violent offenders in State prisons for crimes against intimates were residing with their children (natural, adopted, or stepchildren) under age 18 prior to entering prison," in *Violence by Intimates: Analysis of Data on Crimes by Current or Former Spouses, Boyfriends, and Girlfriends,* U.S. Department of Justice, Bureau of Justice Statistics, revised May 29, 1998

Experts believe that many of these abused children and battered women come from the same homes.

Some government data illustrate that children indeed live in households where domestic violence occurs. NIJ's Spousal Assault Replication Program (SARP), a multicity study of intimate partner violence (from 1981 to 1991) revealed that more than twice as many children were present in homes with domestic violence than in comparable homes in the general population. For example, in Milwaukee, Wisconsin, 8 of 10 (81 percent) of SARP households had children present, compared to just 3 of 10 (32 percent) comparison households. Lawrence A. Greenfeld et al., in *Violence by Intimates: Analysis of Data on Crimes by Current or Former Spouses, Boyfriends, and Girlfriends,* (U.S. Department of Justice, Bureau of Justice Statistics, March 1998), reported that about half of the female victims of

intimate violence lived in households with children under 12. More than one-fifth of the male victims of intimate violence lived in households with young children. Among violent offenders incarcerated in state prisons for crimes against intimates, 40 percent had children under 18 living with them prior to incarceration. These households had an average of 2.2 children. (See Table 5.2.)

Exposure to Domestic Violence and Experiencing Child Maltreatment

According to John W. Fantuzzo and Wanda K. Mohr, in "Prevalence and Effects of Child Exposure to Domestic

Violence" (*The Future of Children: Domestic Violence and Children,* vol. 9, no. 3, Winter 1999), various studies have found that child witnesses to domestic violence are more likely to exhibit aggression and behavior problems. These children experience internalizing behaviors, including depression, anxiety, suicidal tendencies, and low self-esteem. They have problems with schoolwork and attain lower scores in tests that gauge verbal, motor, and cognitive skills.

Linda Spears, in *Building Bridges between Domestic Violence Organizations and Child Protective Services* (Minnesota Center against Violence and Abuse, University of Minnesota, St. Paul, MN, 2000), wrote that aside from seeing their mother being abused, children also witness the injuries resulting from the assault. Children may get hurt as a result of defending their mothers or of being battered themselves. Spears enumerated other effects of a child's exposure to domestic violence, including fearfulness, sleeplessness, withdrawal, anxiety, depression, and externalized problems such as delinquency and aggression.

The Administration for Children and Families of the HHS has found that children whose mothers experience partner battery are twice as likely to be abused as are children whose mothers are not victims of abuse. In addition, children who witness violence at home exhibit many of the symptoms suffered by children who are directly abused. According to the U.S. Advisory Board on Child Abuse and Neglect (*A Nation's Shame: Fatal Child Abuse and Neglect in the United States,* HHS, Washington, DC, 1995), domestic violence is the single major precursor to deaths from child abuse and neglect in the United States.

Azmaira Hamid Maker, Markus Kemmelmeier, and Christopher Peterson, in "Long-Term Psychological Consequences in Women of Witnessing Parental Physical Conflict and Experiencing Abuse in Childhood" (*Journal of Interpersonal Violence,* vol. 13, no. 5, October 1998), found that in distressed families, child witnesses to physical violence between parents experienced other childhood risk factors. In a survey of community college women ages 18 to 43, child maltreatment—specifically sexual abuse and physical abuse—were found to have coexisted with domestic violence.

Women who had witnessed parental violence as children reported being involved in violent dating relationships, both as victims and perpetrators. Witnesses of severe parental violence not only were victims of violence by their dating partners but also exhibited violence toward their dating partners. The risk factors of childhood maltreatment that coexisted with parental violence also accounted for long-term psychological problems, such as depression, antisocial behaviors, and trauma symptoms.

Suzanne Salzinger et al. compared a sample of 100 New York City children, grades four to six, who experienced physical abuse, to a control group of 100 nonabused children ("Effects of Partner Violence and Physical Child Abuse in Child Behavior: A Study of Abused and Comparison Children" *Journal of Family Violence,* vol. 17, no. 1, March 2002). The researchers sought to determine the relationship among family stress, partner violence, caretaker distress, and child abuse. They questioned each caretaker concerning stressful events that had occurred in their family during the lifetime of the child subject. These stress factors included, among other things, separation or divorce, drug abuse, alcohol abuse, deaths, serious illness in the past year, and losing a job in the past year.

Salzinger and her associates found that, in households where partner violence and child maltreatment both occurred, the children suffered physical aggression from both the perpetrator and the victim. The perpetrator and victim could be either parent. In addition, in these households, the mothers who were typically the caretakers reported that they were more likely than the fathers to physically abuse the children. Interestingly, the researchers found that family stress, not partner violence, was responsible for caretaker distress, which in turn increased the risk for child abuse.

Child Protective Services and Domestic Violence

When child protective services (CPS) workers have been involved with children who have witnessed domestic violence, their main concern has been the interests of the children. Critics have charged that CPS further penalizes battered women by taking away their children when their partners have abused the children. Jeffrey L. Edleson, in "The Overlap between Child Maltreatment and Woman Battering" (*Violence against Women,* vol. 5, no. 2, February 1999), observed that, ironically, in child maltreatment reports, CPS records often just list the mother's name and the steps mothers should take to ensure their children's safety. Abusive males are "invisible" in CPS caseload data.

In *Failure to Protect* (Child Welfare Institute, Duluth, GA, February 2002), Thomas D. Morton observed that child welfare agencies need to hold the batterers accountable for their actions. According to Morton, advocates for battered women are concerned that these women are all too often being punished a second time when CPS removes their children.

Morton noted that some CPS caseworkers may equate a mother's victimization to her inability to protect her child, consequently removing the child from the home. Morton asserts that CPS and/or state legislatures should clarify certain CPS practices, including what course of action to take when a nonrelated caregiver in a household is the child abuser. The author asked whether or not CPS should pursue family preservation (keeping the family together) if the abuser is not legally related to the child. He also raised such questions as to whether CPS may require the biological parent to end a relationship with the nonbiological caretaker as a requirement for keeping the child in the family.

ABUSIVE MOTHERS

Straus and Smith, in "Family Patterns and Child Abuse," found that women are as likely, if not more likely, as men to abuse their children. The authors believed child abuse by women could be explained in terms of social factors rather than psychological factors. Women are more likely to abuse their children because they are more likely to have much greater responsibility for raising the children, which means that they are more exposed to the trials and frustrations of child rearing.

Women spend more "time at risk" while tending to their children. "Time at risk" refers to the time a potential abuser spends with the victim. This would apply to any form of domestic violence, such as wife abuse and elder abuse. For example, elderly people are more likely to experience abuse from each other, not from a caregiver, if one is present. This is not because elderly couples are more violent than caregivers, but because they spend more time with each other.

A national survey in the United Kingdom of the childhood experiences of young adults ages 18 to 24 found that mothers were more likely than other household members to be violent to their children. *Child Maltreatment in the United Kingdom—A Study of the Prevalence of Child Abuse and Neglect* (Pat Cawson, Corinne Wattam, Sue Brooker, and Graham Kelly, National Society for the Prevention of Cruelty to Children, London, UK, November 20, 2000) was the most comprehensive report of childhood maltreatment ever conducted in that country, involving 2,869 interviews about young people's childhood experiences. Of the 11 percent of respondents who reported physical abuse, nearly half (49 percent) indicated that their mothers were the perpetrators of violence. Violence took the forms of knocking down the child, burning, threatening with a knife or a gun, kicking hard, shaking, or hitting with a fist or a hard implement. Another 40 percent of the respondents identified their attackers as their fathers.

SIBLING ABUSE

Vernon R. Wiehe, in "Sibling Abuse" (*Understanding Family Violence,* Sage Publications, Inc., Thousand Oaks, CA, 1998), claimed that abusive behavior between brothers and sisters is often considered sibling rivalry and is therefore not covered under mandatory reporting of abuse. The author conducted a nationwide survey of survivors of sibling abuse who had sought professional counseling for problems resulting from physical, emotional, and sexual abuse by a brother or sister.

The respondents were generally victims of more than one type of abuse: 71 percent reported being physically, emotionally, and sexually abused. An additional 7 percent indicated being just emotionally abused, pushing the total of emotionally abused victims to 78 percent. Emotional abuse took the forms of "name-calling, ridicule, degradation, exacerbating a fear, destroying personal possessions, and torturing or destroying a pet."

As far as the victims of sibling incest could remember, they were sexually abused at ages five to seven. The author, however, believed it was possible that the abuse started at an earlier age. The perpetrator was often an older sibling, older by 3 to 10 years. The incest generally occurred over an extended period.

CHILDHOOD MALTREATMENT AND EARLY BRAIN DEVELOPMENT

Increasing research has shown that child abuse or neglect during infancy and early childhood affects early brain development. The National Clearinghouse on Child Abuse and Neglect Information, in *Understanding the Effects of Maltreatment on Early Brain Development* (HHS, Washington, DC, October 2001), defined "brain development, or learning," as "the process of creating, strengthening, and discarding connections among the neurons; these connections are called synapses." Neurons, or nerve cells, send signals to one another through synapses, which in turn form the neuronal pathways that enable the brain to respond to specific environments.

An infant is born with very few synapses formed. These include those responsible for breathing, eating, and sleeping. During the early years of life the brain develops synapses at a fast rate. Scientists have found that repeated experiences strengthen the neuronal pathways, making them sensitive to similar experiences that may occur later on in life. Unfortunately, if these early life experiences are of a negative nature, the development of the brain may be impaired. For example, if an infant who cries for attention constantly gets ignored, his brain creates the neuronal pathway that enables him to cope with being ignored. If the infant continually fails to get the attention he or she craves, the brain strengthens that same neuronal pathway.

Childhood abuse or neglect has long-term consequences on brain development. When children suffer abuse or neglect, their brains are preoccupied with reacting to the chronic stress. As the brain builds and strengthens neuronal pathways involved with survival, it fails to develop social and cognitive skills. Later on in life, maltreatment victims may not know how to react to kindness and nurturing because the brain has no memory of how to respond to those new experiences. They may also have learning difficulties because the brain has focused solely on the body's survival so that the thinking processes may not have been developed or may have been impaired.

Hyperarousal is another consequence of maltreatment on brain development. During the state of hyperarousal, the brain is always attuned to what it perceives as a threatening situation. The brain "has learned" that the world is a dangerous place, and it has to be constantly on the alert. The victim experiences extreme anxiety at any perceived threat, or he or she may use aggression to control the situation. For example, children who have been physically abused may start a fight just so they can control the conflict and be able to choose their adversary. Males and older children are more likely to exhibit hyperarousal.

Researchers have found that, while males and older children tend to suffer from hyperarousal, younger children and females are more likely to show dissociation. In the dissociative state victims disconnect themselves from the negative experience. Their bodies and minds do not react to the abusive experience, "pretending" not to be there.

Childhood maltreatment can result in the disruption of the attachment process, which refers to the development of emotional relationships with others. Under normal circumstances the first relationship that infants develop is with their caretakers. Such relationships form the basis for future emotional connections. In maltreated children, the attachment process may not be fully developed, resulting in the inability to know oneself as well as to put oneself in another's position.

CHILDHOOD MALTREATMENT AND THE RISK FOR SUBSTANCE ABUSE

Studies have shown that childhood abuse increases the risk for substance abuse later in life. A five-year study by McLean Hospital researchers in Belmont, Massachusetts, has uncovered how this occurs (Carl M. Anderson, Martin H. Teicher, Ann Polcari, and Perry F. Renshaw, "Abnormal T2 Relaxation Time in the Cerebellar Vermis of Adults Sexually Abused in Childhood: Potential Role of the Vermis in Stress-Enhanced Risk for Drug Abuse," *Psychoneuroendocrinology,* vol. 27, no. 1–2, January 2002). Anderson et al. found that the vermis, the region flanked by the cerebellar hemispheres of the brain, may play a key role in the risk for substance abuse among adults who have experienced child abuse. The vermis develops gradually and continues to produce neurons after birth. It is known to be sensitive to stress, so that stress can influence its development.

The researchers compared young adults ages 18 to 22, including eight with a history of repeated childhood sexual abuse (CSA) and 16 others as the control group. Using functional magnetic resonance imaging technology, the researchers measured the resting blood flow in the vermis. They found that the subjects who had been victims of CSA had diminished blood flow. Anderson and his colleagues suggested that the stress experienced with repeat-

ed CSA may cause damage to the vermis, which in turn cannot perform its job of controlling irritability in the limbic system. The limbic system in the center of the brain, a collection of connected clusters of nerve cells, is responsible, among other things, for regulating emotions and memory. The damaged vermis, therefore, induces a person to use drugs or alcohol to suppress the irritability.

Since the CSA subjects had no history of alcohol or substance abuse, Anderson and his colleagues wanted to confirm their findings, which linked an impaired cerebellar vermis and the potential for substance abuse in CSA victims. The researchers analyzed test data collected from the 537 college students recruited for the study. They found that students who reported frequent substance abuse showed higher irritability in the limbic system. They also exhibited symptoms usually associated with drug use, including depression and anger.

CHILDHOOD MALTREATMENT AND PROBLEM BEHAVIORS DURING ADOLESCENCE

Barbara Tatem Kelley, Terence P. Thornberry, and Carolyn A. Smith studied the relationship between childhood maltreatment and subsequent adolescent problem behaviors in children involved in a longitudinal study (*In the Wake of Childhood Maltreatment,* U.S. Department of Justice, Office of Juvenile Justice and Delinquency Prevention, Washington, DC, 1997). The *Rochester Youth Development Study* included a sample of 1,000 seventh- and eighth-graders from Rochester, New York, public schools. The students were in grades 11 and 12 when this particular segment of the study was performed.

Demographic Characteristics

Substantiated child maltreatment was reported for 14 percent of the students. While no significant differences were reported in the prevalence of maltreatment by sex or race, the youths' socioeconomic status had a bearing on the prevalence of maltreatment—20 percent of the children from disadvantaged families had been maltreated, compared with 8 percent of those from nondisadvantaged families. (A disadvantaged family was described as one in which the main wage earner was unemployed, welfare was received, or income was below the poverty level.) A marked difference in the prevalence of maltreatment involved the family structure: only 3 percent of the children who lived with both biological parents had been maltreated, while 19 percent of those in other family structures were victims of maltreatment.

Delinquency

The Rochester researchers measured the prevalence of delinquency by examining official police records and self-reported offenses. Self-reported delinquency was determined during face-to-face interviews with the chil-

TABLE 5.3

Interview items for self-reported delinquency indexes

Since we interviewed you last time, have you . . .	Minor Delinquency	Moderate Delinquency	Serious Delinquency	Violent Delinquency
1. Carried a hidden weapon?				
2. Been loud or rowdy in a public place where someone complained and you got in trouble?	X			
3. Been drunk in a public place?		X		
4. Damaged, destroyed, marked up, or tagged somebody else's property on purpose?		X		
5. Set fire or tried to set fire to a house, building, or car on purpose?				
6. Gone into or tried to go into a building to steal or damage something?			X	
7. Tried to steal or actually stolen money or things worth $5 or less?	X			
8. Tried to steal or actually stolen money or things worth $5-$50?		X		
9. Tried to steal or actually stolen money or things worth $50-$100?			X	
10. Tried to steal or actually stolen money or things worth more than $100?			X	
11. Tried to buy or sell things that were stolen?				
12. Taken someone else's car or motorcycle for a ride without the owner's permission?		X		
13. Stolen or tried to steal a car or other motor vehicle?			X	
14. Forged a check or used fake money to pay for something?		X		
15. Used or tried to use a credit card, bank card, or automatic teller card without permission?		X		
16. Tried to cheat someone by selling them something that was not what you said it was or that was worthless?				
17. Attacked someone with a weapon or with the idea of seriously hurting or killing them?			X	X
18. Hit someone with the idea of hurting them?		X		X
19. Been involved in gang or posse fights?			X	X
20. Thrown objects such as rocks or bottles at people?		X		X
21. Used a weapon or force to make someone give you money or things?			X	X
22. Made obscene phone calls?		X		
23. Been paid for having sexual relations with someone?				
24. Physically hurt or threatened to hurt someone to get them to have sex with you?			X	X
25. Sold marijuana/reefer/pot?				
26. Sold hard drugs such as crack, heroin, cocaine, or LSD/acid?				
Total Number of Items	**2**	**9**	**8**	**6**

SOURCE: Barbara Tatem Kelley et al., "Table 3: Interview Items for Self-Reported Delinquency Indexes," in *In the Wake of Childhood Maltreatment*, U.S. Department of Justice, Office of Juvenile Justice and Delinquency Prevention, Washington, DC, August 1997

dren at intervals of six months, for a total of seven interviews, using the questions found in Table 5.3. Figure 5.4 illustrates the relationship between childhood maltreatment and later delinquency.

Other Negative Outcomes

The *Rochester Youth Development Study* also measured other negative outcomes during adolescence as a result of childhood maltreatment. (See Figure 5.5.)

- Pregnancy—there was no difference between the maltreated and nonmaltreated boys in the rates of impregnating a female. Maltreated girls (52 percent), however, were more likely than nonmaltreated girls (34 percent) to get pregnant.

- Drug use—the risk of drug use was higher among maltreated youth (43 percent), compared with nonmaltreated youth (32 percent).

- Low academic achievement—a lower grade point average during middle school or junior high school

was evident in 33 percent of maltreated youth, compared with 23 percent of those who had no history of maltreatment. The researchers found that students performing poorly in middle school were at increased risk for continued academic failure in high school, low educational aspirations, school dropout, and reduced educational and economic opportunities.

- Mental health problems—26 percent of childhood maltreatment victims, compared with 15 percent of nonmaltreated youth exhibited externalized conduct problems (aggression, hostility, hyperactivity) and internalized problems (social isolation, anxiety, physical distress).

MALTREATED GIRLS WHO BECOME OFFENDERS

Researcher Cathy Spatz Widom studied a group of girls who had experienced neglect and physical and sexual abuse from ages 0–11 through young adulthood ("Childhood Victimization and the Derailment of Girls

FIGURE 5.4

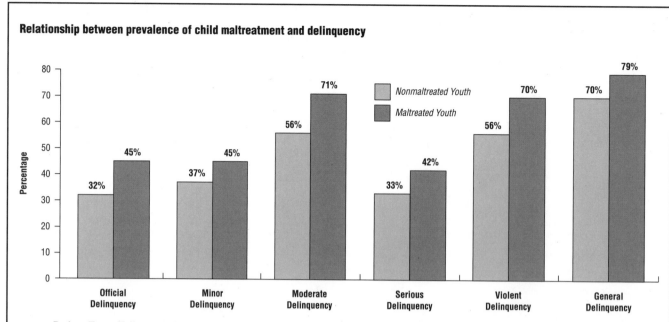

Relationship between prevalence of child maltreatment and delinquency

SOURCE: Barbara Tatem Kelley et al., "Figure 1: Relationship Between Prevalence of Child Maltreatment and Delinquency," in *In the Wake of Childhood Maltreatment,* U.S. Department of Justice, Office of Juvenile Justice and Delinquency Prevention, Washington, DC, August 1997

and Women to the Criminal Justice System," *Research on Women and Girls in the Justice System,* U.S. Department of Justice, Washington, DC, September 2000). The researcher found that abused and neglected girls were almost twice as likely to have been arrested as juveniles (20 percent, compared with 11.4 percent of a matched control group of nonabused girls) and almost twice as likely as the control group to be arrested as adults (28.5 versus 15.9 percent). Additionally, the maltreated girls were also more than twice as likely (8.2 percent) as the nonmaltreated girls (3.6 percent) to have been arrested for violent crimes. Widom, however, noted that although abused and neglected girls were at increased risk for criminal behavior, about 70 percent of the maltreated girls did not become criminals.

Abused and neglected girls who committed status offenses as minors tended to be arrested as adults (49 percent, compared with 36 percent of the nonabused girls). Status offenses are acts that are illegal only when committed by minors: for example, drinking alcohol, skipping school, or violating curfews.

Widom, together with Peter Lambert and Daniel Nagin, found that 8 percent of the maltreated girls developed antisocial and criminal lifestyles that carried over to adulthood ("Does Childhood Victimization Alter Developmental Trajectories of Criminal Careers"; paper presented at the annual meeting of the American Society of Criminology, Washington, DC, November 1998). Among this group, nearly two of five (38 percent) had been arrested for status offenses as juveniles, but a larger percentage

had been arrested for violence (46 percent) and property crimes (54 percent). Almost another third (32 percent) had been arrested for drug crimes. None of the girls in the control group exhibited these tendencies.

LONG-TERM EFFECTS OF CHILD MALTREATMENT

One of the most detailed longitudinal studies of the consequences of childhood maltreatment involved 908 children in a metropolitan area of the Midwest who were ages 6 to 11 when they were maltreated between 1967 and 1971. A control group of 667 children with no history of childhood maltreatment was used for comparison. Each group had about two-thirds white and one-third black persons, with about the same numbers of males and females. Widom examined the long-term consequences of childhood maltreatment on the subjects' intellectual, behavioral, social, and psychological development ("Childhood Victimization: Early Adversity, Later Psychopathology," *National Institute of Justice Journal,* January 2000). When the two groups were interviewed for the study, they had a median age (half were older, half were younger) of about 29 years.

Widom found that, although both abused and control groups finished an average of 11.5 years of school, less than half of the abused group finished high school, compared with two-thirds of the control group. Thirteen percent of the abused group had stable marriages, compared with nearly 20 percent of the control group. The abused group was also more likely to experience frequent separation and divorce.

FIGURE 5.5

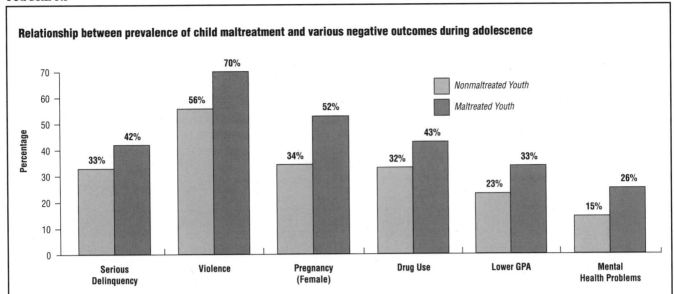

Relationship between prevalence of child maltreatment and various negative outcomes during adolescence

SOURCE: Barbara Tatem Kelley et al., "Figure 2: Relationship Between Prevalence of Child Maltreatment and Various Negative Outcomes During Adolescence," in *In the Wake of Childhood Maltreatment*, U.S. Department of Justice, Office of Juvenile Justice and Delinquency Prevention, Washington, DC, August 1997

The Cycle of Violence

Widom is widely known for her work on the "cycle of violence." The cycle of violence theory suggests that childhood physical abuse increases the likelihood of arrest and of committing violent crime during the victim's later years. Widom found that, although a large proportion of maltreated children did not become juvenile delinquents or criminals, those who suffered childhood abuse or neglect were more likely than those with no reported maltreatment to be arrested as juveniles (31.2 percent versus 19 percent) and as adults (48.4 percent versus 36.2 percent). The maltreated victims (21 percent) were also more likely than those with no reported childhood maltreatment history (15.6 percent) to be arrested for a violent crime during their teen years or adulthood. (See Table 5.4.)

The author noted that the victims' later psychopathology (psychological disorders resulting from the childhood maltreatment) manifested itself in suicide attempts, antisocial personality, and alcohol abuse and/or dependence. Maltreatment victims were more likely than the control individuals to have attempted suicides (18.8 percent versus 7.7 percent) and to have manifested antisocial personality disorder (18.4 versus 11.2 percent). Both groups, however, did not differ much in the rates of alcohol abuse/dependence (54.5 percent for the abused or neglected group and 51 percent for the control group).

Gender played a role in the development of psychological disorders in adolescence and adulthood. Females (24.3 percent) with a history of childhood maltreatment were more likely to attempt suicide, compared with their male counterparts (13.4 percent). A significantly larger

TABLE 5.4

Childhood victimization and later criminality

	Abuse/Neglect Group (676) %	Control Group (520) %
Arrest as juvenile	31.2[2]	19.0
Arrest as adult	48.4[2]	36.2
Arrest as juvenile or adult for any crime	56.5[2]	42.5
Arrest as juvenile or adult for any violent crime	21.0[1]	15.6

[1] $p \leq .05$ [2] $p < .001$
Note: Numbers in parentheses are numbers of cases.
SOURCE: Cathy Spatz Widom, "Table 1: Childhood Victimization and Later Criminality," in "Childhood Victimization: Early Adversity, Later Psychopathology," *National Institute of Justice Journal*, no. 242, January 2000

percentage of male victims (27 percent), however, than female victims (9.8 percent) were at a higher risk for future antisocial personality disorder. Although both male maltreated (64.4 percent) and control (67 percent) subjects had almost similar proportions of alcohol abuse or dependence, females who experienced abuse or neglect were more likely than the control group to have alcohol problems (43.8 percent versus 32.8 percent). (See Table 5.5.)

Cycle of Violence Updated

Another phase of the cycle of violence research was conducted when the maltreated and control groups had a median age of 32.5 years. Aside from collecting arrest records from federal, state, and local law enforcement,

TABLE 5.5

Childhood victimization and later psychopathology, by gender

	Abuse/Neglect Group %	Control Group %
Females	(338)	(224)
Suicide attempt	24.3[3]	8.6
Antisocial personality disorder	9.8[1]	4.9
Alcohol abuse/dependence	43.8[2]	32.8
Males	(338)	(276)
Suicide attempt	13.4[2]	6.9
Antisocial personality disorder	27.0[2]	16.7
Alcohol abuse/dependence	64.4	67.0

[1]$p \leq .05$ [2]$p \leq .01$ [3]$p \leq .001$
Note: Numbers in parentheses are numbers of cases.

SOURCE: Cathy Spatz Widom, "Table 3: Childhood Victimization and Later Psychopathology, by Gender," in "Childhood Victimization: Early Adversity, Later Psychopathology," *National Institute of Justice Journal*, no. 242, January 2000

TABLE 5.6

Involvement in criminality by race, in percent

Type of Arrest	Abused and Neglected Group (n = 900)	Comparison Group (n = 667)
Juvenile		
Black	40.6	20.9[3]
White	21.8	15.2[2]
Adult		
Black	59.8	43.6[3]
White	33.8	26.6[1]
Violent Crime		
Black	34.2	21.8[2]
White	11.0	9.7

[1]$p \leq .05$. [2]$p \leq .01$. [3]$p \leq .001$.

SOURCE: Cathy S. Widom and Michael G. Maxfield, "Exhibit 4: Involvement in criminality by race, in percent," in *An Update on the "Cycle of Violence,"* U.S. Department of Justice, National Institute of Justice, Washington, DC, February 2001

TABLE 5.7

Does only violence beget violence?

Abuse Group	Number of subjects	Percentage Arrested for Violent Offense
Physical Abuse Only	76	21.1
Neglect Only	609	20.2
Sexual Abuse Only	125	8.8
Mixed	98	14.3
Control	667	13.9

SOURCE: Cathy S. Widom and Michael G. Maxfield, "Exhibit 5: Does only violence beget violence?" in *An Update on the "Cycle of Violence,"* U.S. Department of Justice, National Institute of Justice, Washington, DC, February 2001

the researchers also conducted interviews with the subjects (Cathy S. Widom and Michael G. Maxfield, *An Update on the "Cycle of Violence,"* U.S. Department of Justice, National Institute of Justice, February 2001). Overall, the study found that childhood abuse or neglect increased the likelihood of arrest in adolescence by 59 percent and in adulthood by 28 percent. Childhood maltreatment also increased the likelihood of committing a violent crime by 30 percent.

While earlier analysis of the maltreated group found that most of the victims did not become offenders, this study showed that nearly half (49 percent) of the victims had experienced a nontraffic offense as teenagers or adults. Comparison by race showed that, while both white and black maltreated children had more arrests than the control group, there was no significant difference among whites in the maltreated (21.8 percent) and control (15.2 percent) groups. Among black children, however, the maltreated group had higher rates of arrests. Maltreated blacks were nearly twice as likely as the black subjects in the control group to be arrested as juveniles (40.6 percent versus 20.9 percent). (See Table 5.6.)

Widom and Maxfield also examined the type of childhood maltreatment that might lead to violence later in life. They found that physically abused children (21.1 percent) were the most likely to commit a violent crime in their teen or adult years, closely followed by those who experienced neglect (20.2 percent). Although the study showed that just 8.8 percent of children who had been sexually abused were arrested for violence, the researchers noted that the victims were mostly females, and "females less often had a record of violent offenses." (See Table 5.7.)

INMATES REPORT CHILDHOOD ABUSE

A Bureau of Justice Statistics study (Caroline Wolf Harlow, *Prior Abuse Reported by Inmates and Probationers,* U.S. Department of Justice, Washington, DC, 1999) found that male inmates and probationers who reported abuse generally were 17 years old or younger when they experienced the abuse. Their female counterparts reported being abused both as children and as adults. Between 5.8 and 14.4 percent of male offenders and between 23 and 36.7 percent of female offenders in federal and state prisons reported having been physically or sexually abused before age 18. (See Table 5.8.)

Among state prisoners with past or current violent offenses, 70.4 percent of those who had experienced abuse, compared with 60.2 percent of the nonabused, reported serving at least one sentence for a violent crime. More than three-quarters (76.5 percent) of abused male inmates were serving at least one sentence for a violent crime, compared with 61.2 percent of male offenders with no history of abuse. Almost half (45 percent) of abused female inmates were in prison for at least one violent crime, compared with 29.1 percent of females who experienced no childhood maltreatment. (See Table 5.9.)

The study found that a history of past abuse was associated with the commission of sexual assault and homi-

TABLE 5.8

Physical or sexual abuse before admission, by sex of inmate or probationer

Before admission	State inmates Male	State inmates Female	Federal inmates Male	Federal inmates Female	Jail inmates Male	Jail inmates Female	Probationers Male	Probationers Female
Ever abused	16.1%	57.2%	7.2%	39.9%	12.9%	47.6%	9.3%	40.4%
Physically[1]	13.4	46.5	6.0	32.3	10.7	37.3	7.4	33.5
Sexually[1]	5.8	39.0	2.2	22.8	5.6	37.2	4.1	25.2
Both	3.0	28.0	1.1	15.1	3.3	26.9	2.1	18.3
Age of victim at time of abuse								
17 or younger[2]	14.4%	36.7%	5.8%	23.0%	11.9%	36.6%	8.8%	28.2%
18 or older[2]	4.3	45.0	2.7	31.0	2.3	26.7	1.1	24.7
Both	2.5	24.7	1.3	14.2	1.3	15.8	0.5	12.5
Age of abuser								
Adult	15.0%	55.8%	6.9%	39.0%	12.1%	46.0%	8.5%	39.2%
Juvenile only	0.9	1.0	0.2	0.3	0.8	1.3	0.6	
Rape before admission	4.0%	37.3%	1.4%	21.4%	3.9%	33.1%	—	—
Completed	3.1	32.8	1.0	17.9	3.0	26.6	—	—
Attempted	0.8	4.3	0.3	3.2	0.7	5.6	—	—

—Not available.
[1]Includes those both physically and sexually abused.
[2]Includes those abused in both age categories.

SOURCE: Caroline Wolf Harlow, "Table 1: Physical or sexual abuse before admission, by sex of inmate or probationer," in *Prior Abuse Reported by Inmates and Probationers,* U.S. Department of Justice, Bureau of Justice Statistics, 1999

TABLE 5.9

Current and past violent offenses and past alcohol and drug use, by whether abused before admission to state prison, 1997

	Percent of state prison inmates					
	Reported being abused			Reported being not abused		
Offense history and drug and alcohol use	Total	Males	Females	Total	Males	Females
Current or past violent offense	70.4%	76.5%	45.0%	60.2%	61.2%	29.1%
Current violent offense	55.7%	61.0%	33.5%	45.3%	46.1%	20.9%
Homicide	15.9	16.3	13.9	12.7	12.8	7.3
Sexual assault	15.6	18.8	2.0	6.9	7.1	0.4
Robbery	12.5	13.5	7.8	14.5	14.7	6.1
Assault	9.5	9.9	7.6	9.3	9.4	5.7
Used an illegal drug						
Ever	88.6%	88.5%	88.9%	81.8%	81.9%	77.4%
Ever regularly	76.3	75.5	79.7	67.9	67.9	65.0
In month before offense	61.4	59.7	68.6	55.3	55.3	54.0
At time of offense	39.6	38.0	46.2	30.7	30.7	32.0
Drank alcohol						
Ever regularly	66.9%	69.1%	57.5%	59.0%	59.8%	38.2%
At time of offense	41.6	43.6	33.1	36.1	36.6	23.5

SOURCE: Caroline Wolf Harlow, "Table 3: Current and past violent offenses and past alcohol and drug abuse, by whether abused before admission in State prison, 1997," in *Prior Abuse Reported by Inmates and Probationers,* U.S. Department of Justice, Bureau of Justice Statistics, Washington, DC, 1999

cide, illegal drug use, and alcohol use. Some 75.5 percent of abused males and 79.7 percent of abused females had used illegal drugs regularly. Among the nonabused correctional population, a lower proportion of men (67.9 percent) and women (65 percent) had used illegal drugs regularly. About 69.1 percent of abused male inmates and 57.5 percent of abused female inmates had used alcohol regularly at some time in their lives, compared with 59.8 percent of nonabused male inmates and 38.2 percent of nonabused female inmates. (See Table 5.9.)

David Finkelhor and David Ormrod, in *Offenders Incarcerated for Crimes against Juveniles* (U.S. Department of Justice, Office of Juvenile Justice and Delinquency Prevention, Washington, DC, December 2001), reported that one of five inmates incarcerated in state

FIGURE 5.6

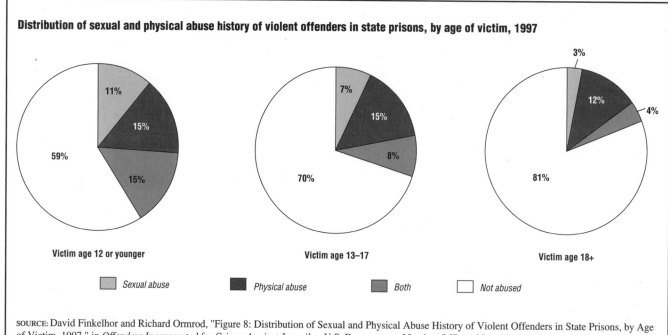

Distribution of sexual and physical abuse history of violent offenders in state prisons, by age of victim, 1997

Victim age 12 or younger

Victim age 13–17

Victim age 18+

Sexual abuse   Physical abuse   Both   Not abused

SOURCE: David Finkelhor and Richard Ormrod, "Figure 8: Distribution of Sexual and Physical Abuse History of Violent Offenders in State Prisons, by Age of Victim, 1997," in *Offenders Incarcerated for Crimes Against Juveniles,* U.S. Department of Justice, Office of Juvenile Justice and Delinquency Prevention, Washington, DC, December 2001

prisons for violent crime in 1997 was an offender who had victimized a child. These violent offenders were more likely to have experienced childhood sexual or physical abuse. Eleven percent of the offenders who victimized younger children ages 12 or under had been sexually abused during childhood. An equal proportion (15 percent each) who had victimized both younger children ages 12 or under and teens ages 13 to 17 reported having been physically abused as children themselves. (See Figure 5.6.)

CHILDHOOD MALTREATMENT, MENTAL HEALTH PROBLEMS, AND DATING VIOLENCE

Researchers in Ontario, Canada, investigated the relationship between childhood maltreatment and mental health problems and dating violence in adolescents with a history of childhood abuse and neglect (David A. Wolfe, Katreena Scott, Christine Wekerle, and Anna-Lee Pittman, "Child Maltreatment: Risk of Adjustment Problems and Dating Violence in Adolescence," *Journal of the American Academy of Child & Adolescent Psychiatry,* vol. 4, no. 3, March 2001). In a sample of 1,419 high school students ages 14 to 19, nearly one-third (462 students) reported having experienced maltreatment as children. The researchers found that maltreated females were more than nine times as likely as nonmaltreated females to suffer from significant anxiety and posttraumatic stress and more than seven times as likely to have problems with anger and depression. Maltreated females were nearly three times as likely to have committed nonviolent offenses, such as vandalism; four and a half

times as likely to have committed violent acts, such as assault; and seven times as likely to have carried a concealed weapon during the past year. They reported being nearly three times as likely to use threatening behaviors with their partners. Maltreated females were also nearly twice as likely to have suffered sexual/physical abuse by a dating partner.

In comparison, maltreated males reported lesser degrees of mental problems. They were more than three times as likely as nonmaltreated males to experience anger and posttraumatic stress and more than twice as likely to report depression. Although maltreated boys did not report significant delinquency, they were more than three times as likely than maltreated males to physically abuse their partners and almost twice as likely to be sexually abusive. They were also nearly three times as likely to threaten their partners. Maltreated males were twice as likely to have been sexually abused, two and a half times as likely to have experienced physical abuse, and three times as likely to have been threatened by their partners.

CORPORAL PUNISHMENT

All 50 states allow parents to use corporal punishment for purposes of disciplining their children. This means that the parent may use objects such as belts as long as the child does not suffer injury. When states passed child abuse laws in the 1960s, provisions allowing parents to use corporal punishment helped facilitate passage of the legislation.

As of November 2002, 23 states allowed corporal punishment in public schools, although in some schools parents can request that their children not be spanked. In August 2000 the Committee on School Health of the American Academy of Pediatrics released its policy statement advocating the abolition of corporal punishment in all schools in the United States (*Pediatrics,* vol. 106, no. 2). The committee claimed that each year corporal punishment is administered 1 million to 2 million times in the nation's schools.

In 1979 Sweden became the first country in Europe to ban all corporal punishment of children. Nine other countries prohibit corporal punishment both in the home and in school: Austria, Croatia, Cyprus, Denmark, Finland, Germany, Israel, Latvia, and Norway.

Past Widespread Practice

The 1985 *National Family Violence Resurvey* found that more than 90 percent of parents of children age three to four years old used some form of corporal punishment, ranging from a slap on the hand to severe spanking. While spanking generally decreased as the child got older, about 49 percent of 13-year-olds were still being physically punished.

Decreasing Use of Physical Punishment

Since 1988 PCA America has surveyed American parents regarding their use of physical punishment (Deborah Daro, *Public Opinion and Behaviors Regarding Child Abuse Prevention: 1999 Survey,* Chicago, IL, November 1999). In 1999, 2 of 5 parents (41 percent) reported having spanked or hit their children during the last year. In comparison, in 1988, 3 of 5 parents (62 percent) indicated having disciplined their children this way.

An October 2002 ABC News poll found that 65 percent of American parents approved of corporal punishment. Half of the parents (50 percent) who had young children at home indicated that they sometimes spanked their children. Respondents in the southern states were more likely to favor corporal punishment, compared with the rest of the country (73 percent versus 60 percent). More parents in the South (62 percent) reported spanking their children, compared to parents in the rest of the states (41 percent).

Public Attitudes Regarding the Effects of Corporal Punishment

Since 1987 the proportion of the American public surveyed by PCA America who thought physical punishment (for example, hitting or spanking) of a child very often or often harms the child has remained stable, at between 30 and 40 percent. In 1999, one-third (34 percent) believed physical punishment very often or often causes injury to a child. Another third (33 percent) thought physical punishment occasionally hurts a child. Just 18 percent felt that physical punishment hardly ever or never leads to injury to a child. (See Table 5.1.) Parents with children under age 18 tended to consider physical punishment as harmful to children (35 percent versus 33 percent of those with no children).

Corporal Punishment Increases the Risk of Physical Abuse

Straus presented a model called "path analysis" to illustrate how physical punishment could escalate to physical abuse ("Physical Abuse," Chapter 6 in *Beating the Devil out of Them: Corporal Punishment in American Families and Its Effects on Children,* 2nd ed., Transaction Publishers, New Brunswick, NJ, 2001). Straus theorized that parents who have been physically disciplined as adolescents are more likely to believe that it is acceptable to use violence to remedy a misbehavior. These parents tend to be depressed and to be involved in spousal violence. When a parent resorts to physical punishment and the child does not comply, the parent increases the severity of the punishment, eventually harming the child.

Corporal punishment experienced in adolescence produces the same effect on males and females. Parents who were hit 30 or more times as adolescents were three times (24 percent) as likely as those who never received physical punishment (7 percent) to abuse their children physically. Straus noted that his model also shows that three-quarters (76 percent) of parents who were hit many times (30 or more) as adolescents did not, in turn, abuse their children.

Prevalence and Chronicity of Corporal Punishment

Straus and Julie H. Stewart, in *Corporal Punishment by American Parents: National Data on Prevalence, Chronicity, Severity, and Duration, in Relation to Child and Family Characteristics* (Family Research Laboratory, University of New Hampshire, Durham, NH; a paper presented at the 14th World Congress of Sociology, Montreal, Canada, 1998), reported on a national survey of American parents regarding their use of corporal punishment.

Overall, based on the chronological age of the children, more than a third (35 percent) of parents surveyed used corporal punishment on their infants, reaching a peak of 94 percent of parents hitting their children who were three and four years old. The prevalence rate of parents hitting their children decreased after age five, with just over 50 percent of parents hitting their children at age 12, one-third (33 percent) at age 14, and 13 percent at age 17. The survey also found that corporal punishment was more prevalent among blacks and parents in the low socioeconomic level. It was also more commonly inflicted on boys, by mothers, and in the South.

Chronicity refers to the frequency of the infliction of corporal punishment during the year. Corporal punishment was most frequently used by parents of two-year-olds, averaging 18 times a year. After age two, chronicity declined, averaging six times a year for teenagers.

Corporal Punishment and Antisocial Behavior of Children

Straus, David B. Sugarman, and Jean Giles-Sims, in "Spanking by Parents and Subsequent Antisocial Behavior of Children" (*Archives of Pediatrics and Adolescent Medicine,* vol. 151, no. 8, August 1997), analyzed more than 900 children ages six to nine whose mothers reported using corporal punishment. The researchers found that, regardless of the child's socioeconomic status, sex, and ethnic group, and regardless of whether the parents provided emotional support, mental stimulation, and satisfactory socialization environment, corporal punishment was linked to an increase in the children's antisocial behavior between the start of the study to two years later. The antisocial behavior included cheating or lying, bullying of or cruelty to others, lack of remorse for misbehavior, deliberate destruction of things, disobedience in school, and trouble in getting along with their teachers.

The researchers pointed out that frequent physical punishment does not always result in a child's exhibiting antisocial behavior. Physical punishment, however, if used through the teen years, has been associated with adult behavior problems.

Corporal Punishment and Criminal Violence

Straus, in "Spanking and the Making of a Violent Society" (a report to the American Academy of Pediatrics, Elk Grove, IL, February 1996), indicated that, while corporal punishment alone does not cause a violent society, it increases the probability of societal violence. In explaining the connection between corporal punishment and criminal violence, Straus pointed out that almost all corporal punishment is carried out to control or correct behavior, and almost all assaults and about two-thirds of homicides are committed to correct a wrong action or behavior.

Straus noted that several studies have shown that the more corporal punishment experienced in middle childhood or early adolescence, the greater the probability of crime and violence. He notes that various studies have linked corporal punishment to delinquency, criminal arrests, and assault of family and nonfamily members. For example, in a 33-year study of individuals who experienced corporal punishment as boys (Joan McCord, "Questioning the Value of Punishment," *Social Problems,* vol. 38, no. 2, May 1991), researchers examined the conviction records of the boys when they reached middle age. Even after controlling for the criminality of the boys' fathers, corporal punishment was linked to the doubling of the proportion of sons who were convicted of serious crimes.

Straus noted the unintended consequences of physical punishment. Because parents are usually the first to hit an infant, the child learns to associate the first people he or she loves with those who hurt him or her. Parents who use physical punishment to train their children or to teach them about which dangerous things they should avoid are also teaching them that it is all right to hit other family members. Children also learn that the use of violence is justified when something is really important. Finally, parents teach their children that when a person is stressed out or angry, it is "understandable" if he or she resorts to hitting.

Corporal Punishment and Cognitive Development

In "Corporal Punishment by Mothers and Child's Cognitive Development: A Longitudinal Study" (Family Research Laboratory, University of New Hampshire, Durham, NH; a paper presented at the 14th World Congress of Sociology, Montreal, Canada, 1998), Straus and Mallie J. Paschall found that corporal punishment was associated with a child's failure to keep up with the average rate of cognitive development.

Straus and Paschall followed the cognitive development of 960 children born to mothers who participated in the *National Longitudinal Study of Youth.* The women were 14–21 years old at the start of the study. In 1986, when the women were between the ages of 21 and 28, those with children were interviewed regarding the way they were raising their children. The children underwent cognitive, psychosocial, and behavioral assessments. Children ages one to four were selected, among other reasons, because "the development of neural connections is greatest at the youngest ages." The children were tested again in 1990.

HIGH INCIDENCE AND LONG DURATION. About 7 in 10 (71 percent) mothers reported spanking their toddlers in the past week, with 6.2 percent hitting the child during the course of their interview for the study. Those who used corporal punishment reported using it an average of 3.6 times per week. This amounted to an estimated 187 spankings a year.

COGNITIVE DEVELOPMENT. Straus and Paschall found that the more prevalent the corporal punishment, the greater the decrease in cognitive ability. (See Figure 5.7.) Considering other studies, which showed that talking to children, including infants, is associated with increased neural connections in the brain and cognitive functioning, the researchers hypothesized that if parents are not using corporal punishment to discipline their child, they are very likely verbally interacting with that child, thus positively affecting cognitive development.

Moreover, corporal punishment has been found to affect cognitive development in other ways. It is believed that experiencing corporal punishment can be very stressful to children. Stress hampers children's ability to process events, which is important for their cognitive development. And since corporal punishment generally occurs over a long period, children's bonding with their parents may be minimized to the point that the children will not be motivated to learn from their parents.

OTHER FINDINGS. Straus and Paschall also found that, contrary to some beliefs that corporal punishment is acceptable if the parent provides emotional support to the child, the adverse effects of physical punishment on cognitive development remained the same whether or not there was maternal support. The results of the study also debunked the general belief among blacks that corporal punishment benefits children. The adverse consequences on cognitive development held true for all racial and ethnic groups.

IS CHILD NEGLECT A LOST CONCERN?

When most Americans think of child maltreatment, they think of abuse and not neglect. Furthermore, research literature and conferences dealing with child maltreatment have generally overlooked child neglect. The congressional hearings that took place before the passage of the landmark Child Abuse Prevention and Treatment Act of 1974 (CAPTA; Public Law 93-247) focused almost entirely on examples of physical abuse. Barely three pages of the hundreds recorded pertained to child neglect.

Nonetheless, every year the federal government reports a very high incidence of child neglect. According to HHS (*Child Maltreatment 2000,* Administration for Children and Families, Washington, DC, 2002), in 2000 more than three times as many children were victims of neglect as of physical abuse (7.3 versus 2.3 children per 1,000 child population). In addition, 34.9 percent of the children who died of child maltreatment died of neglect alone. (See Figure 4.3 and Figure 4.5 in Chapter 4.) It is important to note that these numbers pertain only to children reported to CPS and whose cases had been substantiated. Experts believe these numbers are underreported.

Child Neglect—A Major Social Problem

Neglect is an act of omission, or the absence of action. While the consequences of child neglect can be devastating, it leaves no visible marks. Moreover, it usually involves infants and very young children who cannot speak for themselves.

James M. Gaudin Jr., in "Child Neglect: Short-Term and Long-Term Outcomes" (*Neglected Children: Research, Practice, and Policy,* Sage Publications, Inc., Thousand Oaks, CA, 1999), reported that, compared with nonmaltreated and abused children, neglected children have the worst delays in language comprehension and expression. Psychologically neglected children also score lowest in IQ tests.

Emotional neglect, in its most serious form, can result in the "non-organic failure to thrive syndrome," a condi-

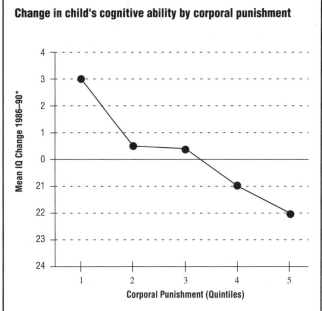

FIGURE 5.7

Change in child's cognitive ability by corporal punishment

*Adjusted for cognitive stimulation and emotional support by mother, mother's age and education, child's race, age and sex, and father in household

SOURCE: Murray A. Straus and Mallie J. Paschall, *Corporal Punishment by Mothers and Child's Cognitive Development: A Longitudinal Study,* Family Research Laboratory, Univeristy of New Hampshire, Durham, NH, 1998

tion in which a child fails to develop physically or even to survive. According to Gaudin, studies have found that, even with aggressive intervention, the neglected child continues to deteriorate. The cooperation of the neglectful parents, which is crucial to the intervention, usually declines as the child's condition worsens. This shows that it is sometimes not that easy to change the parental attributes that have contributed to the neglect in the first place.

NEW INTEREST IN CHILD NEGLECT

Since the mid-1990s child neglect has attracted the interest of government agencies and private researchers. One area of interest involves the link between father involvement and child neglect. In "Fathers and Child Neglect" (*Archives of Pediatrics & Adolescent Medicine,* vol. 154, no. 2, February 2000), Howard Dubowitz et al. examined this link in the first study of its kind. The participants included 244 low-income, inner-city families who were involved in a long-term study of child health and development in families at risk for child maltreatment. The children were under two years old when the study began, and this particular portion of the study was conducted when the children were five years old. A total of 176 children (72 percent) had a father or father figure.

The study found an overall range of 11 to 30 percent of child neglect in the households. The nature of father involvement, however, not the absence of the father, was associated with neglect. The researchers found that less child neglect was associated with the following: a longer duration of father involvement in the child's life, the positive feelings the father had about his parenting skills, the father's greater involvement with household chores, and the father's less involvement with child care. Interestingly, the father's greater involvement with child care resulted in more child neglect. Dubowitz et al. explained that other studies have shown that fathers tended to be more involved in child care when the mothers were unavailable.

HOUSEHOLD COMPOSITION AND RISK OF MALTREATMENT DEATH

In 2000 about 1,200 children died of abuse or neglect in the United States. About 81 percent of these children were five years old or younger, making maltreatment the main cause of injury death in this age group. To determine the role of family composition as a risk factor for fatal child maltreatment, researchers examined all information related to Missouri resident children under five years old who died in that state within a three-year period (Michael N. Stiffman et al., "Household Composition and Risk of Fatal Child Maltreatment," *Pediatrics,* vol. 109, no. 4, April 2002).

Stiffman et al. used the comprehensive data of child deaths (birth through age 17) collected by the Missouri Child Fatality Review Panel (CFRP) system between 1992 and 1994. The CFRP data contained information on all household members and their relationship to the deceased child. For comparison, the researchers used a control group consisting of children under age five who had died of natural causes. Of the 291 injury deaths that were examined, 60 percent (175 children) were determined to have died of maltreatment. Nearly one-third (31 percent, or 55 children) of the deaths resulted from injury caused by a parent or other caregiver. Of this group, 39 of the children died from being shaken, hit, or dropped. Eleven children died from the use of physical objects, including guns. The cause of death for the remaining five children was unknown.

The study found that children living in households with one or more biologically unrelated adult males and boyfriends of the child's mother had the highest risk of death from maltreatment. These children were eight times more likely to die of maltreatment than children living with two biological parents with no other adults. Children residing with foster and adoptive parents, as well as with stepparents, were nearly five times as likely to suffer maltreatment deaths. Those living in households with other adult relatives present were twice as likely to die from maltreatment. Children living with just one biological parent, however, with no other adult present, were not at increased risk for fatal maltreatment.

CHAPTER 6
CHILD SEXUAL ABUSE

A BETRAYAL OF TRUST

Many experts believe that sexual abuse is the most underreported type of child maltreatment. A victim, especially a very young child, may not know what he or she is experiencing. In many cases, the child is sworn to secrecy. Adults who may be aware of the abuse sometimes get involved in a conspiracy of silence.

Child sexual abuse is the ultimate misuse of an adult's trust and power over a child. When the abuser is particularly close to the victim, the child feels betrayed, trapped in a situation where an adult who claims to care for the child is assaulting him or her.

In early 2002 the nation first heard about John Geoghan, a former priest in the Archdiocese of Boston, who was sentenced to 9 to 10 years in prison for sexually abusing a boy. Some 130 more people had brought accusations of sexual abuse against the priest. Church documents, which had previously been sealed, revealed that the church had paid settlements amounting to $15 million to the victims' families. Documents also revealed that Geoghan's superiors, including Boston's Cardinal Bernard Law, had not only been involved in a cover-up of Geoghan's abuse but had reassigned him to different parishes, where he continued to work with children.

FREUD

The first person to present childhood sexual abuse as a source of psychological problems was Austrian psychoanalyst Sigmund Freud (1856–1939). Early in his career, Freud proposed that the hysteria he saw in some of his patients was the result of childhood sexual abuse. He thought his patients' symptoms represented symbolic manifestations of their repressed sexual memories. Freud later changed his mind, denying that he thought sexual abuse had taken place. Instead, he proposed that young children have an unconscious sexual attachment to the parent of the opposite sex and a sense of rivalry with the parent of the same sex. This is called the Oedipus complex in males and the Electra complex in females. In other words, the adult's memories of incestuous experiences were remnants of his or her childhood desires to be seduced by an adult. Freud theorized that, under the normal psychological development process, the child starts to identify with the parent of the same sex. He claimed that if this does not occur, the individual will develop personality disorders in adulthood.

Some scholars have proposed that Freud revised his theory because he was pressured by colleagues to recant. Psychoanalyst Alice Miller claimed that Freud suppressed the truth so that he, his colleagues, and men in Viennese society would be spared having to examine their own histories. Some experts believe that the testimonies Freud originally elicited from his patients were cases of incestuous abuse. Others believe that he changed his theory to preserve his concept of repression, on which he based the whole structure of psychoanalysis.

WHAT IS CHILD SEXUAL ABUSE?

Federal Definition

The Child Abuse Prevention and Treatment Act of 1974 (CAPTA; Public Law 93-247) specifically identified parents and caretakers as the perpetrators of sexual abuse. Sexual molestation by other individuals was considered sexual assault. The 1996 amendments to this law, however, included a more comprehensive definition, one that also included sexually abusive behavior by individuals other than parents and caretakers.

The CAPTA Amendments of 1996 (Public Law 104-235; Sec. 111 [42 U.S.C. 5106g]) defines child sexual abuse as:

• The employment, use, persuasion, inducement, enticement, or coercion of any child to engage in, or assist any other person to engage in, any sexually explicit conduct or simulation of such conduct for the purpose of producing a visual depiction of such conduct; or

- the rape, and in cases of caretaker or interfamilial relationships, statutory rape, molestation, prostitution, or other form of sexual exploitation of children, or incest with children.

Specific Definition Varies by State

Whereas the federal government has established a broad definition of child sexual abuse, it leaves it up to state child abuse laws to specify detailed provisions. All states have laws prohibiting child sexual molestation and generally consider incest illegal. States also specify the age of consent, or the age at which a person can consent to sexual activity with an adult—generally between the ages of 14 and 18. Sexual activity between an adult and a person below the age of consent is against the law.

TYPES OF CHILD SEXUAL ABUSE

Familial abuse, or incest, involves the use of a child for sexual satisfaction by family members—blood relatives who are too close to marry legally. Extrafamilial abuse involves a person outside the family. Extrafamilial predators may be strangers, but they may also be persons in a position of trust, such as family friends, teachers, and spiritual advisers.

Some researchers define incest not in terms of blood ties, but in terms of the emotional bond between the victim and the offender. Suzanne M. Sgroi, an expert on child sexual abuse, believes that the presence or absence of blood relationships is far less important than the kinship roles the abusers play. When live-in help or a parent's lover is the abuser, there may be no blood relationship, but the abuse is still taking place within the context of the family.

HOW FREQUENT IS ABUSE?

Research on the problem of child sexual abuse is contradictory and the more studies that are done, the more researchers find that the extent of the problem is difficult to measure. Because state definitions vary, the number of cases of abuse may not include acts committed by nonfamily members. Therefore, rates of child sexual abuse reported are generally just estimates. In the 1955 *Incest Behavior* (Citadel Press, New York, NY) S. K. Weinberg calculated the average yearly rate to be 1.9 cases per 1 million children.

By 1969 Dr. Vincent De Francis and the American Humane Association had found an annual rate of 40 cases per 1 million children. In 1996 the *Third National Incidence Study of Child Abuse and Neglect* (NIS-3) reported a rate of 3.2 cases of sexual abuse per 1,000 children using the Harm Standard and 4.5 per 1,000 children using the Endangerment Standard.

Some Victims May Not Be Counted

Estimates of the number of sexual abuse cases generally do not include victims of pornographic exploitation and child prostitution. These types of child abuse have only recently become subjects of research, and while they are known to involve multimillion-dollar businesses, little is known about the numbers of child victims involved.

The estimates also do not include stranger abductions, often for sexual purposes, that result in the death of the child. The Second National Incidence Studies of Missing, Abducted, Runaway, and Thrownaway Children (NISMART-2) found that, during the study year 1999, an estimated 58,200 children were victims of nonfamily abductions (David Finkelhor, Heather Hammer, and Andrea J. Sedlak, *Nonfamily Abducted Children: National Estimates and Characteristics,* U.S. Department of Justice, Office of Juvenile Justice and Delinquency Prevention, October 2002). The study also reported an estimated 115 cases of stereotypical kidnapping, the kind that makes it to the news because of its seriousness or duration. The authors noted that the larger number of 58,200 resulted from using a broad definition of nonfamily abduction.

Abduction is typically associated with very serious life-and-death situations involving strangers. Abduction, however, according to legal definition, may involve less serious cases. For its incidence study, NISMART-2 used two definitions: stereotypical kidnapping and nonfamily abduction. Stereotypical kidnapping refers to kidnapping committed by a stranger or a slight acquaintance who keeps the child overnight, transports the child at least 50 or more miles, takes the child for ransom, or takes the child to keep him permanently or to kill him. (A slight acquaintance may be a person the child has known for less than six months. The person may be someone the child has known for more than six months but has seen less than once a month. A slight acquaintance may also be a person the child does not know well enough to have spoken to.) Nonfamily abduction includes stereotypical kidnapping, as well as less serious kidnappings. It may involve luring a child for purposes of collecting ransom or keeping the child permanently. It may also involve the forceful transporting of a child or the detention of a child for at least an hour.

Children ages 12 to 17 accounted for an estimated 81 percent of nonfamily abductions and for about 58 percent of stereotypical kidnappings. About two-thirds of the victims of both nonfamily (65 percent) and stereotypical (69 percent) abductions were girls. The authors noted that, in most cases, abductions were carried out for sexual purposes. Although the sample cases showed that more non-Hispanic black children (42 percent) than non-Hispanic white children (35 percent) were involved in nonfamily abductions, the larger proportion for blacks may just be due to the sample studied. Among child victims of stereo-typical kidnapping, there were nearly four times as many white victims (72 percent) as blacks (19 percent). (See Table 6.1.)

More than half (53 percent) of perpetrators of non-family abductions were people known to the child, including neighbors, authority figures, friends, long-term acquaintances, and caretakers. Strangers made up more than one-third (37 percent) of nonfamily abductors. Most perpetrators of nonfamily (75 percent) and stereotypical (86 percent) kidnapping were males. Almost half of the victims of nonfamily abductions (46 percent) and stereo-typical kidnappings (49 percent) were sexually assaulted.

Is the Federal Count of Sexual Abuse Flawed?

Diana E. H. Russell and Rebecca M. Bolen, in *The Epidemic of Rape and Child Sexual Abuse in the United States* (Sage Publications, Inc., Thousand Oaks, CA, 2000), claimed that the incidence of child sexual abuse reported by the *National Incidence Study of Child Abuse and Neglect* was flawed. The authors noted that the feder-al study counted only abuse committed by parents or care-takers. Sexual abuse by persons not in the caretaking role (for example, siblings, neighbors, and acquaintances), and by peers and strangers was not included in the study.

The Endangerment Standard of the *National Inci-dence Study of Child Abuse and Neglect,* however, count-ed as perpetrators those who allowed sexual abuse to take place. The authors believed that this definition of child sexual abuse perpetrators was out of step with other defin-itions used in research. The authors also considered this practice sexist, because males related to the child were typically the molesters, and mothers were usually blamed for not protecting their children. Finally, the incidence of child sexual abuse was undercounted because only cases substantiated or indicated by child protective services (CPS) were included in the national study.

Adults Who Disclose Sexual Abuse

David Finkelhor, director of the Crimes against Chil-dren Research Center at the University of New Hampshire in Durham, is a national authority on child sexual abuse. In "Current Information on the Scope and Nature of Child Sexual Abuse" (*The Future of Children: Sexual Abuse of Children,* vol. 4, no. 2, Summer/Fall 1994), Finkelhor noted that surveys of adults regarding their childhood experiences (called retrospective studies) probably give the most complete estimates of the actual extent of child sexual abuse. He reviewed 19 adult retrospective surveys and found that the proportion of adults who indicated sex-ual abuse during childhood ranged widely, from 2 to 62 percent for females and from 3 to 16 percent for males.

Finkelhor observed that the surveys that reported high-er levels of abuse were those that asked multiple questions

TABLE 6.1

Characteristics of nonfamily abducted children

Characteristic of Child	All Nonfamily Abduction Victims (n= 58,200)		Stereotypical Kidnapping Victims (n = 115)		Percent of U.S. Child Population* (N = 70,172,700)
	Percent	Estimate	Percent	Estimate	
Age (years)					
0–5	7[1]	4,300[1]	19	20	33
6–11	12[1]	6,800[1]	24	25	34
12–14	22[1]	13,000[1]	38	45	17
15–17	59	34,100	20	20	17
Gender					
Male	35[1]	20,300[1]	31	35	51
Female	65	37,900	69	80	49
Race/ethnicity					
White, non-Hispanic	35	20,500	72	80	65
Black, non-Hispanic	42[1]	24,500[1]	19	20	15
Hispanic	23[1]	13,200[1]	8[1]	10[1]	16
Other	<1[1]	<100[1]	2[1]	<5[1]	5
Region					
Northeast	<1[2]	<100[1]	n/a[2]	n/a	18
Midwest	33	19,300	n/a	n/a	23
South	38[2]	21,900[1]	n/a	n/a	35
West	29[1]	16,900[1]	n/a	n/a	24
No information	<1[2]	100[2]	100	115	—

Note: All estimates are rounded to the nearest 100. Percents may not sum to 100 because of rounding.
* Age, gender, and race for the U.S. population were based on the average monthly estimates of the population ages 0–17 years for 1999 (U.S. Census Bureau, 2000a). The regional distribution of the population was computed from State-by-State estimates of the population ages 0–17 as of July 1, 1999 (U.S. Census Bureau, 2000b).
[1]Estimate is based on too few sample cases to be reliable.
[2]n/a = not available.

SOURCE: David Finkelhor, Heather Hammer, and Andrea J. Sedlak, "Table 2: Characteristics of Nonfamily Abducted Children," in *Nonfamily Abducted Children: National Estimates and Characteristics,* U.S. Department of Justice, Office of Juvenile Justice and Delinquency Prevention, Washington, DC, October 2002

about the possibility of abuse. Multiple questions are more effective because they provide respondents various "cues" about the different kinds of experiences the researchers are asking about. Multiple questions also give the respondents ample time to overcome their embarrassment. Many experts accept the estimate that 1 of 5 (20 percent) Ameri-can women and 1 of 10 (10 percent) American men were subjected to some form of sexual abuse as children.

Do some adults exaggerate trivial incidents or fab-ricate experiences that inflate abuse statistics? Finkel-hor believed that there was no evidence to suggest that fabrication had distorted the validity of surveys, and yet no study has ever been done that examined the actu-al circumstances of alleged abuse reported in any large-scale study.

While the actual numbers of sexual abuse can only be roughly estimated, experts do agree that demographic trends suggest that more children are in situations of risk than ever before. More mothers are working outside the home, more children are in day care centers, and more parents are divorcing and remarrying, bringing stepfami-lies together in much greater numbers than ever before.

FIGURE 6.1

Substantiated cases of child sexual abuse, 1990–98

Note: Extrapolated to the U.S. child population.

SOURCE: Lisa Jones and David Finkelhor, "Figure 1: Substantiated Cases of Child Sexual Abuse, 1990-98," in *The Decline in Child Sexual Abuse Cases,* U.S. Department of Justice, Office of Juvenile Justice and Delinquency Prevention, Washington, DC, January 2001

ARE CHILD SEXUAL ABUSE CASES DECLINING?

CPS agencies across the United States report that, following the great numbers of child sexual abuse cases of the 1980s and early 1990s, reported and substantiated cases have declined since 1992. Finkelhor and Lisa Jones (*The Decline in Child Sexual Abuse Cases,* U.S. Department of Justice, Office of Juvenile Justice and Delinquency Prevention, Washington, DC, January 2001) examined the possible factors responsible for the decline.

Reported child sexual abuse cases declined 26 percent from an estimated 429,000 in 1991 to 315,400 in 1998. Substantiated, or confirmed, cases dropped from a peak of 149,800 in 1992 to 103,600 in 1998, a 31 percent decrease. (See Figure 6.1). Between 1990 and 1992 just three states experienced a decrease in cases of substantiated child sexual abuse, compared to 14 states reporting increases of 20 percent or more. The decreasing trend started between the 1992–94 period, with 22 states reporting a decline of 20 percent or more, followed by 18 states reporting declines between 1994 and 1996. From 1996 to 1998, 13 states showed decreases of 20 percent or more substantiated child sexual abuse cases. (See Figure 6.2.)

According to the authors, several factors may influence the decline in substantiated cases of child sexual abuse. (See Figure 6.3.) Since the 1990s the incidence of child sexual abuse may have been reduced by such factors as child victimization prevention programs, incarceration of sexual offenders, treatment programs for sex offenders, as well as other variables that may cause child sexual abuse. These variables include female victimization by intimate partners and poverty. In other words, declining trends in these causal variables may play a role in the decreasing cases of child sexual abuse. Experts have

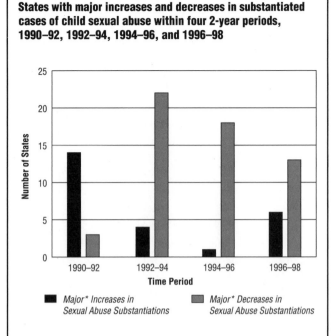

FIGURE 6.2

States with major increases and decreases in substantiated cases of child sexual abuse within four 2-year periods, 1990–92, 1992–94, 1994–96, and 1996–98

*Twenty percent or more.

SOURCE: Lisa Jones and David Finkelhor, "Figure 2: States With Major Increases and Decreases in Substantiated Cases of Child Sexual Abuse Within Four 2-Year Periods," in *The Decline in Child Sexual Abuse Cases,* U.S. Department of Justice, Office of Juvenile Justice and Delinquency Prevention, Washington, DC, January 2001

shown a 30 to 60 percent overlap in the victimization of children and the victimization of their mothers. Since 1993 a 21 percent decrease in female victimization by intimate partners has been reported. Poverty, down 18 percent between 1993 and 1998, while more often linked to cases of neglect and physical abuse, has also been found to contribute to child sexual abuse.

Jones and Finkelhor suggested that the drop in reports of child sexual abuse between 1991 to 1998 may be due to people's reluctance to report their suspicions because of widely publicized cases of false accusations. The public and mandated reporters, such as health care professionals, may have learned accurate identification of the signs of abuse. In addition, the large numbers of sexual abuse cases that had surfaced as a result of increased vigilance starting in the 1980s may have been exhausted.

The investigation of child sexual abuse may have changed in scope. The authors noted that some CPS agencies may not be screening certain cases, such as sexual abuse by nonfamily members. Agencies with large caseloads may be investigating just cases they deemed serious enough to warrant their time. These factors also affect the sexual abuse count. Changes in agency criteria of which investigated cases are substantiated may also affect the final count of substantiated cases.

Jones and Finkelhor pointed out that, if declining numbers of child sexual abuse resulted from intimidation of child abuse reporters or changes in CPS investigative and substantiating policies, more research is needed. They suggested better training of professionals in identifying abuse. They also suggested exploring the cases that had not been investigated or substantiated and the changes in CPS procedures that caused the decline.

A LANDMARK STUDY OF CHILD SEXUAL ABUSE

One of the early landmark studies of child sexual abuse was conducted by sociologist Diana E. H. Russell in 1978. She surveyed 930 adult women in San Francisco about their early sexual experiences (*The Secret Trauma: Incest in the Lives of Girls and Women,* Basic Books, New York, NY, 1986). Russell reported that 38 percent of the women had suffered incestuous and extrafamilial sexual abuse before their eighteenth birthday. About 16 percent had been abused by a family member.

Russell's study is still frequently cited by experts who believe that much more abuse occurs than is officially reported by government studies. They suggest the high results recorded in her study reflect the thoroughness of her preparation. While other studies have asked one question concerning childhood sexual abuse, she asked 14 different questions, any one of which might have set off a memory of sexual abuse.

In 2000, in *The Epidemic of Rape and Child Sexual Abuse in the United States,* Russell and Bolen revisited the prevalence rates reported in Russell's 1978 survey. The authors believed those rates to be underestimates. The 1978 survey subjects did not include two groups regarded to be at very high risk for child sexual abuse: females in institutions and those not living at home. The authors also found that some women were reluctant to reveal experiences of abuse to survey interviewers, while others did not recall these experiences.

MULTIPLE ABUSE AND POLYINCEST

M. Sue Crowley and Brenda L. Seery sought to address what they believed to be a gap in studies on childhood sexual abuse—the study of multiple abuse and polyincest. In "Exploring the Multiplicity of Childhood Sexual Abuse with a Focus on Polyincestuous Contexts of Abuse" (*Journal of Child Sexual Abuse,* vol. 10, no. 4, 2001), the authors found that, in a sample of 88 adult women undergoing treatment for childhood sexual abuse, 43 percent reported having been sexually molested by multiple (three or more) abusers and 23 percent reported having experienced polyincest. The authors described a polyincestuous situation as one in which more than one family member related by blood, adoption, or marriage is involved in the sexual abuse of other family members.

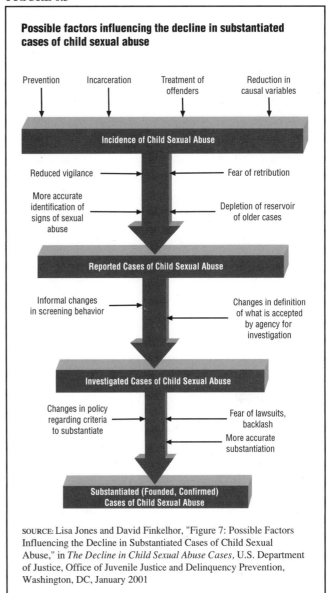

FIGURE 6.3

Possible factors influencing the decline in substantiated cases of child sexual abuse

SOURCE: Lisa Jones and David Finkelhor, "Figure 7: Possible Factors Influencing the Decline in Substantiated Cases of Child Sexual Abuse," in *The Decline in Child Sexual Abuse Cases,* U.S. Department of Justice, Office of Juvenile Justice and Delinquency Prevention, Washington, DC, January 2001

Of the 88 women, 30 agreed to extensive interviews. Among this group, 14 women reported polyincestuous abuse, including six who were molested by female relatives in addition to experiencing sexual abuse by other perpetrators. Upon disclosure of abuse, all single-abuse, multiple-abuse, and polyincest victims suffered different forms of silencing, including minimizing and denying of the abuse. Compared to single-abuse and multiple-abuse victims, victims of polyincest received very little or no support from friends and authorities. They also suffered threats from family members for revealing their abuse, therefore allowing the perpetrator to revictimize the child over time.

THE VICTIMS

Gender

Virtually all studies indicate that girls are far more likely than boys to suffer sexual abuse. Under the Harm and Endangerment Standards of NIS-3, girls were sexually abused about three times more often than boys.

GIRLS SUFFER ABUSE BY DATING PARTNERS. In the most comprehensive study of dating abuse among adolescents, researchers found that one of five adolescent females ages 14 to 18 had been a victim of physical or sexual abuse, or both, by dating partners (Jay G. Silverman, Anita Raj, Lorelei A. Mucci, and Jeanne E. Hathaway, "Dating Violence against Adolescent Girls and Associated Substance Use, Unhealthy Weight Control, Sexual Risk Behavior, Pregnancy, and Suicidality," *Journal of the American Medical Association,* vol. 286, no. 5, August 1, 2001).

The researchers analyzed the responses of Massachusetts public high school students grades 9 through 12 to the 1997 and 1999 *Youth Risk Behavior Survey,* a national assessment survey conducted by states. Massachusetts was the first state to include a question about sexual and physical abuse from dating partners. Female respondents to the two surveys consisted of more than 4,100 students. The survey found that about one of five female high school students (20.2 percent in 1997 and 18 percent in 1999) in Massachusetts had been sexually and/or physically abused by a date. Silverman et al. suggested that the same proportions may be applied to the students' counterparts in the rest of the states.

IS SEXUAL ABUSE OF BOYS UNDERREPORTED? Dr. William C. Holmes of the University of Pennsylvania School of Medicine claimed that sexual abuse of boys is not only common but also underreported and undertreated. In "Sexual Abuse of Boys: Definition, Prevalence, Correlates, Sequelae, and Management" (*Journal of the American Medical Association,* vol. 281, no. 21, December 2, 1998), Dr. Holmes reviewed 149 studies of male sexual abuse. These studies, conducted between 1985 and 1997, included face-to-face interviews, telephone surveys, medical chart reviews, and computerized and paper questionnaires. The respondents included adolescents (ninth-through twelfth-graders, runaways, non-sex-offending delinquents, and detainees), college students, psychiatric patients, Native Americans, sex offenders (including serial rapists), substance-abusing patients, and homeless men. Dr. Holmes found that, overall, one in five boys had been sexually abused.

Dr. Holmes found that boys younger than 13 years of age, nonwhite, of low socioeconomic status, and not living with their fathers were at a higher risk for sexual abuse. Boys whose parents had abused alcohol; had criminal records; and were divorced, separated, or remarried were more likely to experience sexual abuse. Sexually abused boys were 15 times more likely than boys who had never been sexually abused to live in families in which some members had also been sexually abused.

TABLE 6.2

Age profile of the victims of sexual assault, 1991–96

Victim age	All sexual assault	Forcible rape	Forcible sodomy	Sexual assault with object	Forcible fondling
Total	100.0%	100.0%	100.0%	100.0%	100.0%
0 to 5	14.0%	4.3%	24.0%	26.5%	20.2%
6 to 11	20.1	8.0	30.8	23.2	29.3
12 to 17	32.8	33.5	24.0	25.5	34.3
18 to 24	14.2	22.6	8.7	9.7	7.7
25 to 34	11.5	19.6	7.5	8.3	5.0
Above 34	7.4	12.0	5.1	6.8	3.5

SOURCE: Howard N. Snyder, "Table 1: Age profile of the victims of sexual assault," in *Sexual Assault of Young Children as Reported to Law Enforcement: Victim, Incident, and Offender Characteristics,* U.S. Department of Justice, Bureau of Justice Statistics, Washington, DC, July 2000

Start and Duration of Abuse

Kathleen Kendall-Tackett and Roberta Marshall, in "Sexual Victimization of Children" (*Issues in Intimate Violence,* Raquel Kennedy Bergen, ed., Sage Publications, Inc., Thousand Oaks, CA, 1998), reported that studies have found that the age of victims at the start of the abuse could be anywhere between 7 and 13, although there had been cases of sexual abuse among children 6 years of age or younger. The sexual abuse may be a one-time occurrence or it may last for several years. The authors found durations of abuse ranging from 2.5 to 8 years.

In *Sexual Assault of Young Children as Reported to Law Enforcement: Victim, Incident, and Offender Characteristics* (U.S. Department of Justice, Bureau of Justice Statistics, Washington, DC, 2000), Howard N. Snyder found that 34.1 percent of all victims of sexual assault reported to law enforcement from 1991 to 1996 were under age 12, with 14 percent (1 of 7 victims) under age 6. (See Table 6.2.) (Some researchers distinguish between child sexual abuse as perpetrated by parents or caretakers and sexual assault as committed by other individuals. In this report, the term "sexual assault" included child sexual abuse.)

MALE VICTIMS. In his research on male child victims, Dr. Holmes found that sexual abuse generally began before puberty. About 17 to 53 percent of the respondents reported repeated abuse, with some victimization continuing over periods of less than 6 months and some victimization enduring for 18- to 48-month periods.

THE PERPETRATORS

Howard N. Snyder (*Sexual Assault of Young Children as Reported to Law Enforcement: Victim, Incident, and Offender Characteristics*) found that the abusers of young victims were more likely than the abusers of older victims to be family members. Sexual abusers whose victims were children five years old and younger were family members nearly half the time (48.6 percent), a number

TABLE 6.3

TABLE 6.4

Victim-offender relationship in sexual assault, 1991–96

	Offenders			
Victim age	Total	Family member	Acquaintance	Stranger
All victims	**100.0%**	**26.7%**	**59.6%**	**13.8%**
Juveniles	**100.0%**	**34.2%**	**58.7%**	**7.0%**
0 to 5	100.0	48.6	48.3	3.1
6 to 11	100.0	42.4	52.9	4.7
12 to 17	100.0	24.3	66.0	9.8
Adults	**100.0%**	**11.5%**	**61.1%**	**27.3%**
18 to 24	100.0	9.8	66.5	23.7
Above 24	100.0	12.8	57.1	30.1

SOURCE: Howard N. Snyder, "Table 6: Victim-offender relationship in sexual assault," in *Sexual Assault of Young Children as Reported to Law Enforcement: Victim, Incident, and Offender Characteristics,* U.S. Department of Justice, Bureau of Justice Statistics, Washington, DC, July 2000

Victim-offender relationship in sexual assault, by victim gender, 1991–96

	Offenders			
Victim age	Total	Family member	Acquaintance	Stranger
Female victims	**100.0%**	**25.7%**	**59.5%**	**14.7%**
Juveniles	100.0%	33.9	58.7	7.5
0 to 5	100.0	51.1	45.9	3.0
6 to 11	100.0	43.8	51.4	4.8
12 to 17	100.0	24.3	65.7	10.0
Adults	100.0%	11.5	61.0	27.5
18 to 24	100.0	9.8	66.4	23.8
Above 24	100.0	12.9	56.9	30.2
Male victims	**100.0%**	**32.8%**	**59.8%**	**7.3%**
Juveniles	100.0%	35.8	59.2	5.0
0 to 5	100.0	42.4	54.1	3.5
6 to 11	100.0	37.7	57.7	4.6
12 to 17	100.0	23.7	68.7	7.6
Adults	100.0%	11.3	63.9	24.8
18 to 24	100.0	10.7	68.4	20.9
Above 24	100.0	11.8	60.3	27.9

SOURCE: Howard N. Snyder, "Table 7: Victim-offender relationship in sexual assault, by victim gender," in *Sexual Assault of Young Children as Reported to Law Enforcement: Victim, Incident, and Offender Characteristics,* U.S. Department of Justice, Bureau of Justice Statistics, Washington, DC, July 2000

that decreased for 6- to 11-year-olds (42.4 percent), and further decreased for victims ages 12 to 17 (24.3 percent). (See Table 6.3.) More female victims (51.1 percent of those 5 years old and younger and 43.8 percent of those ages 6–11) were abused by family members, compared with their male counterparts (42.4 percent of those 5 years old and younger and 37.7 percent of those ages 6–11). (See Table 6.4.)

Fathers

Finkelhor, in "The Sexual Abuse of Children: Current Research Reviewed" (*Psychiatric Annals: The Journal of Continuing Psychiatric Education,* April 1987), found that, while case reports from child welfare systems were dominated by sexual abuse by fathers and stepfathers, such cases actually made up no more than 7–8 percent of all sexual abuse cases. Other family members (usually uncles and older brothers) accounted for 16–42 percent, while nonrelatives known to the child (for example, neighbors, family friends, child care workers) accounted for 32–60 percent of perpetrators.

Finkelhor and Linda Meyer Williams, in *The Characteristics of Incestuous Fathers* (Family Research Laboratory, University of New Hampshire, Durham, NH, 1992), found that, generally, incestuous fathers had lonely childhoods (82 percent). Almost half (47 percent) had not lived with their own fathers and had changed living arrangements (43 percent), perhaps as a result of parental divorce or remarriage. Their own parents' alcohol problem, however, was no different from that of the nonabused comparison group. Incestuous fathers were far more likely to have been juvenile delinquents and to have been rejected by their parents. The researchers also found that the sex education of incestuous fathers while growing up did not come from friends or peers, but from being victims of sexual abuse. About 70 percent had a history of sexual

abuse, with 45 percent having multiple abusers. Nearly three of five were sexually abused by nonfamily adults.

Women Who Abuse

Until recently, experts thought female sex abusers were uncommon. When women were involved in abuse, it was thought to be a situation in which a man had forced the woman to commit the abuse. Some experts postulate that women are more maternal and, therefore, less likely to abuse a child. Women are also thought to have different attitudes toward sex. While a man ties his feelings of self-worth to his sexual experiences, a woman is supposedly less concerned with sexual prowess and tends to be more empathetic toward others.

Some researchers have proposed that the abusive behavior of women is influenced by severe psychiatric disturbance, mental retardation, brain damage, or male coercion. C. Allen studied female offenders in *A Comparative Analysis of Women Who Sexually Abuse Children* (Final Report to the National Center on Child Abuse and Neglect, Iowa State University, 1990) and found that their lives involved particularly harsh childhoods marked by instability and abuse.

Comparing male and female offenders, Allen found that the women reported more severe incidents of physical and emotional abuse in their pasts, had run away from home more often, were more sexually promiscuous than male offenders, and had more frequent incidents of being paid for sex. Both male and female offenders reported that their victims were most often members of their own families.

Because they perceived child sexual abuse as a great social deviance, female offenders were less likely to admit guilt. They were less cooperative than men during the investigations and were angrier with informants and investigators. Following disclosure, they also appeared to experience less guilt and sorrow than male offenders.

MOTHERS. Sexual abuse by mothers may remain undetected because it occurs at home and is either denied or never reported. Mothers generally have more intimate contact with their children, and the lines between maternal love and care and sexual abuse are not as clear-cut as they are for fathers. Furthermore, society is reluctant to see a woman as a perpetrator of incest, portraying the woman as someone likely to turn her pain inward into depression, compared with the man who acts out his anger in sexually criminal behavior.

Sibling Sexual Abusers

Sibling incest is another form of abuse that has not been well studied. Some experts, however, believe that sibling sexual abuse is more common than father–daughter incest. Vernon R. Wiehe ("Sibling Abuse," *Understanding Family Violence: Treating and Preventing Partner, Child, Sibling, and Elder Abuse,* Sage Publications, Inc., Thousand Oaks, CA, 1998) believed that the problem of sibling incest has not received much attention because of the families' reluctance to report to authorities that such abuse is happening at home, the parents' playing down of the fact that "it" is indeed a problem, and the perception that it is normal for brothers and sisters to explore their sexuality.

The author also felt that a very serious factor is that the victim may be living with threats of real harm from the abusive sibling. Indeed, in the author's nationwide survey of survivors of sibling abuse, the incest victims reported an interaction of physical abuse and incest, such as threats of physical harm, or even death, if the parents were told. An interaction of emotional abuse and incest might involve constant humiliation of the victim from the sibling perpetrator, such as comments that the victim was no longer a virgin.

Wiehe believed that sexual abuse by a sibling should be considered a crime of rape because the perpetrator uses aggression, force, or threats. Moreover, the consequences to the victim are the same whether the sexual abuse takes the form of fondling or intercourse.

Babysitters

As more and more working parents depend on outside help to care for their children, law enforcement has recognized the importance of collecting information about these caretakers. Although the Federal Bureau of Investigation National Incident-Based Reporting System will eventually replace its Uniform Crime Report program as the national statistical database of crimes reported to law enforcement, it has not yet evolved into a complete national system. Nonetheless, its four-year (1995 through 1998) compiled data about the offenses against children committed by babysitters showed more than 1,435 babysitter victimizations.

In *Crimes against Children by Babysitters,* (U.S. Department of Justice, Office of Juvenile Justice and Delinquency Prevention, Washington, DC, September 2001), Finkelhor and Richard Ormrod reported that, about two-thirds (65 percent) of babysitter offenses reported to police were sex offenses. Forcible fondling comprised 41 percent of the sex offenses, followed by 11 percent of sodomy and 9 percent of rape. Another 3 percent were made up of sexual assault with an object. (See Figure 6.4.) In comparison, simple assault accounted for approximately 25 percent of babysitter offenses, and aggravated assault accounted for another 9 percent.

Overall, 63 percent of babysitters reported for offenses against children were male and 37 percent were females. Among male offenders, 77 percent were sex offenders. A majority (71 percent) of male sex offenders victimized females and more than half (54 percent) victimized children under six years of age. Female sex offenders, however, nearly equally victimized female (46 percent) and male (54 percent) children; and more than two-thirds (68 percent) of their victims were younger children ages 0 to 6. (See Figure 6.5.) Babysitter sex offenders were generally teens (48 percent). Nevertheless, while female sex offenders were more likely to be adolescents ages 13 to 15 (67 percent), male sex offenders tended to be adults (58 percent).

Sexual Abusers of Boys

Dr. Holmes's review of 149 studies of boys and young male adolescents who experienced sexual abuse revealed that more than 90 percent of their abusers were male ("Sexual Abuse of Boys: Definition, Prevalence, Correlates, Sequelae, and Management"). Male abusers of older male teenagers and young male adults, however, made up 22 to 73 percent of perpetrators. This older age group also experienced abuse by females, ranging from 27 to 78 percent. Adolescent babysitters accounted for up to half of female sexual abusers of younger boys.

More than half of those who sexually abused male children were not family members, but were known to the victims. Boys younger than six years old were more likely to be sexually abused by family and acquaintances, while those older than 12 were more likely to be victims of strangers. While male perpetrators used physical force, with threats of physical harm increasing with victim age, female perpetrators used persuasion and promises of special favors. One study reviewed by Dr. Holmes found that up to one-third of boys participated in the abuse out of curiosity.

FIGURE 6.4

Types of crime committed against juveniles by babysitters, 1995–98

Forcible fondling
Forcible sodomy
Forcible rape
Sexual assault with object
Nonforcible offenses
Simple assault
Aggravated assault
Kidnaping
Homicide

Percentage of all offenses
(*N*=1,435 offenses)

Legend:
■ Sex offenses ■ Physical assaults ▨ Other crimes

SOURCE: David Finkelhor and Richard Ormrod, "Figure 3: Types of Crime Committed Against Juveniles by Babysitters," in *Crimes Against Children by Babysitters,* U.S. Department of Justice, Office of Juvenile Justice and Delinquency Prevention, Washington, DC, September 2001

FIGURE 6.5

Gender and age of juvenile victims of sex offenses committed by babysitters, by offender gender, 1995–98

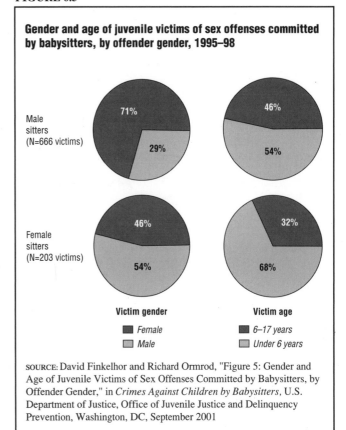

Male sitters (N=666 victims): 71%, 29% (victim gender); 46%, 54% (victim age)

Female sitters (N=203 victims): 46%, 54% (victim gender); 32%, 68% (victim age)

Victim gender
■ Female
▨ Male

Victim age
■ 6–17 years
▨ Under 6 years

SOURCE: David Finkelhor and Richard Ormrod, "Figure 5: Gender and Age of Juvenile Victims of Sex Offenses Committed by Babysitters, by Offender Gender," in *Crimes Against Children by Babysitters,* U.S. Department of Justice, Office of Juvenile Justice and Delinquency Prevention, Washington, DC, September 2001

Pedophiles

At one time, a pedophile was stereotyped as a lonely, isolated man who generally sought employment that permitted contact with children. Experts now know that men or women, heterosexual or gay, married or single, may be pedophiles. Examples include the pediatric dentist who anesthetized his patients and photographed them in lewd positions. Another molester was a high school teacher who had sex with her students during tutoring sessions at her home. Still another was a police officer who made more than 1,000 videotapes of young boys performing sex acts.

Many pedophiles have found that the Internet gives them easy access to vulnerable children. They target and recruit potential victims through electronic conversations. Pedophiles also contact one another through the Internet and computer online services, transmitting electronic images and sharing experiences.

FIRST NATIONAL SURVEY ON THE ONLINE VICTIMIZATION OF CHILDREN. In 1999 Congress directed the National Center for Missing & Exploited Children (NCMEC) to conduct the *Youth Internet Safety Survey,* the first national survey on the risks children face on the Internet. NCMEC contracted with the Crimes Against Children Research Center of the University of New Hampshire to undertake the research.

In *Online Victimization: A Report on the Nation's Youth* (David Finkelhor, Kimberly J. Mitchell, and Janis

Wolak, Crimes against Children Research Center, University of New Hampshire, Durham, NH, and NCMEC, Alexandria, VA, June 2000), the researchers reported that nearly one of five (19 percent) youths using the Internet in the last year had received an unwanted sexual solicitation or approach. Sexual solicitations involved requests to do sexual things the children did not want to do, while sexual approaches involved incidents in which persons tried to get children to talk about sex when they did not want to or asked them intimate questions. One in four of those solicited (5 percent of child Internet users) reported distressing incidents in which they were very or extremely afraid or upset. Another 3 percent reported aggressive solicitations in which attempts had been made to contact them through regular mail, by telephone, or in person. (See Figure 6.6; solicitations include sexual approaches.)

Twice as many females (66 percent) as males (34 percent) received a sexual solicitation or approach, and more than three-quarters were age 14 or older. Persons age 18 and older accounted for 24 percent of perpetrators of sexual solicitations and approaches. Twice as many solicitors (48 percent) were under 18. About two-thirds (67 percent) of the solicitors were males, and 19 percent were females. Interestingly, one-quarter of the aggressive incidents involved female solicitors.

FIGURE 6.6

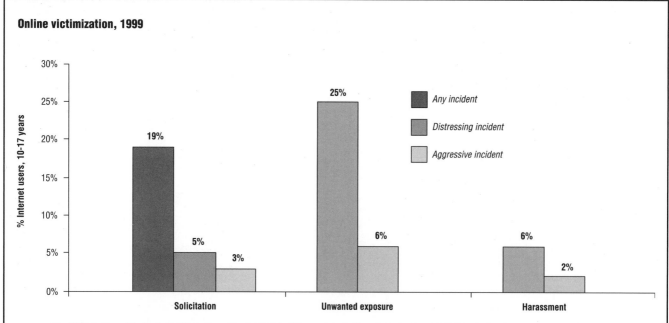

Online victimization, 1999

SOURCE: David Finkelhor, Kimberly J. Mitchell, and Janis Wolak, "Figure 1-1: Online victimization, 1999," in *Online Victimization: A Report on the Nation's Youth,* Crimes Against Children Research Center, University of New Hampshire, Durham, NH, and National Center for Missing & Exploited Children, Alexandria, VA, June 2000

One in four children (25 percent) reported unwanted exposure to sexual material (pictures of naked people or people having sex). Six percent of the regular Internet users indicated distressing exposures in which they were very or extremely upset. (See Figure 6.6.) About 7 in 10 youths (71 percent) were exposed to unwanted sexual material while surfing the Web or doing online searches. Nearly 3 of 10 (28 percent) were exposed to sexual material while opening e-mail or e-mail links.

Based on the estimated 23.8 million regular Internet users between the ages of 10 and 17, Finkelhor et al. noted that about 4.5 million of these users had experienced sexual solicitations and approaches. Nearly 6 million had experienced unwanted exposure to sexual material. (See Table 6.5.)

The survey found that few parents and children were familiar with places to which they could report offensive Internet incidents. Although almost a third (31 percent) of the parents realized there are places to report these incidents, just 10 percent could name the specific places that receive such reports. Among the children, only 24 percent had heard of places to report Internet incidents. Of these children, most (9 percent) cited their Internet service provider, while just 1 percent cited the Federal Bureau of Investigation (FBI) as a place that receives such reports. (See Figure 6.7.)

When asked by the interviewers if they knew about CyberTipline, almost 10 percent of parents and 2 percent of youth responded that they had heard of it. CyberTipline

was established in 1998 as a cooperative effort among the NCMEC, the FBI, the U.S. Postal Inspection Service, and the U.S. Customs Service to receive reports on missing children and children in harm's way.

The CyberTipline also serves as the Child Pornography Tipline. Through these toll-free tiplines, the NCMEC has received telephone calls nationwide and from Canada (1-800-843-5678), as well as from Mexico (001-800-843-5678) and Europe (00-800-843-5678). Since October 1984 the NCMEC has received more than 1.3 million calls.

TEENS COMMUNICATE WITH STRANGERS ONLINE. A June 20, 2001, a study released by the Pew Internet & American Life Project (Amanda Lenhart, Lee Rainie, and Oliver Lewis, *Teenage Life Online: The Rise of the Instant-Message Generation and the Internet's Impact on Friendships and Family Relationships,* Washington, DC) found that adolescents who have Internet access do communicate with strangers they meet online. About three of five (60 percent) of online teens, ages 12 to 17, surveyed by Pew reported that they had received e-mails or instant messages from strangers. About 63 percent of those who had received e-mails or instant messages from strangers had answered such messages. Teens also said that they had lied about their age to get on a Web site with pornography. Boys (19 percent) were more likely than girls (11 percent) to have done so.

INTERNET PORNOGRAPHERS. Law enforcement agencies worldwide have arrested increasing numbers of

TABLE 6.5

Population estimates and confidence intervals for online victimization of youth[1], 1999

Online Victimization	% Regular Internet Users	95% Confidence Interval	Estimated Number of Youth[2]	95% Confidence Interval[2]
Sexual Solicitations and Approaches				
• Any	19%	17%-21%	4,520,000	4,050,000–4,990,000
• Distressing	5%	4%-6%	1,190,000	930,000–1,450,000
• Aggressive	3%	2%-4%	710,000	510,000–910,000
Unwanted Exposure to Sexual Material				
• Any	25%	23%-27%	5,950,000	5,430,000–6,470,000
• Distressing	6%	5%-7%	1,430,000	1,140,000–1,720,000
Harassment				
• Any	6%	5%-7%	1,430,000	1,140,000–1,720,000
• Distressing	2%	1%-3%	480,000	310,000–650,000

[1]Estimates and confidence intervals are based on an estimated number of 23,810,000 regular Internet users between the ages of 10 and 17.
[2]Estimates and confidence intervals are all rounded to the nearest ten thousand.
SOURCE: David Finkelhor, Kimberly J. Mitchell, and Janis Wolak, "Table 7-2: Population estimates and confidence intervals for online victimization of youth," in *Online Victimization: A Report on the Nation's Youth,* Crimes Against Children Research Center, University of New Hampshire, Durham, NH, and National Center for Missing & Exploited Children, Alexandria, VA, June 2000

FIGURE 6.7

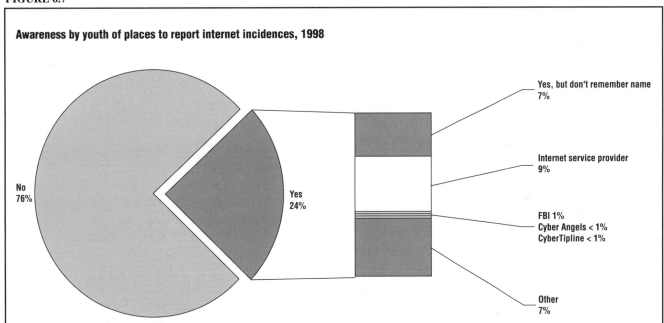

Awareness by youth of places to report internet incidences, 1998

SOURCE: David Finkelhor, Kimberly J. Mitchell, and Janis Wolak, "Figure 4-4: Has youth heard of places to report Internet incidents?" in *Online Victimization: A Report on the Nation's Youth,* Crimes Against Children Research Center, University of New Hampshire, Durham, NH, and National Center for Missing & Exploited Children, Alexandria, VA, June 2000

Internet child-pornography businesses and subscribers to these Web sites. In March 2002 federal investigators charged 90 members of a U.S. child-sex ring called the Candyman with possession, production, or distribution of child pornography. The group—which included law enforcement personnel, clergy members, Little League coaches, and others—had more than 7,000 subscribers all over the world. Sexually explicit images of children, some of whom were toddlers, were depicted in Web sites. Investigators found that at least 36 victims had been molested.

A new form of child pornography involves parents trading pictures of their own children being sexually abused. In August 2002, 10 Americans and 10 Europeans were arrested for such child pornography. Eighty percent of the images showed parents molesting their children. As of September 2002 law enforcement authorities continued investigation of the global customer list of the largest child-pornography enterprise ever uncovered in the United States. About 300,000 subscribers to more than 5,700 online pornography sites operated by Landslide Productions, Inc., of Fort

Worth, Texas, were from such countries as Ireland, England, Canada, Sweden, and Norway.

CHALLENGES IN FIGHTING INTERNET CRIMES AGAINST CHILDREN. The Office for Victims of Crime of the U.S. Department of Justice reported that, by 2005, about 77 million children would be using the Internet (*Internet Crimes against Children,* February 2001). Authorities compare the Internet to places, such as playgrounds and shopping malls, where children typically congregate and where predators are likely to find victims. For predators, the Internet presents an even more attractive venue because they can commit their crime anonymously and are able to contact the same child on a regular basis. Predators may groom children online for the production of child pornography. They have been known to prey on vulnerable children, gaining their confidence online, and then traveling for the purpose of engaging their victims in sex acts.

The dangers presented by the Internet, especially in the sexual exploitation of children, have presented new challenges for law enforcement. To help states fight cyberspace predators, the Justice Department created the Internet Crimes against Children (ICAC) Task Force Program. Regional ICAC task forces help the community develop programs to combat child pornography and child enticement. They provide assistance to parents, educators, law enforcement, and other professionals with victim services, training programs, as well as investigation of Internet crimes.

Pedophile Priests

Following the arrest and conviction of defrocked priest John Geoghan for child molestation in early 2002, other victims of pedophile priests have come forward. In September 2000 the Archdiocese of Boston paid $10 million in settlement to 86 people who had been victims of Geoghan. Other dioceses have since settled abuse cases for millions of dollars. At least 800 priests had been removed from office because of allegations of sexual abuse. Four bishops had resigned after being accused of sexual abuse.

On December 13, 2002, Cardinal Bernard Law, a major figure in the abuse scandal, resigned as archbishop of Boston. Cardinal Law was the highest-ranking Roman Catholic official in the United States. Some Catholic organizations, priests, and parishioners had called for his resignation since church files released during the Geoghan trial revealed that he not only knew of the abuses by Geoghan and other priests but also proceeded to move the abusers from parish to parish.

On July 12, 2002, the *Dallas Morning News* (Brooke Egerton and Reese Dunklin, Dallas, TX) reported that about 111 of 178 Catholic leaders in 40 states allowed priests accused of child sexual abuse to continue working. Eight of these leaders were cardinals. Some bishops let the offenders stay in their parishes or transferred them out to other parishes. The bishops did not inform law enforcement agencies about the sexual misconducts and, in some cases, told the victims not to report the molestation. Some of the molesters were transferred to treatment centers where they monitored recent offenders. The reporters also found that some priest molesters in Boston were moved to the diocese headquarters where they assisted in deciding the fate of recent offenders.

THE EFFECTS OF CHILD SEXUAL ABUSE

According to the American Psychological Association (APA), children who have been sexually abused exhibit a range of symptoms (*Understanding Child Sexual Abuse: Education, Prevention, and Recovery,* Washington, DC, October 1999). The immediate effects may include thumb sucking and/or bed wetting; sleep disturbances; eating problems; and school problems, including misconduct, problems with performing schoolwork, and failure to participate in activities.

The APA also detailed long-term effects of childhood sexual abuse. Adult victims of childhood sexual abuse may suffer from depression, sexual dysfunction, and anxiety. Anxiety may manifest itself in such behaviors as anxiety attacks, insomnia, and alcohol and drug abuse. Adult survivors of childhood sexual abuse also report revictimization, as rape victims or as victims of intimate physical abuse.

Teen Pregnancy, High-Risk Sexual Behaviors, and Other Effects

Jacqueline L. Stock, Michelle A. Bell, Debra K. Boyer, and Frederick A. Connell, in "Adolescent Pregnancy and Sexual Risk-Taking among Sexually Abused Girls" (*Family Planning Perspectives,* vol. 29, no. 5, September/October 1997), analyzed a health-behavior survey of female adolescents in grades 8, 10, and 12. Of the 3,128 respondents, 18 percent of eighth-grade, 24 percent of tenth-grade, and 28 percent of twelfth-grade participants reported having been sexually abused. The authors found that female adolescents with a history of sexual abuse were 3.1 times as likely as those with no such history to report that they had ever been pregnant. Moreover, female victims of sexual abuse were also more likely to have had sexual intercourse by the time they were 15 years old, to have not used birth control during their last intercourse, and to have had more than one sexual partner.

Compared with girls who reported no sexual abuse, those with a history of sexual abuse indicated having also experienced physical abuse. They were more likely to have a poor body image, to have used drugs and alcohol, and to have contemplated or attempted suicide. They were not performing well in school, had considered dropping out of school, and were not all that interested in pursuing college.

Adolescent and Adult Males Who Impregnate Adolescent Girls

More than 4,100 men in a primary care setting were interviewed regarding whether or not they had ever impregnated an adolescent girl (Robert F. Anda, "Abused Boys, Battered Mothers, and Male Involvement in Teen Pregnancy," *Pediatrics,* vol. 107, no. 2, February 2001). The study found that men with a history of childhood sexual or physical abuse or witnessing physical abuse of their mother were more likely to have been involved in teenage pregnancy. About 19 percent of the men reported ever getting a girl pregnant during adolescence and adulthood. The girls were between 12 and 19 years old. About 59 percent of the men were age 20 or younger at the time they impregnated the girls.

One-fourth (25.5 percent) of men who experienced childhood sexual abuse indicated having impregnated teen girls, compared to 17.8 percent of those who had not been sexually abused as children. Those whose sexual abuse was characterized by physical force or threat of harm were about twice as likely to have impregnated a teenage girl. Those who were abused at age 10 and under showed an 80 percent increased risk of getting a teenage girl pregnant.

Adult Survivors of Childhood Sexual Abuse

Dr. Holmes's review of studies of male child sexual abuse ("Sexual Abuse of Boys: Definition, Prevalence, Correlates, Sequelae, and Management," *Journal of the American Medical Association,* vol. 281, no. 21, December 2, 1998) found that only 15–39 percent of victims who responded to the studies thought that they were adversely affected by the sexual abuse. The victims stressed that the adverse effects were linked to the use of force, a great difference in victim–perpetrator age, or cases in which the perpetrator was much older, or the victim was very young. Dr. Holmes noted, however, that negative clinical results (in contrast to what the studies' subjects reported) included posttraumatic stress disorder, major depression, paranoia, aggressive behavior, poor self-image, poor school performance, and running away from home.

Dr. Holmes also found a connection between sexual abuse and subsequent substance abuse among male victims. Sexually abused males were also more likely to have sex-related problems, including sexual dysfunction, hypersexuality, and the tendency to force sex on others. He surmised that the discrepancy between the respondents' perceptions of the negative consequences of their sexual victimization and those discovered in clinical outcomes may be due to several factors. Dr. Holmes observed that perhaps abused males believe they have failed to protect themselves as society expects them to do.

Instead of owning up to their failure, they resort to not giving much gravity to their experiences. Moreover, if the victims had experienced pleasure while being abused, they may be confused by their feelings about it.

Diane N. Roche, Marsha G. Runtz, and Michael A. Hunter studied female undergraduate students who had suffered child sexual abuse ("Adult Attachment: A Mediator between Child Sexual Abuse and Later Psychological Adjustment," *Journal of Interpersonal Violence,* vol. 14, no. 2, February 1999). Overall, the women who were victims of child sexual abuse were less secure and more fearful in their adult relationships, compared with the control group. Moreover, those who suffered family abuse exhibited more negative attachment relationships than those abused by nonfamily offenders.

According to the authors, when a child is abused by a family member, he or she loses trust in what should have been a safe relationship. The abuse interrupts the child's developing sense of self. This development, which, under normal circumstances, continues to early adulthood, is derailed. Consequently, the victim's damaged perception of self may keep him or her from sustaining healthy relationships.

CHILDHOOD SEXUAL ABUSE AND DRUG USE AMONG WOMEN AT A RISK FOR ILLICIT DRUG USE. A total of 1,478 noninjecting female sexual partners of male injection-drug users were the subjects of a study by Robert C. Freeman, Karyn Collier, and Kathleen M. Parillo ("Early Life Sexual Abuse as a Risk Factor for Crack Cocaine Use in a Sample of Community-Recruited Women at High Risk for Illicit Drug Use," *American Journal of Drug and Alcohol Abuse,* vol. 28, no. 1, February 2002). Nearly two-thirds (64 percent) of the women reported having used crack cocaine. The researchers found that an equal proportion of all women had suffered sexual abuse before age 12 (39.5 percent) and during adolescence (38.8 percent). Overall, nearly 22 percent were sexually abused during both childhood and adolescence.

While Freeman et al. found a relationship between childhood sexual abuse and lifetime crack use, they found no direct link between sexual abuse during adolescence and lifetime crack use. They did find, however, some indirect connections between the two. Female teens who were victims of sexual abuse were more likely to run away, and these runaways were more likely to use crack because of the type of people with whom they associated.

ADULT SEXUAL REVICTIMIZATION. Carolyn M. West, Linda M. Williams, and Jane A. Siegel interviewed female, African American victims of child abuse about 17 years after their abuse ("Adult Sexual Revictimization among Black Women Sexually Abused in Childhood: A Prospective Examination of Serious Consequences of Abuse," *Child Maltreatment,* vol. 5, no. 1, February

2000). The research subjects were 113 black women, ages 19 to 31, who were 10 months to 12 years of age at the time of the abuse. The researchers found that 30 percent of the women experienced revictimization as adults, with physical force during childhood abuse as the only predictor of adult abuse. The women reported between one and six episodes of revictimization, with the majority (79 percent) experiencing one incident of abuse, and 18 percent indicating two such incidents.

The researchers found that revictimized women were three times more likely to have engaged in prostitution (27 percent, compared with 8 percent of nonrevictimized women) and to be 1.5 times as likely to have been involved in partner violence (73 percent, compared with 48 percent of nonrevictimized women). Although revictimized women did not have first consensual intercourse at a younger age or more sexual partners compared with their nonrevictimized counterparts, they tended to have more health problems. They had more problems conceiving and experienced more vaginal infections, sexually transmitted diseases, and painful intercourse.

Jeremy Coid et al. surveyed a larger sample of women to determine whether childhood sexual and physical abuse increases the risk of revictimization ("Relation between Childhood Sexual Abuse and Physical Abuse and Risk of Revictimization in Women: A Cross-Sectional Survey," *The Lancet,* vol. 358, no. 9280, August 11, 2001). A survey involving more than 1,200 women ages 16 to 85 was conducted in primary care practices in London, United Kingdom. Fifty-four percent of the respondents were white.

The researchers found that women who had a history of unwanted sexual intercourse before age 16 were more likely to experience intimate partner violence and rape. Those who had been severely beaten before age 16 by their parents or caretakers reported adult abuse in the form of intimate partner violence, rape, and other traumatic experiences. The women also reported a co-occurrence of sexual and physical abuse both during childhood and adulthood.

RITUAL CHILD ABUSE

Many child care experts believe that the phenomenon "ritual child abuse" started with the release of the book, *Michelle Remembers* (Pocket Books, New York, NY, 1980). The book was the story of Michelle Smith of British Columbia, Canada. While in therapy she told her psychiatrist how, as a young child, she had been offered to Satan by her own mother. She recounted stories of murder and the sacrifice of babies and animals. Dr. Lawrence Pazder and Smith collaborated on the book that experts say fueled the hysteria about an alleged underground movement of Satanists who were engaged in ritual sexual abuse of children during the 1980s and early 1990s.

A Study of Ritual Abuse Reports and Evidence

Concerned over allegations of ritual child abuse during the 1980s and early 1990s, especially since the much-publicized McMartin Preschool case in California, the federal government commissioned four studies to investigate the characteristics and sources of such allegations (Gail S. Goodman, Jianjian Qin, Bette L. Bottoms, and Phillip R. Shaver, *Characteristics and Sources of Allegations of Ritualistic Child Abuse,* Final Report to the National Center on Child Abuse and Neglect, Washington, DC, 1994). For comparison, the investigators also looked into allegations of religion-related abuse (for example, withholding of medical care, abuse by religious officials, and corporal punishment "to beat the devil out of the children").

The first study surveyed clinicians who might have worked with ritual and religion-related abuse cases. A total of 720 clinical psychologists, psychiatrists, and social workers provided information on 1,548 such cases. These cases had been reported to them by victims who were either adult survivors or children. About 31 percent of clinicians each reported one or two cases of ritual abuse. More than 1 percent reported having more than 100 cases each.

Claims of adult ritual cases were the most extreme and involved more severe types of abuse, such as murder, cannibalism, and baby breeding for ritual sacrifice. No hard evidence, however, of these incidents could be found. Moreover, victims in adult ritual cases were most likely to be diagnosed with multiple personality disorders. The only evidence reported in ritual abuse cases was the patients' disclosure during hypnotherapy and, in a few cases, the presence of scars. Goodman and colleagues noted, however, that even when scars were found, it was not determined whether the victims themselves had caused them.

Overall, the clinicians accepted the allegations of abuse, as well as the characteristics of both ritual and religion-related cases. They reported finding evidence of harm and abuse in religion-related cases and very rare cases of ritual abuse of children involving satanic themes that were perpetrated by one or two people. They also reported, however, that hard evidence for satanic ritual abuse, especially that involving large cults, was "scant to nonexistent."

In the second study, Goodman et al. surveyed different agencies that were involved with child abuse allegations: offices of district attorneys, departments of social services, and law enforcement agencies. About 23 percent (1,079 respondents) reported that they had encountered at least one ritual or religion-related case, while three-quarters (77 percent) reported no cases. More than 2 percent reported having seen more than 100 victims of alleged ritual abuse.

As with the clinicians, the various agencies reported that victims of alleged ritual abuse cases experienced severe abuse. In addition, ritual cases involved more types of abuse than religion-related cases. The agencies also found that allegations of ritual abuse involved multiple perpetrators and victims, with relatively high numbers of female perpetrators and male victims. Most religion-related cases were committed by parents or persons in a position of trust, while ritual abuses were committed by acquaintances or strangers. The agencies believed the allegations of both ritual abuse and religion-related abuse, although they were more likely to accept the validity of allegations of religion-related abuse than of ritual abuse.

The third study examined repression and recovery of memories of early abuse, analyzing 490 cases from the first study. Of these cases, 43 were repressed memory (RM) cases and 447 were nonrepressed memory (NRM) cases. RM cases were characterized by more types of abuse and a larger number of perpetrators than those not based on RM. More than two-thirds (68 percent) of RM cases were diagnosed with multiple personality disorder. The alleged abuse started earlier and lasted longer and was more likely to involve ritual abuse than NRM cases. According to Goodman, there was no evidence to indicate the existence of the satanic ritual abuse scenarios that allegedly occurred in many of the RM cases.

The fourth study examined children's knowledge of satanic topics. Some professionals believe that children are incapable of reporting ritual abuse if they have not experienced the abuse. Other professionals, however, feel that children's suggestibility makes them vulnerable to making false reports of such abuse. The researchers investigated whether children have the necessary knowledge base to make up details of ritual abuse.

Of the children surveyed, those ages 3 to 12, while knowing about the devil and crime, did not have any knowledge of activities associated with satanic sexual abuse. The researchers noted that just because younger children had little knowledge of ritual abuse, this did not mean that their reports of satanic abuse were true. The researchers felt it meant that children were unlikely to have made up such reports. They also warned that the results of the fourth study must be interpreted cautiously.

For ethical reasons, the children were not asked about satanic ritual abuse. Instead, they were asked about God, the devil, heaven, hell, symbols, and pictures.

An Expert's Opinion

Kenneth V. Lanning, a supervisory special agent at the Behavioral Science Unit at the National Center for the Analysis of Violent Crime of the FBI Academy, Quantico, Virginia, is one of the foremost national experts on child molestation. Lanning claims that satanic or ritual abuse is rare and that the FBI has never found evidence or credible witnesses indicating the existence of Satanists who ritually abuse children sexually.

The FBI National Center for the Analysis of Violent Crime often assists local and state law enforcement across the country. Lanning admitted that, in the early 1980s, when news about ritual child abuse first surfaced, he tended to believe the stories. He believed it was possible that a few people in the country might have been conducting satanic ritual and, in the process, murdering people. The numbers of people, however, claiming victimization in such rituals kept on growing. Yet the FBI and other authorities could find no corroborative evidence to substantiate the alleged atrocities. They could not find the thousands of supposedly murdered bodies nor the places of sacrifice. In *Investigator's Guide to Allegations of "Ritual" Child Abuse* (FBI Academy, Quantico, Virginia, 1992) Lanning wrote:

> Any professional evaluating victims' allegations of "ritual abuse" cannot ignore or routinely dismiss the lack of physical evidence (no bodies or physical evidence left by violent murders); the difficulty in successfully committing a large-scale conspiracy crime (the more people involved in any crime conspiracy, the harder it is to get away with it); and human nature (intragroup conflicts resulting in individual self-serving disclosures are likely to occur in any group involved in organized kidnapping, baby breeding, and human sacrifice). If and when members of a destructive cult commit murders, they are bound to make mistakes, leave evidence, and eventually make admissions in order to brag about their crimes or to reduce their legal liability.

CHAPTER 7
CHILD ABUSE AND THE LAW

JUVENILE COURTS

As early as the mid-seventeenth century in colonial America, adults accused of child abandonment, of excessive physical abuse, and of depriving their children of basic necessities faced criminal trials. In 1899 Cook County, Illinois established the first juvenile court system, not so much to protect abused and neglected children but mainly to keep the abandoned children and runaways off the streets. In 1944 the U.S. Supreme Court held, in *Prince v. Massachusetts* (321 U.S. 158), that the government has the authority to protect children from child labor (in this case, a girl under 18 whose Jehovah's Witness guardian furnished the child with periodicals to sell in the streets in violation of state child labor law).

Today all 50 states have authorized juvenile family courts to intervene in child abuse cases, and all 50 states consider child abuse of any kind to be a felony and a civil crime. A felony could result in a prison term; a loss of a civil suit could result in the payment of a fine or in losing custody of the child. (While many states have distinct and separate juvenile courts, some states try juvenile or family cases in courts of general jurisdiction, where child protection cases are given priority over other cases on the court's docket.)

Government child protective services (CPS) initiates a civil court proceeding (after consultation with CPS lawyers) if it seeks to remove the child from the home, provide in-home protective services, or require the abuser to get treatment. Criminal proceedings are initiated by a government prosecutor if the abuser is to be charged with a crime, such as sexual abuse.

In civil child protection cases, the accused has the right to a closed trial (a hearing with no jury and closed to the public), in which court records are kept confidential, although a few states permit jury trials. In criminal child protection cases, however, the person charged with abuse is entitled to the Sixth Amendment right to an open trial (a jury trial opened to the public), which can be waived only by the defendant.

In 1967 *In re Gault* (387 U.S.1) substantially changed the nature of juvenile courts. Initially, children were not subject to constitutional due process rights or legal representation, and judges presiding over these courts were given unlimited power to protect children from criminal harm. *In re Gault* established that children—whether they have committed a crime or are the victims of a crime—are entitled to due process and legal representation. These rights, however, are interpreted differently among the states.

Court-Appointed Special Advocate

In the past, for many abused and neglected children who could not be reunited with their families, foster care became a permanent placement. In the 1970s David W. Soukup, presiding judge of the King County Superior Court in Seattle, Washington, realized that judges did not always have enough information to make the right decision to serve the best interests of the child.

Traditionally the child's advocate in court had been the guardian *ad litem* (literally, for the lawsuit). In other words, the guardian *ad litem* is an attorney appointed by the court for the lawsuit being prosecuted. The lawyers, however, usually did not have the time or training to conduct a thorough review of each child's case. Consequently, Judge Soukup recruited and trained community volunteers to serve as the children's long-term guardians *ad litem*. The role of the court-appointed special advocate (CASA) was born on January 1, 1977, and Seattle's program has since been adopted nationwide.

In 1984 the National CASA Association was formed in Seattle, Washington. Congress passed the Victims of Child Abuse Act of 1990 (Public Law 101-647) to require that a CASA volunteer be provided to every child maltreatment victim who needs such an advocate. More than 950 CASA programs, with more than 58,000 volunteers, have been established in all 50 states and the District of Columbia and the U.S. Virgin Islands.

Typically the judge appoints a CASA volunteer, who then reviews all records pertaining to the maltreated child, including CPS reports and medical and school records. The volunteer also meets with the child, parents and family members, social workers, health care providers, school officials, and other people who may know of the child's history. The research compiled by the CASA volunteer helps the child's lawyer in presenting the case. It also helps the court in deciding what is best for the child. Each trained volunteer works with one or two children at a time, enabling the volunteer to research and monitor each case thoroughly.

PROBLEMS FOR THE PROSECUTOR

For the prosecutor's office, child abuse can present many problems. The foremost is that the victim is a child. This becomes an even greater problem when the victim is very young (from birth to age six), since the question of competency arises. More and more studies have examined children's reliability in recalling and retelling past events. Researchers have found that different settings and interview techniques may result in children remembering different details at different times.

The prosecutor may also worry about the possible harm the child may suffer, having to relive the abuse and being interrogated by adversarial defense attorneys. If the child is an adolescent making accusations of sexual abuse, the defendant's attorney may accuse the teenage victim of seducing the defendant or having willingly taken part in the acts.

Other factors that prosecutors must consider include the slowness of the court process and the possibility that the case may be delayed, not just once, but several times. This is hard enough for adults to tolerate, but it is particularly difficult for children. The delay prolongs the child's pain. Children may become more reluctant to testify or may no longer be able to retell their stories accurately. There is a far greater difference between a 31-year-old testifying about something that happened when he or she was 26 and an 11-year-old retelling an event that happened at 6 years of age. Prosecutors are also obliged to keep the child's best interests in mind and to try and preserve the family.

Prosecuting Child Sexual Abuse

Prosecuting a child sexual abuse case is particularly challenging. A child who has been physically abused will often display unmistakable signs of the abuse, such as broken bones. Sexual abuse does not necessarily leave such visible marks. So the abuse is less likely to have been noticed by others and is more difficult to verify once an accusation has been made.

Many other difficulties exist. For example, physical abusers will sometimes admit to having "disciplined" their children by striking them, or have actually been seen committing abusive acts in public. Sexual abusers almost never admit to their actions when confronted, and their abuse always takes place in secret. Another major difficulty is that young children who have little or no knowledge of sex may have trouble understanding, let alone explaining in a court room, what was done to them.

DISCLOSURE

What should parents do when their children claim to have been abused? It may come as an offhand remark, as if the child is testing to see what a parent's reaction will be. Perhaps the child is engaged in sexual behavior, a common symptom of sexual abuse. For example, the child may go through the motions of sexual intercourse and then say that this is what a parent, stepparent, relative, or a teacher at school has done. A major preschool sexual abuse case against Margaret Kelly Michaels, a teacher at the Wee Care Day Nursery in Maplewood, New Jersey, began when a boy who was having his temperature taken rectally at the pediatrician's office remarked that his teacher had been doing the same thing to him while he napped at school. The remark ultimately led to Michaels's being charged with various forms of sexual abuse, and a nine-month trial at which several children testified. (The case, discussed in more detail later in this chapter, was dropped by the prosecution in 1994.)

Sometimes a parent realizes that something is wrong when the child's behavior changes. Some young children have an especially hard time expressing themselves verbally and may instead begin having sleep difficulties, such as nightmares and night terrors; eating problems; a fear of going to school (if that is the site of the abuse); regression; acting out, such as biting, masturbating, or sexually attacking other family members; and withdrawing. These behavior changes, however, do not necessarily mean that the child is being sexually abused. Children may also express themselves in their drawings.

The abuse may have occurred for a long time before children tell. Why do children keep the abuse a secret? Children who reveal their abuse through the nonverbal ways listed above may be afraid to speak out because they believe the threats of death or punishment made by their abusers. Child Abuse Listening and Mediation (CALM), a Santa Barbara, California, counseling organization, lists some of the reasons children do not tell:

• Children feel responsible for what has happened to them.

- Children fear adults will not believe them.

- Children believe threats from the offender.

- Children do not know how to describe what has happened to them.

- Children are taught to be respectful of adults.

- Children fear getting an adult in trouble or disobeying an adult who has requested secrecy.

  According to CALM, children tell:

- when they come in contact with someone who appears to already know

- when they come in contact with someone who does not appear to be judgmental, critical, or threatening

- when they believe a continuation of the abuse will be unbearable

- when physical injury occurs

- when they receive sexual abuse prevention information

- if pregnancy is a threat

- when they come into contact with someone who may protect them

If parents believe their child, particularly if the abuser is not a family member, their first reaction may be to file charges against the alleged perpetrator. Parents rarely realize how difficult and painful the process can be. Some experts claim that children psychologically need to see their abuser punished, while others feel children are victimized by the court process, only this time by the very people who are supposed to protect them.

THE CHILD'S STORY

Some experts believe children do not lie about abuse. They point out that children cannot describe events unfamiliar to them. For example, the average six-year-old has no concept of how forced penetration feels or how semen tastes. Experts also note that children lie to get themselves out of trouble, not into trouble, and reporting sexual abuse is definitely trouble. Children sometimes recant, or deny that any abuse has happened, after they have disclosed it. Perhaps the reaction to the disclosure was unfavorable or the pain and fear of talking about the experience were too great. The child's recanting under interrogation in a court of law may prove damaging to the case and may encourage claims that the child has made false accusations.

Not a Lie but Not the Truth Either

Kenneth V. Lanning, a supervisory special agent at the Behavioral Science Unit at the National Center for the Analysis of Violent Crime of the Federal Bureau of Investigation Academy, Quantico, Virginia, claimed that children rarely lie about sexual abuse ("Criminal Investigation of Sexual Victimization of Children," *The APSAC Handbook on Child Maltreatment,* 2nd ed., Sage Publications, Inc., Thousand Oaks, CA, 2002). Some children, however, may recount what they believe in their minds to be the truth, although their accounts may turn out to be inaccurate. Lanning gave the following explanations for these inaccuracies:

- The child may be experiencing distorted memory due to trauma.

- The child's story might be a reflection of normal childhood fears and fantasy.

- The child may have been confused by the abuser's use of trickery or drugs.

- The child's testimony may be influenced by the suggestive questions of investigators.

- The child's account might reflect urban legends and cultural mythology.

The Pressure of the Judicial System

Once the child becomes enmeshed in the courts, his or her testimony may become muddled. Children, by definition, are immature in their physical, reasoning, and emotional development. In "Early and Long-Term Effects of Child Sexual Abuse" (*Professional Psychology,* no. 21, 1990) David Finkelhor, an expert on child sexual abuse, pointed out that the child's story may decrease in validity as the abuse becomes a distant past occurrence. Therapists who believe children do not invent abuse feel that if a child's story changes, then psychological progress is being made because the child is dealing with the emotional trauma. For the courts, however, changing stories raise doubts.

Often, the goals of the therapist and the judicial system are at odds. The therapist's goal is to protect the best interests of the child. If, to encourage the child to speak out, a therapist asks leading questions (questions that suggest a specific answer—"Did daddy take his clothes off?"—rather than, "What did daddy look like? What was he wearing?"), the purpose is to help the child remember painful events that need to be expressed. The courts, however, look at such questions as leading the witness. Cases have fallen apart when it appeared that therapists put words in the children's mouths. Critics charge that an alleged abuse may go to trial because an overzealous therapist or investigator has implanted the occurrence of abuse into the child's impressionable mind.

By the time a case makes it to the courtroom, most children are under a great deal of stress. Many will have undergone a thorough genital/rectal examination by a physician and relentless interrogations by innumerable strangers. A child may have been interviewed more than 30 times by therapists, lawyers, the police, CPS workers, and the parents. Some of these people may have experience with sexual abuse cases; many may not, and their goals will be very different. How can a child possibly handle all this? Nonetheless, the U.S. legal system demands this process in order to give every accused person a fair trial and a chance to be cleared of the charges.

Sexual abuse cases are different from most trials in that the question is not just who did it, but did it actually happen? In cases where there is frequently no physical evidence of the crime, it is crucial for the jury to hear the children testify. Many people, however, feel that children are not able to present credible evidence to a jury. Testimony by others, such as the parents, is often excluded by hearsay rules (rules that prevent a witness from repeating in court those statements someone else has made about the case).

THE CHILD AS A COMPETENT WITNESS

Traditionally, judges protected juries from incompetent witnesses, which in early America were considered to include women, slaves, and children. Children in particular were believed to live in a fantasy world, and their inability to understand such terms as "oath," "testify," and "solemnly swear" denied them the right to appear in court. In 1895 the U.S. Supreme Court, in *Wheeler v. United States* (159 U.S. 523), established the rights of child witnesses. The court explained:

> There is no precise age which determines the question of competency. This depends on the capacity and intelligence of the child, his appreciation of the difference between truth and falsehood, as well as of his duty to tell the former. The decision of this question rests primarily with the trial judge, who sees the proposed witness, notices his manner, his apparent possession or lack of intelligence, and may resort to any examination which will tend to disclose his capacity and intelligence as well as his understanding of the obligation of an oath. To exclude [a child] from the witness stand would sometimes result in staying the hand of justice.

As a result of this ruling, the courts formalized the *Wheeler* decision, requiring judges to interview all children to determine their competency. It was not until 1974 that the revised Federal Rules of Evidence abolished the competency rule so that children may testify at trial in federal courts regardless of competence.

In state courts, judges sometimes still apply the competency rule regardless of state laws that may have banned it. In the 1987 Margaret Kelly Michaels case, the judge chatted with each child witness before he or she testified, holding a red crayon and asking questions like, "If I said this was a green crayon, would I be telling the truth?"

Children Can Be Unreliable Witnesses if Subjected to Suggested Events

A new study shows that children may not be able to distinguish fact from fiction when subjected to suggested events prior to formal interviews. Psychologists Debra Ann Poole and D. Stephen Lindsay examined children's eyewitness reports after the children were given misinformation by their parents ("Children's Eyewitness Reports after Exposure to Misinformation from Parents," *Journal of Experimental Psychology: Applied,* vol. 7, no. 1, March 2001).

A total of 114 children three to eight years old participated, on a one-to-one basis, in four science activities with a man called "Mr. Science." Three interviews were conducted afterward. The first interview occurred right after the science activities in which an interviewer asked each child nonsuggestive questions about the activities. About 3.5 months later the children's parents read them a story, in three instances, about their science experience. The story included two science activities they had experienced and two others that they had not experienced. The story also included an event in which the child experienced unpleasant touching by Mr. Science. In reality this event did not happen. The children were then interviewed. The final step in the interview consisted of a source-monitoring procedure, in which the children were reminded of their actual experiences, as well as the story, to help them distinguish fact from fiction. A final interview was conducted after another month. This time the children were not given any misinformation.

The interview conducted soon after the science activities showed that the children recalled their experiences, with the amount of events reported increasing with the age of the child. When prompted for more information, the amount of new information reported also increased with age. The reports resulting from the promptings remained accurate.

In the interview that occurred soon after the children were read the storybook with misleading suggestions, 35 percent (40 of the 114 children) reported 58 suggested events in free recall (without prompting from the interviewer), including 17 events relating to the unpleasant touching by Mr. Science. In the last interview a month later, with no additional misinformation given the children, 21 percent (24 children) reported 27 suggested events, including 9 suggested events that involved unpleasant touching. Even when the children were prompted to provide more information about their experiences, they continued to report false events. The researchers concluded that, since children's credibility as eyewitnesses depends on their ability to distinguish their memories from other sources, interviewers will have to develop better procedures to help them do so.

INNOVATIONS IN THE COURT

Anatomically Detailed Dolls

Many legal professionals use dolls with sexual organs made to represent the human anatomy to help children explain what has happened to them in court. Advocates of the use of dolls report that they make it easier to get a child to talk about things that can be very difficult to discuss. Even when children know the words, they may be too embarrassed to say them out loud to strangers. The dolls allow these children to point out and show things difficult or even impossible for them to say. Some experts claim dolls work because children find them easier to use, as they are age-appropriate and familiar to them.

Lori S. Holmes, training coordinator for CornerHouse, a child abuse evaluation and training center in Minneapolis, Minnesota, noted that the use of anatomical dolls helps the child demonstrate internal consistency. A child who has made allegations of abuse can show the interviewer exactly what happened to him or her, thus confirming the oral disclosure ("Using Anatomical Dolls in Child Sexual Abuse Forensic Interviews," *American Prosecutors Research Institute Update,* vol. 13, no. 8, 2000).

Potential problems, however, exist in using dolls. Critics of this method believe that dolls suggest fantasy to children, and the exaggerated sexual organs on a doll (they are proportionally larger than life-size) may suggest improper sexual activity. Since most children's dolls do not have such sexual parts, the appearance of such parts on a doll might bring to a child's mind things he or she might not have thought of otherwise. According to the "affordance phenomenon," children will experiment with any opportunities provided by a new experience. Some experts believe that what might appear to be sexual behavior, like putting a finger in a hole in the doll, may have no more significance than a child putting a finger through the hole in a doughnut. Such exploratory play can have disastrous effects when it is misinterpreted as the re-creation of a sexual act.

CHILDREN INTERACT WITH DOLLS DIFFERENTLY. In the 1990s most research of children's interaction with anatomically detailed dolls was concentrated on white, middle-class children. Lane Geddie, Brenda Dawson, and Karl Weunsch, in "Socioeconomic Status and Ethnic Differences in Preschoolers' Interactions with Anatomically Detailed Dolls" (*Child Maltreatment,* vol. 3, no. 1, February 1998), found that cultural differences may influence the manner in which children interact with dolls.

A study of a sample of nonabused preschoolers confirmed the findings of previous studies that nonabused children are not likely to exhibit sexualized behavior with dolls. The researchers found, however, that black children who were of low socioeconomic status were more likely to demonstrate sexualized behavior with the dolls.

Black families are more likely than white families to have older siblings and other family members supervising the children. This means the children are exposed to a variety of experiences, such as watching an explicit movie with an older sibling. Children in low-income families are also more likely to share their parents' bedroom, which may account for inadvertent exposure to parental relations

and nudity. This study shows that professionals have to be cautious in their interpretations of children's interaction with anatomically detailed dolls.

Videotaped Testimony and Closed-Circuit Television Testimony

It is difficult for children to deal with the fear and intimidation of testifying in open court. The person who has allegedly abused and threatened them may be sitting before them, while the serious nature of the court can be intimidating to them. Videotaped testimony and closed-circuit television testimony have become common methods used to relieve the pressure on the child who must testify. The federal government and 37 states allow the use of closed-circuit television testimony instead of in-court testimony for children under age 18. States vary in their requirements regarding the use of closed-circuit television testimony. In some states the jury stays in the courtroom while the child, the judge, the prosecutor, the defendant, and the defense attorney are in a different room. In some states the child alone is in a room separate from the jury and other participants.

The federal government and 16 states recognize the right to use videotaped testimony taken at a preliminary hearing or deposition (testimony given under oath to be used in court at a later date) for children under age 18. A videotape of the pretrial interviews shows the jury how the child behaved and whether the interviewer prompted the child. Often prepared soon after the abuse, videotaped interviews preserve the child's memory and emotions when they are still fresh. Because a videotaped interview presents an out-of-court statement, which the alleged abuser cannot refute face to face, it can be admitted only as a hearsay exception.

Whereas the videotapes generally pertain to oral statements by the child victims, Missouri allows both verbal and nonverbal statements. Nonverbal assertions include the child's actions, facial expressions, or demonstrations of the abuse using anatomical dolls or other visual aids. In Rhode Island and Wisconsin, child witnesses are required to swear under oath regarding their statements. Prior to taking the oath, the significance of the oath is explained to the child—that is, false statements are punishable under the law and that it is important to tell the truth. Some state laws also say that, even with the videotaped testimony, the child may still be called to testify and be cross-examined.

Videotaping can cut down on the number of interviews the child must undergo, and prosecutors indicate that this method encourages guilty pleas. Videotapes can be powerful tools to deal with the problem of the child who recants his or her testimony when put on the witness stand. The case can still be prosecuted, with the jury witnessing the child's opposing statements. Experts believe that a videotape statement containing sufficient details from the child and elicited through nonleading questions makes for very compelling evidence.

Depositions, however, can be as demanding and difficult as a trial. They often take place in small rooms, forcing the child and defendant closer together than they might have been in a courtroom. The judge might not be there to control the behavior of the defendant or his or her attorney. Individuals who might offer the child support, such as victim advocates, may not be permitted to attend.

Furthermore, if the prosecutor claims the child is unable to handle the emotional trauma of the witness stand, the child may have to undergo medical or psychiatric tests by the state or defense attorney in order to permit videotaped testimony. This could be as traumatic as going through with a personal appearance at the trial. Some states permit the child to sit behind a one-way mirror so that the defendant can see the child and communicate with the defense attorney, but the child is shielded from direct confrontation with the defendant.

Critics of videotaping have suggested other possible problems:

- It is possible that people "perform" for the camera instead of communicating.

- Victims are placed under subjective scrutiny by juries when every gesture, change in voice or speech pattern, and eye movement are judged.

- There is no accountability for the videotapes. Multiple copies of tapes are sometimes made and given to various attorneys and witnesses. Some tapes are used at training sessions, often without concealing the victims' names.

THE CONFRONTATION CLAUSE

Use of closed-circuit television testimony or videotape testimony has been challenged on the grounds that the defendant's Sixth Amendment constitutional right permits him or her to confront an accuser face to face. The Confrontation Clause of the Sixth Amendment states, "In all criminal prosecutions, the accused shall enjoy the right . . . to be confronted with the witnesses against him."

Several court rulings in the 1990s have upheld the introduction of closed-circuit television, but only when it was used carefully and with full recognition of the rights of the accused. Those who disagree with these rulings claim that this method unfairly influences the jury to think that the accused is guilty simply because the procedure is permitted, and, worse, it deprives the defendant of his or her constitutional right to confront the accuser face to face.

State Rulings on the Confrontation Clause

STATE V. LOMPREY. In 1992 Mark Lomprey appealed a conviction for sexually abusing his niece (*State of Wiscon-*

sin v. Lomprey, 496 N.W.2d 172 [Wis.App. 1992]). The defendant maintained that his right to cross-examine the child in a videotaped interview that was shown to the court was denied because when he entered the room, she curled herself up into a ball ("withdrew into her shell") and refused to speak. The trial court made two more efforts to provide both sides with opportunities to interrogate the child, but she would not respond. She was so withdrawn that the defendant's attorney did not even attempt to question her. The appeals court found that the child's behavior was "in fact, a statement." A statement includes "nonverbal conduct of a person if it is intended by him as an assertion." The court found that the child asserted through her conduct that she feared the defendant.

COMMONWEALTH V. WILLIS. Leslie Willis, who was indicted for the sexual abuse of a five-year-old child, claimed that the child was an incompetent witness and should not therefore be allowed to testify in his trial. The trial judge conducted a private hearing to determine the child's competency, but the child was unresponsive.

The prosecution proposed that, pursuant to the Kentucky statute allowing a child abuse victim age 12 or younger to testify by videotape or closed-circuit television, the trial should proceed using such method. The state statute permits such testimony if there is "substantial probability that the child would be unable to reasonably communicate because of serious emotional distress produced by the defendant's presence." The trial judge ruled to exclude the child's testimony because he was of the opinion that the provisions of the Kentucky statute allowing such testimony were unconstitutional. He held that the statute not only violated the Sixth Amendment Confrontation Clause and Section Eleven of the Kentucky Constitution "to meet the witnesses face to face," but also the separation of powers doctrine of the state constitution.

Without the testimony of the child witness to the alleged crime, the case could not go to trial. Therefore, the prosecution appealed the case. The Kentucky Supreme Court, in *Commonwealth v. Willis* (Ky., 716 S.W.2d 224 [1986]), upheld the state law permitting the child to testify by videotape or closed-circuit television. It ruled that the law did not violate the defendant's state and federal rights of confronting his witness. The court pointed out that the defendant's right to hear and see the witness testify remained intact. He could "object to and seek exclusion of all portions of a tape which he consider[ed] unfair or unduly prejudicial." He also had the right of cross-examination through consultation with his lawyer. Moreover, the jury could assess the credibility of the witness.

The court also ruled that the state law did not violate the separation of powers doctrine of the Kentucky Constitution, because the law left it up to the judge to use his discretion in applying the law. The court concluded:

The strength of the State and Federal Constitutions lies in the fact that they are flexible documents which are able to grow and develop as our society progresses. The purpose of any criminal or civil proceeding is to determine the truth. [The law] provides such a statutory plan while protecting the fundamental interests of the accused as well as the victim.

Federal Rulings on the Confrontation Clause

COY V. IOWA. In June 1988 the U.S. Supreme Court ruled on a case similar to *Commonwealth v. Willis.* An Iowa trial court, pursuant to a state law enacted to protect child victims of sexual abuse, allowed a screen to be placed between the two child witnesses and the alleged abuser. The lighting in the courtroom was adjusted so that the children could not see the defendant, Coy, through the screen. Coy, however, was able to see the children dimly and hear them testify. The trial judge cautioned the jury that the presence of the screen was not an indication of guilt. Coy was convicted.

In *Coy v. Iowa* (397 N.W.2d 730, 1986) Coy appealed to the Iowa Supreme Court, arguing that the screen denied him the right to confront his accusers face to face as provided by the Sixth Amendment. In addition, he claimed that due process was denied because the presence of the screen implied guilt. The Iowa Supreme Court, however, upheld the conviction of the trial court, ruling that the screen had not hurt Coy's right to cross-examine the child witnesses, nor did its presence necessarily imply guilt.

The U.S. Supreme Court, however, in a 6-2 decision, reversed the ruling of the Iowa Supreme Court and remanded the case to the trial court for further proceedings. In *Coy v. Iowa* (487 U.S. 1012, 1988) the High Court maintained that the right to face-to-face confrontation was the essential element of the Sixth Amendment's Confrontation Clause. It held that any exceptions to that guarantee would be allowed only if needed to further an important public policy. The Court found no specific evidence in this case that these witnesses needed special protection that would require a screen.

The two dissenters, Justice Harry A. Blackmun and Chief Justice William Rehnquist, argued that the use of the screen is only a limited departure from the face-to-face confrontation, justified by a substantially important state interest that does not require a case-by-case scrutiny.

MARYLAND V. CRAIG. In June 1990, in a 5-4 decision, the U.S. Supreme Court upheld the use of one-way closed-circuit television. In *Maryland v. Craig* (497 U.S. 836), a six-year-old child alleged that Sandra Craig had committed perverted sexual practices and assault and battery on her in the prekindergarten run by Craig. In support of its motion to permit the child to testify through closed-circuit television, the state presented expert testimony that the child "wouldn't be able to communicate effectively,

would probably stop talking and would withdraw, and would become extremely timid and unwilling to talk."

The High Court decision, written by Justice Sandra Day O'Connor, noted that, although "it is always more difficult to tell a lie about a person 'to his face' than 'behind his back,'" the Sixth Amendment Confrontation Clause does not guarantee *absolute* right to a face-to-face meeting with the witness. The closed-circuit television does permit cross-examination and observation of the witness's demeanor. "We are therefore confident," Justice O'Connor declared, "that use of the one-way closed-circuit television procedure, where necessary to further an important state interest, does not impinge upon the truth-seeking or symbolic purposes of the Confrontation Clause."

Justice Antonin Scalia, dissenting, felt that the Constitution had been juggled to fit a perceived need when the Constitution explicitly forbade it. He stated, "We are not free to conduct a cost-benefit analysis [comparison of the benefits] of clear and explicit constitutional guarantees and then to adjust their meaning to comport [agree] with our findings."

HEARSAY EVIDENCE

Together with the Sixth Amendment Confrontation Clause, hearsay rules are intended to prevent the conviction of defendants by reports of evidence offered by someone they would be unable to challenge. Certain exceptions to the ban on hearsay have always been allowed. A dying person's reported last words are often permitted in court, for example. Whether or not to accept the hearsay evidence from a child's reports of abuse to a parent has been frequently debated.

Hearsay evidence is especially important in cases of child sexual abuse. Cases often take years to come to trial, by which time a child may have forgotten the details of the abuse or may have made psychological progress in dealing with the trauma. The parents may be reluctant to plunge the child back into the anxious situation suffered earlier. Hearsay evidence can be crucial in determining the validity of sexual abuse charges in custody cases. In these cases juries need to know when the child first alleged abuse, to whom, under what circumstances, and whether the child ever recanted.

In *Ohio v. Roberts* (448 U.S. 56, 1979), the U.S. Supreme Court established the basis for permitting hearsay: the actual witness has to be unavailable and his or her statement has to be reliable enough to permit another person to repeat it to the jury. Many judges have chosen to interpret unavailability on physical standards rather than the emotional unavailability that children who are afraid to testify may exhibit. Furthermore, legal experts insist that the reliability of a statement does not refer to whether the statement appears to be truthful, but only that it has sufficient reliability for the jury to decide whether it is true.

Hearsay Exceptions

Some courts consider spontaneous declarations or excited utterances made by a person right after a stressful experience as reliable hearsay. Courts also allow statements children have made to physicians and other medical personnel for purposes of medical treatment or diagnosis. In this case, it is generally assumed that people who consult with physicians are seeking treatment and, therefore, tell the physicians the truth about their illness. Josephine A. Bulkley, Jane Nusbaum Feller, Paul Stern, and Rebecca Roe cited the example of the case *State v. Nelson* (406 N.W.2d 385 [Wis. 1987], *cert. denied* 110 S. Ct. 835, 1990), in which the court permitted a psychologist to repeat his patient's statements because the child believed she was being treated by the doctor ("Child Abuse and Neglect Laws and Legal Proceedings," *APSAC Handbook on Child Maltreatment,* Sage Publications, Inc., Thousand Oaks, CA, 1996). The authors observed that some states have concluded that younger children do not understand that seeing a psychologist will help make them better. Therefore, the child's statements to the physician cannot be considered reliable and truthful so as to constitute a hearsay exception.

The Greenbrook Preschool case (reported in *On Trial: America's Courts and Their Treatment of Sexually Abused Children,* Beacon Press, Boston, 1989), with all identifying details changed to protect the families, was lost largely because of the judge's strict interpretation of hearsay. The parents of the children were not permitted to tell the jury anything the children had revealed in conversations during the year between the discovery of the abuse and the trial. Illogical court testimony ensued.

At one point the defense asked one of the parents to relate a conversation she had had with the school's teacher and director. "I asked if they [the teacher and director] had any explanation for the sexual detail that Laurie had gone into." (The jury had no knowledge of the sexual detail because the court had not permitted Laurie's mother to talk about it.) The defense objected, and the judge sustained the objection, saying, "The jury will not assume that she went into sexual detail because that would be hearsay."

The Validity of Hearsay Evidence

In *United States v. Inadi* (475 U.S. 387, 1986), the U.S. Supreme Court clarified its intentions on hearsay evidence that did not concern child sexual abuse. The Court explained that "unavailability" (of a witness) was not a required criterion for the admission of hearsay. In fact, the Court wrote that some statements "derive much of their value from the fact they are made in a context very different from trial and, therefore, are usually irreplaceable as substantive evidence." The Arizona Supreme Court, in *State v. Robinson* (735 P.2d 801, 1987), permitted hearsay evidence from a 10-year-old girl to her psychologist. The court stated:

An additional factor of great weight in this case is the unlikelihood that more trustworthy or probative evidence could have been produced by [the child's] in-court testimony. A young child's spontaneous statements about so unusual a personal experience, made soon after the event, are at least as reliable as the child's in-court testimony, given months later, after innumerable interviews and interrogations may have distorted the child's memory. Indeed, [her] statements are valuable and trustworthy in part because they were made in circumstances very different from interrogation or a criminal trial.

WHITE V. ILLINOIS. In *White v. Illinois* (502 U.S. 346, 1992), the U.S. Supreme Court dealt with both the hearsay rules and the Confrontation Clause of the Sixth Amendment. Randall White was charged with sexually assaulting a four-year-old girl, S. G., in the course of a residential burglary. The child's screams attracted the attention of her babysitter, who witnessed White leaving the house. S. G. related essentially the same version of her experience to her babysitter, her mother (who returned home shortly after the attack), a police officer, an emergency room nurse, and a doctor. All of these adults testified at the trial. S. G. did not testify, being too emotional each time she was brought to the courtroom.

White was found guilty and appealed on the grounds that, because the defendant had not been able to face the witness who had made the charges of sexual assault, her hearsay testimony was invalid under the Confrontation Clause. The High Court, in a unanimous decision, rejected linking the Confrontation Clause and the admissibility of hearsay testimony.

S. G.'s statements fulfilled the hearsay requirements in that they were either spontaneous declarations or made for medical treatment and, therefore, in the eyes of the High Court, "may justifiably carry more weight with a [court] than a similar statement offered in the relative calm of the courtroom." The Supreme Court concluded that whether the witness appeared to testify had no bearing on the validity of the hearsay evidence. Furthermore, because the hearsay statements in this case fit the "medical evidence" and "spontaneous declaration" exceptions, its decision upheld hearsay evidence as valid.

This decision, coupled with the *Inadi* decision, has affected hundreds of child abuse cases. More prosecutors can now risk taking on abuse cases without having to rely on a frightened child's testimony to reveal the full story.

EXPERT WITNESSES

Videotaping and closed-circuit television permit juries to see and hear child witnesses, but it does not mean that the juries will understand or believe them. Prosecutors often request permission to bring in an expert witness to clarify an abused child's behavior, particularly to explain why a child might have waited so long to make an accusation or why the child might withdraw an accusation made earlier.

The danger of bringing in an expert witness is that the expert often lends an unwarranted stamp of authenticity to the child's truthfulness. If an expert states that children rarely lie about sex abuse, that expert might be understood by the jury to be saying that the defendant must be guilty, when the expert has no way of knowing if that is the case. In some highly contested cases, expert witnesses swayed the jury in their decision. In the Margaret Kelly Michaels case, an expert witness explained how the children's problems were symptomatic of their abuse. In the Eileen Franklin case (see Chapter 8), the expert witness convinced the jury of the validity of repressed memory and explained that inconsistencies in Eileen Franklin's story were symptoms of her trauma.

Rules Governing the Use of Expert Testimony

The states have their own rules when it comes to expert testimony. Federal courts, however, follow the Federal Rules of Evidence. On December 1, 2000, the Federal Rules of Evidence were amended because of concerns that experts in the past had lacked the proper qualifications. The new rule requires that before the jury can hear expert testimony, the trial judge first has to determine that the expert has the proper "knowledge, skill, experience, training, or education" to help the jury understand the evidence.

For expert testimony to be acceptable in court, the statements made must be very general and explain only psychological tendencies, never referring specifically to the child witness. The U.S. Court of Appeals, in *United States v. Azure* (801 F.2d 336, 1986), reversed the conviction of the defendant because an expert's testimony was too specific. During trial an expert witness had testified that the alleged victim was believable. According to the court, "by putting his stamp of believability on [the young girl's] entire story, [the expert] essentially told the jury that [the child] was truthful in saying that [the defendant] was the person who sexually abused her. No reliable test for truthfulness exists and [the expert witness] was not qualified to judge the truthfulness of that part of [the child's] story."

JUDICIAL REFORMS

The National Council of Juvenile and Family Court Judges (NCJFCJ) of Reno, Nevada, the nation's oldest organization of judges, has always sought to improve the way courts handle child maltreatment cases. In 1995 NCJFCJ developed and published *Resource Guidelines Improving Court Practices in Child Abuse and Neglect Cases,* which provides step-by-step recommendations on how to improve court practice. Begun in 1995, the nationwide initiative by the NCJFCJ, the Victims Act Model Courts, seeks to shorten children's time in foster care and bring about an early permanent resolution of maltreatment cases.

The NCJFCJ provides training and education to judges and other practitioners through its Permanency Planning for Children Department. In light of the recognition that child maltreatment and domestic violence often co-occur, the NCJFCJ established a committee to develop guidelines to improve how the courts, CPS, domestic violence services, and community groups can help families experiencing those problems. The committee recommendations were published in *Effective Intervention in Domestic Violence & Child Maltreatment Cases: Guidelines for Policy and Practice.* Just as Model Courts across the country have served as "models" for reforming the handling of children in foster care, the Green Book Initiative (named for the color of the publication) was being tested in various sites in the nation.

FALSE ACCUSATIONS OF CHILD SEXUAL ABUSE

The willingness of people to believe children's accusations of sexual abuse has varied greatly since the mid-twentieth century. At one time, people were simply unwilling to believe that sexual abuse of children was happening or happening with any frequency. Once society accepted the fact that child sexual abuse was occurring regularly, responses to accusations of child sexual abuse went from disbelief to almost total acceptance by experts, who claimed children do not lie about these things.

Some observers noted that since approximately the 1990s, parents and other persons of authority have tried to educate children about sexual abuse. Hence, children are more knowledgeable about such offenses. Some people believe that, in some cases, children make false accusations. The consequences could be irreparable. *Baltimore Sun* reporter Todd Richissin wrote that in Montgomery County, Maryland, one of five cases of child sexual abuse accusations had been proven false. In "Legacy of a Lie" (*Baltimore Sun,* December 17, 2000), Richissin recounted the story of a physical education teacher who was accused of sexual abuse by seven sixth-graders. The girls accused the teacher of going to their locker room, watching them dress, and touching their bodies. The girls also had a male classmate corroborate their story. In the end, the girls admitted they had made up the story because they were displeased with the teacher "for insisting on good sportsmanship." In the end, after his name was cleared, the teacher decided to give up his 32-year career. The court ordered the accusers to perform community service for their false accusations.

Types of False Accusations

Edwin Mikkelsen et al. examined studies of sexual abuse allegations to determine how many initial reports of abuse were later determined to be false. They found rates that ranged from 2 to 8 percent of abuse cases referred to child abuse clinics, to 6 percent of emergency room referrals, to much higher rates (36.4 to 55.5 percent) in cases arising out of custody disputes ("False Sexual Abuse Allegations by Children and Adolescents: Contextual Factors and Clinical Subtypes," *American Journal of Psychotherapy,* vol. 46, no. 4, 1992).

Mikkelsen et al. defined four types of false allegations, although many cases involve a combination of the four types.

Subtype I is the most common and appears in the context of a custody dispute. This is the conscious manipulation on the part of one parent or caregiver to obtain custody of children from another parent or caregiver. The parent may coerce the child into alleging abuse. In these cases, the description of the abuse may be on a more sophisticated level than a child would be expected to know at that age. In one case an 11-year-old boy related sexual activity but could not explain the meaning of the sophisticated language he used to describe it.

Subtype II is an allegation that results from the accuser's psychological disturbance. The accuser may be a child or a parent/caregiver. When it comes from a child, the child is unable to differentiate fantasy from reality; in a parent, it is a delusional (a strong belief maintained despite evidence to the contrary) process in an individual who otherwise appears to be functioning adequately. For example, a mother who had been sexually abused by her 14-year-old brother when she was 12 became convinced her own daughters were being abused by her brother when the children reached the ages of 12 and 14, respectively.

Subtype III is an allegation that is a conscious manipulation by the child. In these cases, the child makes an allegation as a means to obtain a specific goal out of vindictiveness or desire for revenge or rage. Children who are in a living situation they dislike are the most common accusers. An example is a child who lives with a parent and stepparent and would rather live with the other natural parent.

Subtype IV is iatrogenic (induced in a client/patient by a professional, such as a therapist or social worker). For example, a pediatrician in England insisted she could detect sexual abuse based on subtle physical symptoms that she could see even when the person did not claim he or she had been abused. Based on this, charges were made against several parents in one English village.

Suing Child Protective Services

In 1993 David Tyner III was accused by his wife of sexually abusing their four-year-old daughter. The couple was in the process of a divorce. CPS did not uncover any abuse but continued to prohibit the father from seeing his children. Tyner sued CPS for mishandling the investigation.

In June 2000 the Washington Supreme Court, in *Tyner v. the State of Washington Department of Social and Health Services, CPS* (No. 67602, Supreme Court of Washington, June 15, 2000, Filed 2000 Wash. LEXIS 387), ruled that CPS could be sued for negligent handling of investigations. The court held that "CPS owes a duty of care to a child's parents, even those suspected of abusing their own children, when investigating allegations of child abuse." The court reinstated a jury verdict of more than $200,000 against the department.

Suing the Police

In September 2000 the Washington Supreme Court, in *Rodriguez v. City of Wenatchee* (No. 69614-4, Supreme Court of Washington, Sept. 2000, Wash. LEXIS 578), unanimously ruled that the police can be held financially liable for negligence in child abuse investigations. This first court decision of its kind stemmed from a lawsuit filed by Pastor Robert Robertson, his wife, and others accused of child molestation.

In 1994 a nine-year-old foster child was placed in the home of Bob Perez, Wenatchee's chief sex-crimes investigator. The following year the girl told her foster father about being sexually abused by her parents. After the parents were convicted, the child made allegations of a sex-ring involving the Robertsons and 43 adults since 1988. Based on the girl's testimony and that of her 13-year-old friend and a former member of Robertson's church, Robertson, his wife, and 19 others were arrested on 30,000 counts of sexual abuse against 60 children. In December 1995 the Robertsons were acquitted. In 1996 Perez's foster daughter recanted, denying her sexual abuse allegations and saying that Perez had pressured her. Her friend had also recanted her testimony. In a September 2000 hearing, the Washington Supreme Court reinstated the $30 million lawsuit brought by the Wenatchee defendants.

THE REGISTRATION OF SEX OFFENDERS

At a national conference on sex offender registries in 1998, director of Bureau of Justice Statistics Jan M. Chaiken reported that nearly two-thirds of the 95,000 sex offenders in state prisons that year committed their violent sex crimes against children under age 18. The victims of the majority of the violent sex offenders were children younger than 12. The number of sex offenders in state prisons has since risen to 113,900 (Paige M. Harrison and Allen J. Beck, *Prisoners in 2001,* U.S. Department of Justice, Bureau of Justice Statistics, July 2002). Three federal laws have been enacted to track sex offenders after their release from prison:

The Jacob Wetterling Act

The Jacob Wetterling Crimes against Children and Sexually Violent Offender Registration Act, also known as the Jacob Wetterling Act, was signed into federal law on September 13, 1994, as part of the Violent Crime Control and Law Enforcement Act of 1994 (Public Law 103-322). The act provides funding to states to establish registration systems for sex offenders. States must require abusers who have committed a criminal offense against a minor to register every year for 10 years after release from prison, parole, or probation. Sexually violent predators must report their addresses to the state every 90 days until it is determined they are no longer threats to public safety. Sexually violent predators include those who have committed sexually violent crimes, as well as those who may not have committed sexual crimes but suffer from mental abnormalities or personality disorders that may predispose them to commit predatory or violent sex offenses.

Jacob Wetterling was an 11-year-old boy kidnapped near his home in St. Joseph, Minnesota, by an armed, masked man on October 22, 1989. His abduction was similar to a case involving a boy from a nearby town who was kidnapped and sexually assaulted earlier that year. Jacob has never been found, but police believed the cases were linked and encouraged the creation of a database so that police departments could share information.

Megan's Law

"Megan's Law" (Public Law 104-145), signed May 17, 1996, amended the Jacob Wetterling Act by requiring states to release information on registered sex offenders if needed to protect the public. In 1994 the nation's first notification law was enacted in New Jersey after seven-year-old Megan Kanka was raped and murdered by a convicted sex offender who lived across the street from her family. Since then every state has enacted legislation ("Ashley's Law" in Texas and "Polly Klass's Law" in California, for instance) that requires the registration and tracking of sex offenders.

The Pam Lychner Act

The Pam Lychner Sexual Offender Tracking and Identification Act (Public Law 104-236), signed on October 3, 1996, also amended the Jacob Wetterling Act by requiring the Federal Bureau of Investigation (FBI) to establish a National Sex Offender Registry to help state-to-state tracking and management of released sex offenders. It further allows the FBI to conduct sex offender registration and community notification in states that do not have "minimally sufficient" systems in place for such purposes. The Pam Lychner Act was named after a victim's rights activist who was killed in an airplane crash in 1988.

State Sex Offender Registries

As of February 2001 a total of 386,112 convicted sex offenders were registered in 49 states and the District of Columbia, up from 263,166 in 1998. California reported the largest number of sex offenders in its registry (88,853),

TABLE 7.1

Number of offenders in state sex offender registry, 1998 and 2001

State	Offenders in registry 1998	Offenders in registry 2001	Percent change in the number of registrants, 1998-2001
Alabama	440	3,338	659%
Alaska*	3,535	4,107	16
Arizona	9,200	11,500	25
Arkansas	958	2,935	206
California*	78,000	88,853	14
Colorado	4,326	8,804	104
Connecticut	N/A	2,030	
Delaware	800	1,688	111
District of Columbia	50	303	506
Florida	9,000	20,000	122
Georgia	1,200	4,564	280%
Hawaii	1,000	1,500	50
Idaho	1,710	1,778	4
Illinois*	14,300	16,551	16
Indiana	9,500	11,656	23
Iowa	2,240	3,921	75
Kansas	1,200	1,794	50
Kentucky	800	2,000	150
Louisiana	3,455	5,708	65
Maine	275	473	72
Maryland	400	1,400	250%
Massachusetts**	7,004		
Michigan	19,000	26,850	41
Minnesota	7,300	10,610	45
Mississippi	1,063	1,512	42
Missouri	2,800	7,500	168
Montana***	1,739	2,088	20
Nebraska	640	1,120	75
Nevada	1,500	2,519	68
New Hampshire	1,500	2,168	45
New Jersey	5,151	7,495	46%
New Mexico	450	1,171	160
New York	7,200	11,575	61
North Carolina	2,200	5,922	169
North Dakota	683	766	12
Ohio	1,294	5,423	319
Oklahoma	2,303	4,020	75
Oregon	7,400	9,410	27
Pennsylvania	2,400	4,533	89
Rhode Island	273	1,424	422
South Carolina	2,500	4,924	97
South Dakota	800	1,182	48%
Tennessee	2,800	4,561	63
Texas	18,000	29,494	64
Utah	4,733	5,192	10
Vermont	877	1,509	72
Virginia	6,615	9,306	41
Washington	1,400	15,304	993
West Virginia	600	950	58
Wisconsin	10,000	11,999	20
Wyoming	552	682	24
Total	263,166	386,112	

*Number includes more than just registered offenders (for example, never registered but required to do so, offenders in jail, registered but not in compliance).
**The 2001 count is not included due to a superior court injunction against the Sex Offender Registry Board, prohibiting registration without first providing the offender a hearing. Massachusetts estimated about 17,000 sex offenders to be qualified to register at the time of the survey.
***Also includes offenders who must register for certain violent offenses.

SOURCE: Devon B. Adams, "Appendix table 2: Number of offenders in State SOR's, 1998 and 2001," in *Summary of State Sex Offender Registries, 2001*, U.S. Department of Justice, Bureau of Justice Statistics, Washington, DC, March 2002

followed by Texas (29,494), Michigan (26,850), and Florida (20,000). (See Table 7.1.) Massachusetts, with an estimated 17,000 sex offenders, was not included in the

February 2001 count because of a superior court injunction against inclusion in the registry prior to a hearing. Since then the superior court has ruled that sex offender information may be shared with law enforcement but not with the public until the offenders are afforded court hearings in which they can challenge their sex offender classification. Twenty-nine states and the District of Columbia had Internet sites where the public could access information about the offenders. According to 22 states, DNA samples had been collected as part of registration.

CHILD PORNOGRAPHY LAWS

Although the First Amendment protects pornography, it does not protect child pornography. Under the definition established in *Miller v. California* (413 U.S. 15 [1973]), pornography may be banned if it is deemed legally obscene. To be considered obscene, material "taken as a whole" must:

- appeal to a prurient interest in sex;

- be patently offensive in light of community standards; and

- lack serious literary, artistic, political, or scientific value.

Since 1982 child pornography has been banned by the U.S. Supreme Court ruling, *New York v. Ferber* (458 U.S. 747), which held that pornography depicting children engaged in sexually explicit acts can be banned, whether or not it is obscene, because of the state's interest in protecting children from sexual exploitation. In other words, such images are not protected by the First Amendment. The Child Pornography Prevention Act of 1996 (Public Law 104-208) added a definition of child pornography, stating that an actual minor need not be used in creating a depiction in order for the depiction to constitute child pornography.

In October 1998, in an effort to further protect children from sexual predators who target minors through the Internet, Congress enacted the Protection of Children from Sexual Predators Act (Public Law 105-314). The bill provides punishment for any individual who knowingly contacts, or tries to contact, children under 18 in order to engage in criminal sexual activity, or who knowingly transfers obscene material to children.

Protecting Children from Pornography on the Internet

Congressional debate continues on how the government should enforce obscenity standards in cyberspace. Some policy makers believe any obscenity standards could interfere with free speech and would be difficult to enforce, while others believe this is an issue relating to child protection, not to the First Amendment.

COMMUNICATIONS DECENCY ACT. In 1996 Congress first attempted to protect minors from Internet material that,

judged under contemporary community standards, would be considered "obscene or indecent" for them. Congress passed the Communications Decency Act, or Title V of the Telecommunications Act (Public Law 104-104), which makes it a federal crime to use any facility or means of interstate or foreign commerce to entice or force any person under age 18 to engage in prostitution or any sexual act.

On June 26, 1997, the U.S. Supreme Court, in *Reno v. American Civil Liberties Union* (521 U.S. 844), held by a 7-2 decision that the Communications Decency Act "abridges the freedom of speech protected by the First Amendment" because "In order to deny minors access to potentially harmful speech, the CDA effectively suppress[ed] a large amount of speech that adults ha[d] a constitutional right to receive and to address to one another."

CHILD ONLINE PROTECTION ACT. In October 1998 Congress enacted the Child Online Protection Act (COPA; Public Law 105-277). In light of the Supreme Court's ruling on the CDA, Congress narrowed the scope of COPA to include just the material published on the World Wide Web. In comparison, the CDA included all communications over the Internet. COPA applied only to persons who are in the business of distributing pictures, articles, images, and video and audio recordings for the purpose of making a profit. In addition, COPA limited the materials to those that are considered harmful to children, unlike the CDA, which bans all "indecent" and "patently offensive" communications.

Persons liable to COPA violations include all those who place such obscene material on the Internet in order to earn a profit (although it is not necessary that they make a profit). The person may be a Web site administrator who creates and maintains a Web site, a content provider such as an online bookstore or magazine, or a content contributor who writes or creates graphics for communications media. COPA requires all commercial sites on the Internet to obtain credit card numbers or adult identification numbers from users. Violation of COPA entails heavy fines ($50,000–$150,000 per day) and up to six months in jail.

COPA, however, exempts the following persons from liability:

- a telecommunications carrier who provides telecommunications services

- a person who provides an Internet access service

- a person who provides an Internet information location tool

- a person engaged in the transmission, storage, retrieval, hosting, formatting, or translation (or any combination of these functions) of a communication made by another person, without alteration or deletion of some parts of the communication content

COPA was set to be put into effect on November 20, 1998, but that same day, commercial World Wide Web providers and Web site users who used the materials described by COPA filed a complaint with the U.S. District Court for the Western District of Pennsylvania, challenging the constitutionality of the law. The plaintiffs argued that they would be forced to either establish age-verification barriers or delete materials from their Web sites that may be perceived to violate COPA. The plaintiffs asked the court to issue a temporary restraining order prohibiting the U.S. attorney general from enforcing COPA.

In *American Civil Liberties Union v. Reno* (Civil Action No. 98-5591, 1998), Federal District Judge Lowell A. Reed Jr., issued a preliminary injunction against the enforcement of COPA. Judge Reed ruled:

> The Supreme Court has repeatedly stated that the free speech rights of adults may not be reduced to allow them to read only what is acceptable for children.
>
> While the public certainly has an interest in protecting its minors, the public interest is not served by the enforcement of an unconstitutional law. Indeed, to the extent that other members of the public who are not parties to this lawsuit may be affected by the statute, the interest of the public is served by the preservation of the status quo until such time that this Court . . . may more closely examine the constitutionality of this statute.

On February 1, 1999, with the restraining order he imposed against COPA set to expire, Judge Reed again issued a preliminary injunction against the enforcement of the law (No. 99-1324). On June 22, 2000, the U.S. Court of Appeals for the Third Circuit, in *American Civil Liberties Union. v. Reno* affirmed Judge Reed's ruling.

Upon appeal by the U.S. attorney general, the U.S. Court of Appeals ruled that COPA violated the First Amendment because it relies, in part, on "contemporary community standards" (per *Roth v. United States,* 354 U.S. 476, [1957]), to determine whether or not certain materials are harmful to children. According to the appellate court, the *Roth* decision could not be applied to the Internet or the World Wide Web because juries across the country would have different community standards. Some juries might apply the "most puritan" community standards, which would put too much burden on First Amendment freedoms. The court also found it unnecessary to review the rest of the law.

In 2001 the government appealed its case to the U.S. Supreme Court. On May 13, 2002, in *Ashcroft v. American Civil Liberties Union et al.* (217 F.3d 162), the Supreme Court limited its decision to ruling that COPA's use of community standards to identify material harmful to children does not necessarily make it unconstitutional as far as First Amendment freedoms are concerned. It further found the appellate court decision incomplete and sent the case back for further proceedings. The court did not lift the injunction against the COPA enforcement.

CHILD PORNOGRAPHY PREVENTION ACT. On April 16, 2002, the U.S. Supreme Court resolved the question of whether another 1996 law, the Child Pornography Prevention Act (CPPA; Public Law 104-208), is unconstitutional because it prohibits free speech that is not obscene based on *Miller* nor child pornography based on *Ferber.* The CPPA, in part, bans any visual depiction that "is, or appears to be, of a minor engaging in sexually explicit conduct." Such depiction, called virtual child pornography, includes computer-generated images and images using youthful-looking adults. The CPPA also prohibits the advertisement or promotion of any sexually explicit image that "conveys the impression" that children are performing sexual acts.

The Supreme Court, in *Ashcroft v. Free Speech Coalition et al.* (No. 00-795), ruled 6-3 that banning virtual child pornography is unconstitutional because, unlike *Ferber,* actual children are not used in its production. Moreover, the Court claimed that the government cannot prohibit material fit for adults just because children might get hold of it. The Court also struck down the government's argument that child pornography whets the appetites of pedophiles and encourages them to commit unlawful acts. On the part of the law that bans material that "conveys the impression" it contains children performing sexual acts, the justices noted that anyone found in possession of such "mislabeled" material could be prosecuted.

CHILDREN'S INTERNET PROTECTION ACT. The Children's Internet Protection Act (CIPA; Public Law 106-554), enacted by Congress in 2000, requires all public libraries receiving federal funds to install software that blocks visual depictions of obscenity, child pornography, and material harmful to children. Libraries, library associations, library patrons, and some Web sites filed lawsuits challenging the law.

Two lawsuits in Philadelphia, which were consolidated, were tried on May 31, 2002. In *American Library Association v. United States* (Civil Action No. 01-1303) and *Multnomah County Public Library v. United States* (Civil Action No. 01-1322), the U.S. District Court for the Eastern District of Pennsylvania unanimously ruled that CIPA abridges the First Amendment rights of library patrons. The court found that limitations in filtering programs might also block access to other material protected by First Amendment speech. A group of libraries, library associations, library patrons, and Web sites across the country filed lawsuits challenging the law.

PROSECUTION FOR DRUG USE DURING PREGNANCY

In November 1997 the South Carolina Supreme Court, in *Whitner v. South Carolina* (492 S.E.2d 777 [S.C. 1997]), ruled that pregnant women who use drugs can be criminally prosecuted for child maltreatment. The court found that a viable (potentially capable of surviving outside the womb) fetus is a "person" covered by the state's child abuse and neglect laws. The ruling was handed down in a case appealed by Cornelia Whitner, who was sentenced to eight years in prison in 1992 for pleading guilty to child neglect. This was the first time the highest court of any state upheld the criminal conviction of a woman charged with such an offense. Whitner's newborn tested positive for cocaine.

In March 1998 Malissa Ann Crawley, charged with the same criminal offense, began serving a five-year prison sentence in South Carolina. In June 1998 the U.S. Supreme Court refused to hear appeals by Whitner and Crawley.

Whitner's lawyer had argued that if a woman could be prosecuted for child abuse for having used drugs while pregnant, what was to keep the law from prosecuting her for smoking or drinking or even for failing to obtain prenatal care? Other critics claimed that women who are substance abusers, fearing prosecution, might not seek prenatal care and counseling for their drug problems, which would further endanger the child.

Cases similar to *Whitner v. South Carolina* had been brought before other state courts, but none had convicted a substance-ingesting pregnant woman. These included Florida, Kentucky, Michigan, Nevada, Ohio, Washington, and Wyoming.

Mandatory Reporting of Child Abuse by Pregnant Women

Many states require the mandatory reporting of substance-abusing pregnant women and newborns exposed to drugs. Social services agencies then come to the mother's aid, sometimes removing the infant from her custody on a temporary or permanent basis. Currently, South Dakota has a statute that mandates the reporting of substance-ingesting pregnant women for "child abuse" to law enforcement instead of to social services. Failure to report such cases of child abuse would constitute a crime punishable by up to six months in prison.

In 1988 the Charleston public hospital run by the Medical University of South Carolina (MUSC) collaborated with city officials and police to test pregnant women suspected of drug use. Ten women who were arrested after testing positive for cocaine filed a lawsuit, charging that "warrantless and nonconsensual drug tests conducted for criminal investigatory purposes were unconstitutional searches" prohibited by the Fourth Amendment. The U.S. Supreme Court agreed. On March 21, 2001, the Court ruled 6-3 that the MUSC's policy was unconstitutional (*Ferguson v. City of Charleston;* No. 99-936). The Court recognized that the hospital policy was "designed to obtain evidence of criminal conduct by the tested patients that would be turned over to the police and that could be admissible in subsequent criminal prosecutions." The Court noted that the Fourth Amendment's ban against nonconsensual, warrantless, and suspicionless searches applies to such a policy.

CHILD ABUSE LAWS RELATING TO DOMESTIC VIOLENCE

Some local laws that have been passed impose penalties for domestic violence when children are present. For example, Salt Lake County, Utah, and Houston County, Georgia, enacted statutes creating a new crime of child maltreatment when domestic violence is witnessed by a child. Multnomah County, Oregon, passed legislation upgrading some assault offenses to felonies (serious crimes) when a child is present during domestic violence. Debra Whitcomb conducted a study involving a survey of prosecutors to determine their responses to cases where children witness domestic violence ("Prosecutors, Kids, and Domestic Violence Cases," *National Institute of Justice Journal,* no. 248, March 2002).

The survey asked 128 prosecutors across the country how they would respond to three domestic violence cases in which children were present. A majority of prosecutors (94 percent) would report a battered mother to CPS if she were found abusing the child. All indicated they would prosecute the abusing mother. Prosecutors would more likely report a battered mother if she failed to protect her child from abuse (63 percent) than if she failed to protect the child from witnessing the domestic violence (40 percent). More than three times as many prosecutors would charge the mother with a crime for the child's abuse (77.5 percent) than for exposure to family violence (25 percent). (See Table 7.2.)

Court Sides with Battered Women Whose Children Are Removed

Battered women with children are often further penalized by CPS's removal of their children. On December 21, 2001, Jack B. Weinstein, a federal judge, ruled that New York City's Administration for Children's Services (ACS) violated the constitutional rights of mothers and their children by removing the children simply because the mothers were victims of domestic violence. In the first case of its kind, 15 battered women brought the class action suit *Nicholson v. Scoppetta.*

On January 3, 2002, the judge issued an injunction ordering ACS to stop separating a child from his or her battered mother unless the child "is in such imminent danger." The injunction holds that "the government may not penalize a mother, not otherwise unfit, who is battered by her partner, by separating her from her children; nor may children be separated from the mother, in effect visiting upon them the sins of their mother's batterer."

MAJOR PRESCHOOL ABUSE CASES

In the 1980s and early 1990s alleged incidents of mass molestation of preschool children in the United States triggered hysteria not only among the parents of the children involved in the cases but also among the public. Some of these cases continued into the late 1990s. Some have not been resolved. While these cases are unusually famous, they demonstrate many of the typical issues and problems that the legal system faces in dealing with child abuse cases.

The McMartin Preschool Case

The McMartin Preschool case is often considered as the case that started a string of cases involving preschool sexual abuse. In 1983 Judy Johnson, the mother of a two-and-one-half-year-old child enrolled at the McMartin Preschool in Manhattan Beach, California, told police that her son had been molested by Raymond Buckey, the adult grandson of the preschool director, Virginia McMartin. Police sent letters to 200 parents of current and former students, informing them of the molestation investigation. Soon other parents claimed to remember strange happenings, such as their children sometimes coming home in underwear and clothes that were not their own. The parents also reported behavior changes for which they could find no explanation.

Raymond Buckey was arrested, but charges of sexual abuse were later dropped for lack of evidence. In 1984 he was rearrested. His grandmother Virginia, his mother Peggy McMartin Buckey, his sister Peggy Ann, and three other female teachers were also arrested. In 1986 Virginia, Peggy Ann, and the teachers were released for lack of evidence.

The prosecution's primary investigator was Kee MacFarlane, director of the Children's Sexual Abuse Diagnostic Center of the Children's Institute International (CII; Los Angeles), an organization that dealt with maltreated children. CII personnel interviewed the children who had allegedly been abused. The children began to tell stories about being drugged, sodomized, penetrated with sharp objects, and used in a game called "Naked Movie Star." The interviewers used anatomically correct dolls to help the children explain what happened. The interviews were videotaped.

When the case finally went to trial in 1986, the children were 8 to 12 years old and were recounting events that occurred when they were 3 to 5 years old. Defense attorneys used the videotapes to show how the interviewers elicited the desired replies from the children by asking leading questions. They also claimed that the use of anatomically correct dolls put ideas into the children's heads.

As the trial wore on, the allegations grew more fantastic (drinking blood in a church, riding in a van with a half-dead baby). The children turned out to be unreliable

TABLE 7.2

Prosecutors' responses to scenarios involving children and abuse

Scenario	Would Report At Least Sometimes	Would Prosecute At Least Sometimes
Mom Abuses Children	94% (n=90)	100% (n=82)
Mom Fails to Protect from Abuse	63% (n=87)	77.5% (n=80)
Mom Fails to Protect from Exposure	40% (n=86)	25% (n=73)

SOURCE: Debra Whitcomb, "Table 1: Prosecutors' Responses to Scenarios Involving Child and Abuse," in "Prosecutors, Kids, and Domestic Violence Cases," *National Institute of Justice Journal*, Issue 248, March 2002

witnesses and many recanted their earlier statements. On January 18, 1990, the trial involving Raymond and his mother Peggy ended with acquittals on some counts and a jury deadlocked on other charges. Pressured by the parents, however, the prosecutor immediately retried Raymond Buckey on the deadlocked charges. The hung jury voted for acquittal. The prosecutor decided not to retry him. Raymond had already spent five years in jail and Peggy two years.

The McMartin case has turned out to be the longest (seven years) and most expensive ($16 million) criminal trial in U.S. history. Some people observe that the McMartin case is an example of how a case can be mishandled by everyone involved. They argue that MacFarlane, the child sex abuse expert who headed the investigation, was not licensed to practice therapy in California. Critics point out that the children's testimonies were the results of events suggested to them by their parents who were caught up in the mass hysteria and by the therapists who conducted the interviews. It was later discovered that Judy Johnson, the mother who made the initial allegations of child molestation, was suffering from paranoid schizophrenia. She was also drinking a lot. After her first accusation, she continued to recount bizarre stories to investigators about her son's behavior, such as his having also been molested by a Los Angeles School Board member. The prosecution did not share this information with the defense for nearly a year. Johnson died of alcohol poisoning in 1986.

The Fells Acres Case

In 1984 a five-year-old boy told his uncle that Gerald Amirault, the son of the owner of the Fells Acres Day School in Malden, Massachusetts, had touched his private parts. He also told his mother of other incidents of abuse. Police notified parents about the situation, instructing them to question their children and watch for behaviors related to sexual abuse. Forty-one children, ages three to six, eventually told stories of being raped by a clown, of being forced to watch animals being killed, and of having their pictures taken naked. Although the children testified about a "secret" or "magic" room they visited daily, no child could show the police the location of the room, nor could the police find it. Violet Amirault and her children, Cheryl Amirault LeFave and Gerald Amirault, were convicted of sexual abuse. The mother and daughter received a sentence of 8–20 years, and Gerald, 30–40 years.

Violet and Cheryl were released in 1995 after the Massachusetts Superior Court overturned their convictions because the seating arrangement of the child witnesses (facing the jury but not the defendants) violated their right to "face-to-face" confrontations with their accusers as guaranteed by Article 12 of the Massachusetts Declaration of Rights. Two years later the state's highest court reinstated their convictions, claiming that the accused had not offered sufficient proof that justice had been miscarried. Violet Amirault died of cancer later that year.

In June 1998 a Superior Court judge overturned Cheryl's conviction, noting that the accusers, now teenagers, who have never recanted their allegations of abuse, could not testify. The judge claimed that, due to investigators' leading interview methods, it could not be determined if the accusers were telling the truth. In October 1999, after eight years in prison, Cheryl Amirault LeFave was set free. Her conviction for child molestation stood, but the court commuted her sentence to time served.

On July 6, 2001 the Massachusetts Parole Board voted 5-0, recommending that Gerald's sentence be commuted. On February 20, 2002, Governor Jane Swift rejected the board's recommendation. Gerald Amirault remains in prison.

The Margaret Kelly Michaels Case

In 1985 a four-year-old boy was being examined at a pediatrician's office. When the nurse took his temperature rectally, the boy remarked that his teacher had done the same thing to him while he napped. The mother went to the authorities. Police charged Margaret Kelly Michaels,

the boy's teacher at the Wee Care Day Nursery in Maplewood, New Jersey, with child molestation. A child sexual abuse expert advised the parents of the preschool children to look for changes in their children's behavior as evidence of abuse.

In 1988 Michaels was found guilty of 115 counts of sexual abuse against 19 children, and sentenced to 47 years in prison. She was charged with inserting objects, including serrated eating utensils, into the children's genital organs, forcing them to eat a cake made of feces, and playing the piano naked. The state's evidence consisted of the children's allegations during the pretrial period. No medical evidence was found, and none of the other teachers noticed the alleged abuse that supposedly went on for seven months.

In 1993 the New Jersey Appellate Division reversed the conviction, remanding the case for a retrial. The court concluded:

> Certain questions [by investigators] planted sexual information in the children's minds and supplied the children with knowledge and vocabulary, which might be considered inappropriate for their age. Children were encouraged to help the police "bust this case wide open." Peer pressure and even threats of disclosing to the other children that the child being questioned was uncooperative were used.

The New Jersey Supreme Court affirmed the appellate court's ruling and ordered a hearing to determine if the children's testimony was tainted. According to the court:

> The interrogations of the child sex abuse victims were improper and there is a substantial likelihood that the evidence derived from them is unreliable. Therefore, if the State seeks to reprosecute Margaret Kelly Michaels, a pretrial hearing must be held in which the State must prove by clear and convincing evidence that the statements and testimony elicited by the improper interview techniques nonetheless retain a sufficient degree of reliability to warrant admission at trial.

The prosecution decided to drop the case. In 1994 Michaels was released after serving five years in prison.

CHAPTER 8
FALSE MEMORIES?

In the early 1900s Austrian psychoanalyst Sigmund Freud first proposed the theory of repression, which hypothesizes that the mind can reject unpleasant ideas, desires, and memories by banishing them into the unconscious. Some clinicians believe that memory repression explains why a victim of a traumatic experience, such as childhood sexual abuse, may forget the horrible incident. Some clinicians also believe that forgotten traumatic experiences can be recovered later.

Memory researchers do not agree, saying that children who have suffered serious psychological trauma do not repress the memory; rather, they can never forget it. They cite the examples of survivors of concentration camps or children who have witnessed the murder of a parent who never forget. These researchers believe that memory is inaccurate and that it can be manipulated to "remember" events that never happened.

Although allegations of recovered repressed memories have declined since their peak in the early 1990s, the controversy over the validity of repressed memories of childhood sexual abuse has not abated. For many, there is no room for the possibility that perhaps the other side might be right. Nonetheless, there are clinicians and memory researchers who believe that the workings of the mind have yet to be fully understood. They agree that, while it is possible for a trauma victim to forget and then remember a horrible experience, it is also possible for a person to have false memories.

Psychologist Elizabeth F. Loftus (a memory expert and leading opponent of the recovered-memory movement) wrote that if repression consists of avoiding in one's consciousness the terrible past experiences that come back to a person, then she believed in repression (*The Myth of Repressed Memory: False Memories and Allegations of Sexual Abuse,* St. Martin's Press, New York, NY, 1994). Dr. Loftus, however, could not accept that the mind could block out experiences of recurrent traumas, with the person unaware of them, and then recover them years later.

IS THERE EVIDENCE OF FALSE MEMORIES IN THE BRAIN?

Research has tried to find evidence of false memory in the brain. Daniel L. Schacter et al. showed volunteers an initial list of words and then a second list incorporating words that were similar but had not appeared in the original list (*Neuron,* August 1996). More than half the words the volunteers "remembered" were not on the first list. Using positron emission tomography scans (PET scans measure changes in blood flow, and blood flow indicates neural activity), Schacter found that parts of the brain involved in memory (the hippocampus) became active regardless of whether the memories were true or false.

In cases of true memories, however, Schacter et al. found that an area that processes information about sounds of recently heard words also lit up. False memories, however, showed more activity in portions of the brain that had been found to struggle to recall the context of an event.

Implanting Memories

Many scientific studies have shown that false memories can be implanted in a person's mind, leading the subject to "remember" events that never happened. Hypnosis, especially, has been cited for producing "memories" that may or may not be true. Once these memories have been introduced, they become as real to that person as what happened the previous week.

Memory researchers have shown that false memories can be implanted fairly easily in the laboratory. In *The Myth of Repressed Memory: False Memories and Allegations of Sexual Abuse,* Dr. Loftus recounted assigning a term project to students in her cognitive psychology class. The project involved implanting a false memory in someone's mind. One of the students chose his 14-year-old brother as his test subject. The student wrote four events his brother had supposedly experienced. Three of the experiences really happened, but the fourth one was a fake event of the boy getting lost at the mall at age five. For the next five days the brother was asked to read about his experiences and then write down details that he could remember about them. The brother "remembered" his shopping-mall experience quite well, describing details elaborately.

Recovered-memory advocates insist that while it may be easy to implant memories of common emotions (in this case, that of being lost), it is not possible to implant memories of something traumatic like sexual abuse. Researchers cannot experiment with implanting sexual abuse memories because of the obvious ethical considerations and possible repercussions.

In an unusual situation, Richard Ofshe, social psychologist and expert on cults, successfully implanted a memory of abuse in the mind of Washington resident Paul Ingram. In 1988, returning home from a religious retreat, Ingram's two daughters accused him and several men in the community of extensive sexual and satanic abuse. After months of interrogations and pressure from a psychologist and police detectives, Ingram began to confess to all kinds of horrific behavior. As his children brought up new charges, he would search his memory until he finally "remembered" and could even supply details of the events. The daughters' accusations included the murder of infants, abortions, and satanic orgies, even involving their mother.

Dr. Ofshe, who had been hired by the prosecution, did not believe Ingram's memories were genuine. Dr. Ofshe told Ingram he had spoken to one of Ingram's sons and one of his daughters, and they related the time Ingram forced them to have sex in front of him. This was one of the few charges that had not been brought against Ingram, and never was, but within a day Ingram submitted a written confession with details of the memory of the event. When Dr. Ofshe informed Ingram he was mistaken, Ingram protested, saying that the event was as real as anything else.

Although he was not sure about his memories, Ingram, a very religious man, was convinced that his daughters would not lie and that he had a dark side he had not known. His pastor, who was counseling his daughters, told him that the abuse had indeed happened. The pastor exorcised him and admonished him to pray to God to bring back memories of his evil acts. Later on Ingram claimed remembering the abuse. Before Dr. Ofshe could submit his report to the prosecution, Ingram pleaded guilty to the charges of rape.

Richard Ofshe reported to the prosecution that "my analysis of this interrogation is that it is quite likely that most of what Mr. Ingram reports as recollections of events

are products of social influence rather than reports based on his memory of events." Ingram later realized his false recollections and withdrew his guilty plea. The Washington State Supreme Court rejected his appeal. Ingram received a 20-year prison sentence. In 1996 Ingram, having exhausted all of his appeals, applied for a pardon from then-governor Mike Lowry through the Washington pardons board. Memory experts Elizabeth Loftus and Richard Ofshe, as well as the county prosecutor, sheriff, and Ingram's son testified on his behalf. The board denied Ingram's request for pardon. He remains in jail.

ARE THERE SYMPTOMS THAT INDICATE REPRESSED MEMORIES OF CHILDHOOD SEXUAL ABUSE?

In 1988 Ellen Bass and Laura Davis wrote a book that many consider a survivor's guide for adult victims of childhood abuse. *The Courage to Heal: A Guide for Women Survivors of Child Sexual Abuse* (HarperCollins, New York, NY, 1988) has often been described as the "bible" of the recovered-memory movement. The authors claimed that Freud was right about his first theory that the physical symptoms of hysteria in his patients were indicative of childhood sexual abuse.

In *The Courage to Heal,* the authors ask women readers how often they suffer the following symptoms, which they consider signs of childhood sexual abuse:

- You feel that you are bad, dirty, or ashamed.
- You feel powerless, like a victim.
- You feel that there is something wrong with you deep down inside or that if people really knew you, they would leave.
- You feel unable to protect yourself in dangerous situations.
- You have no sense of your own interest, talents, or goals.
- You have trouble feeling motivated.
- You feel you have to be perfect.

On one side of the repressed-memory controversy are some clinical therapists who believe that repressed sexual trauma can be determined from a checklist of symptoms such as those stated earlier and that treatment is required to uncover the abuse. They believe that memories rediscovered through hypnosis and other recovery techniques are true and that they must be acknowledged in order for treatment to be successful. They are concerned that questioning the validity of these memories provides offenders with an easy way to avoid responsibility for their actions. Some more-skeptical experimental psychologists, however, wonder how therapists can be so sure of their diagnosis from a list of symptoms that could be the result of many different conditions.

Many mental health professionals warn the public about unscrupulous therapists and persons who have no training in mental health. For example, they note that the authors Bass and Davis were not licensed therapists. Bass was a creative writing teacher, and Davis was a student in one of her writing workshops.

Looking for Answers to Symptoms

When an anxious, unhappy patient seeks help, she (most patients are female) is looking for an explanation for what are often vague symptoms that do not appear to have a source. Some therapists feel it is imperative to ask about sexual abuse in the first meeting with every new patient.

Critics of repressed-memory theories suggest that therapists who believe in repressed memory may encourage patients to "remember" that they had been sexually abused in childhood. For example, some of these therapists have been known to recommend that patients cut off all ties with their families to speed up recovery. This leaves the patients highly dependent on their therapists for emotional support and vulnerable to suggestion, sometimes for many years.

Michael Yapko, a clinical psychologist and a memory expert, believes that many therapists do not really understand how easy it is to convince people that they remember events that never actually happened. He fears that many therapists who believe in repressed memory treat their patients based on these personal beliefs and philosophy, rather than an objective assessment of the facts (*Suggestions of Abuse: True and False Memories of Childhood Sexual Abuse*, Simon and Schuster, New York, NY, 1994). Carolyn Zerbe Enns warned against condemning all therapists just because some are poorly informed or unscrupulous ("Counselors and the Backlash: 'Rape Hype' and 'False Memory Syndrome,'" *Journal of Counseling and Development*, vol. 74, March/April 1996). She argued that there are real victims out there who have survived abuse and may fear that others may not believe them. Enns believes, however, that therapists who try to force their patients to remember things are abusing their power and may hurt rather than help their patients.

Recovered-Memory Therapy

Some critics claim that recovered-memory therapists are convinced their patients cannot heal until they confront their memories. They often suggest that the patient sue the offending parent in court. Critics charge that such therapy does not heal and often destroys.

In 1996 Dr. Loftus presented a study of the Washington State Crime Victims Compensation Program to the Southwestern Psychological Association. Dr. Loftus found that all 30 claimants in the study were still in therapy three years after their first recovered memory; 18 were still in therapy after five years. While only 3 thought about suicide or attempted suicide before recovering their first memory, 20 killed themselves after therapy. Two had been hospitalized prior to their first recovered memory, compared with 11 after they retrieved memories. Before therapy, 25 had been employed; after therapy, only 3 still had jobs. Of the 23 who had been married, 11 divorced. Seven lost custody of their children.

Verification

People have questioned whether the repressed-memory movement would have attained epidemic proportions had psychotherapists verified their patients' "memories" of past abuse. Many psychotherapists wonder why some of their colleagues have not only failed to corroborate their patients' stories, but have accepted them as realities. The False Memory Syndrome Foundation claims that, in not a single case of alleged childhood abuse that has come to its attention, has the therapist sought the patient's pediatrician's records. Plus, in only a few of the 2,800 cases was there any attempt to consult school records, other family members, or any independent sources. David Spiegel, in the *Harvard Mental Health Letter* (September 1998), observed that repressed memory, whether retrieved with or without the help of hypnosis, cannot be proven to be true without external verification.

A report by the Council on Scientific Affairs by the American Medical Association stated, "The AMA considers recovered memories of childhood sexual abuse to be of uncertain authenticity, which should be subject to external verification. The use of recovered memories is fraught with problems of potential misapplication" (Sub. Res. 504, A-93; Modified by: CSA Rep. 5-A-94).

TRAUMA AND DISSOCIATION

Some psychologists believe sexual abuse can be so psychologically traumatic that the victim dissociates from full awareness of the horrible experience. In other words, dissociation is the mind's defense mechanism against the trauma. Other scientists disagree, however. For example, Schacter (*Searching for Memory: The Brain, the Mind, and the Past*, BasicBooks, New York, NY, 1996) questioned how a patient could dissociate so much of her past, and yet function in society for years without her problems being obvious in her behavior before she consults a therapist. Schacter argued that patients who have really experienced many episodes of dissociation should also have a documented history of the manifestations of such disorder before ever having recovered repressed memories of long-term abuse.

Dissociative Amnesia for Childhood Abuse Memories

According to James A. Chu, Lisa M. Frey, Barbara L. Ganzel, and Julia A. Matthews, although research has shown that memories can be inaccurate and can be influenced by outside factors such as overt suggestions, most research has shown that memory tends to be accurate when it comes to remembering the core elements of important events ("Memories of Childhood Abuse: Dissociation, Amnesia, and Corroboration," *American Journal of Psychiatry,* vol. 156, no. 5, May 1999). The authors conducted a study of 90 female patients, ages 18 to 60, who were undergoing treatment in a psychiatric hospital. Dissociative amnesia, discussed in this study, is a type of dissociation, or dissociative disorder.

A large proportion of patients reported childhood abuse: 83 percent experienced physical abuse, 82 percent were victims of sexual abuse, and 71 percent witnessed domestic violence. Those who had a history of any kind of abuse reported experiencing partial or complete amnesia. The occurrence of physical and sexual abuse at an early age accounted for a higher level of amnesia. Contrary to the popular belief that recovered memory of childhood abuse typically occurs under psychotherapy or hypnosis, most of the patients who suffered complete amnesia for their physical and sexual abuse indicated first recalling the abuse when they were alone or at home. Most patients did not recover memory of childhood abuse as a result of suggestions. Critics of recovered memories have noted the lack of corroboration (confirmation that the abuse really occurred) in many instances of recovered memories. In this study, the researchers found that, among patients who tried to corroborate their abuse, more than half found physical evidence such as medical records. Nearly 9 of 10 of those who suffered sexual abuse found verbal validation of such abuse.

BETRAYAL TRAUMA THEORY

Psychologist Jennifer J. Freyd used the betrayal trauma theory to explain how children who experience abuse may process that betrayal of trust by mentally blocking information about it (*Betrayal Trauma: The Logic of Forgetting Childhood Abuse,* Harvard University Press, Cambridge, MA, 1996). Dr. Freyd explained that people typically respond to betrayal by distancing themselves from the betrayer. Children, however, who have suffered abuse in the hands of a parent or a caregiver might not be able to distance themselves from the betrayer. Children need the caregiver for their survival so that they "cannot afford *not* to trust" the betrayer. Consequently, the children develop a "blindness" to the betrayal.

In 2001 Dr. Freyd, Anne P. DePrince, and Eileen L. Zurbriggen reported on their preliminary findings relating to the betrayal trauma theory ("Self-Reported Memory for Abuse Depends upon Victim–Perpetrator Relationship," *Journal of Trauma & Dissociation,* vol. 2, no. 3). The researchers found that persons who had been abused by a trusted caregiver reported greater amnesia, compared with those whose abusers were not their caregivers. Greater amnesia was also more likely to be associated with the

fact that the perpetrator was a caregiver than with the repeated trauma of abuse.

A LONGITUDINAL STUDY OF MEMORY AND CHILDHOOD ABUSE

Between 1986 and 1998 Catherine Cameron conducted a long-term study of child sexual abuse survivors (*Resolving Childhood Trauma,* Sage Publications, Inc., Thousand Oaks, CA, 2000). The researcher interviewed 72 women, ages 25–64, during a 12-year period. The women comprised a group of sexual abuse survivors who sought therapy for the first time in the 1980s. On average, it had been 30 years since their first abuse occurred (36 years for those who suffered amnesia). The women were in private therapy, were better educated, and were more financially well off than most survivors. Twelve imprisoned women were included in the survey. They came from a low socioeconomic background, were serving long sentences, and had participated only in brief group therapy sessions, lasting less than a year.

Cameron sought to study amnesia as both an effect and a cause—what was it about the abuse that resulted in amnesia and how did the amnesia affect the victim later on in life? Twenty-five women were amnesiac, having no awareness of the abuse until recently. Twenty-one were nonamnesiac, unable to forget their abuse, and 14 were partially amnesic about their abuse. The imprisoned women were not assigned a specific category because they were part of a therapy group.

About 8 of 10 of the amnesic and partially amnesic women believed that they did not remember the sexual abuse because the memories were too painful to live with (82 percent) and they felt a sense of guilt or shame (79 percent). More than half of each group believed the amnesia served as a defense mechanism resulting from their desire to protect the family (58 percent) and love for, or dependence on, the perpetrator (53 percent). About three-quarters (74 percent) thought the amnesia occurred because they felt no one would believe them or help them. More than one-third (37 percent) thought the amnesia had come about because they needed to believe in a "safe" world.

During the years between the abuse and the recall of the abuse, the amnesiacs reported experiencing the same problems as the nonamnesiacs, including problems with relationships, revictimization, self-abuse, and dependency on alcohol. Because the amnesiacs, however, had no conscious knowledge of their childhood abuse, they could not find an explanation for their problems. The author claimed that the conflict between the amnesia and memories that needed release left the amnesic victims depressed and confused.

Cameron addressed the allegations that some therapists implant false memories of sexual abuse in their clients. She noted that 72 percent of the amnesic women in her study had begun to recall their abuse prior to seeking therapy. Once the survivors in her study confronted their traumatic past, they took charge of how they wanted their therapy handled. Cameron also observed that, since it is evident that recovered memories of childhood abuse are common, they should not be labeled as "false memories" nor accepted as "flawless truth," but should instead be explored by proponents of the opposing views.

SCIENTIFIC PROOF OF REPRESSED MEMORY?

While some repressed memory experts such as Lenore Terr, a clinical professor of psychiatry, dismiss all laboratory experiments on memory as invalid, others have tried to prove scientifically that memories can be forgotten. Linda Meyer Williams, of the Family Research Laboratory of the University of New Hampshire in Durham, studied the recall of women who had been abused in childhood, for whom there were medical records proving the abuse ("Recall of Childhood Trauma: A Prospective Study of Women's Memories of Child Sexual Abuse," *Journal of Consulting and Clinical Psychology,* vol. 62, no. 6, 1994).

Williams used data gathered between 1973 and 1975 on 206 girls (ages 10 months to 12 years) who had been examined for sexual abuse in a city hospital emergency room. In 1990 and 1991, 129 of these women were included in a study that was, they were told, a follow-up on the lives and health of women who had received health care as children at the hospital. The women, now between the ages of 18 and 31, were not told of their history of child sexual abuse, although some women suspected the reason for their hospital visit.

Of the 129 women, 38 percent failed to report the sexual abuse documented by the hospital; of this group, however, 68 percent reported other childhood sexual abuses. Williams doubted that the women were simply unwilling to discuss the abuse because other personal subjects—such as abortions, prostitution, or having sexually transmitted diseases—were not withheld.

Twelve percent (15 respondents) of the total sample reported that they were never abused in childhood. Williams suggested that this was an undercount of the likely number of women who had forgotten childhood abuse. Because the abuse these women suffered was known to at least one other person (the person who brought the child to the hospital), it was less likely to have been repressed than abuse that was always kept a secret.

Williams concluded that if it is possible that victims do not remember having been abused, their recovery of repressed memory later on in life should not come as a surprise. In fact, 16 percent of the women who recalled the sexual victimization that brought them to the hospital reported there were periods when they "forgot" the abuse.

In a second paper on the same research ("Recovered Memories of Abuse in Women with Documented Child Sexual Victimization Histories," *Journal of Traumatic Stress,* October 1995), Williams described the interviews with some of the women who had forgotten. It is not clear whether the women were truly amnesiac or whether the abuse was simply not a part of their conscious lives for a time.

Most reported that they recalled the abuse when a television movie or some other event jogged their memory. None had sought therapy to uncover repressed memories. Williams suggested that these women (inner-city, mainly black, women) did not have the financial resources or knowledge to get professional help.

A Rebuttal

Critics of Williams's conclusions pointed out that one of the reasons women in the study had forgotten their abuse was that the trauma had occurred in infancy. (Experts contend that events that happen before the acquisition of language at two to three years of age are forgotten because there is no way to express the event.) Williams disagreed, noting that, while 55 percent of those who had been abused at three years or younger had no memory of the occurrence, 62 percent of those who were four to six years old also did not remember.

In addition, critics questioned how Williams could be certain that those who claimed not to remember were actually telling the truth. The researchers never confronted the women who did not report abuse by showing them their hospital records.

The American Psychological Association Report

The American Psychological Association (APA) assembled a group of clinicians and researchers to produce "The Final Report of the APA Working Group on the Investigation of Memories of Childhood Abuse" (1996). The group was split between practitioners who supported the concept of recovered memories and scientists who studied memory. The report included a list of final conclusions, which stated that most abused children remember all or part of their abuse; it is possible, however, for the victims to remember long-time memories of abuse that have been forgotten. The group also reported that it is also possible to construct convincing false memories, but there are gaps in understanding the processes that lead to accurate and inaccurate memories of childhood abuse. The bulk of the 293-page report, however, was a battle between the clinicians and scientists, each citing research and evidence to support their group's position.

GOING TO COURT

Suing Alleged Abusers

Between 1983 and 1996 many individuals who had "recovered" memories of childhood sexual abuse sued their alleged abusers, many at the instigation of their therapists. During those years a total of 517 civil (85 percent) and criminal (15 percent) suits based on repressed memory were filed. Following a sharp rise in 1992, the year the False Memory Syndrome Foundation (FMSF) was created, was a steep drop since 1994. An informal tally of cases by the FMSF has found that two-thirds of the civil suits had been dropped, dismissed, or concluded in favor of the alleged abusers.

While the courts readily accepted some early cases of child sexual abuse, courts in more and more states are becoming increasingly suspicious of accounts of outrageous abuse. Therapists are being held liable for malpractice not only by their patients, but often by third parties (usually the accused parents of someone who has allegedly recovered memories of sexual abuse).

The Case of Eileen Franklin

In 1990 George Franklin was convicted of killing his daughter Eileen's friend 20 years earlier. Eileen claimed to have recovered memories of her father's murderous act as she was gazing into her own daughter's eyes. She told her secret to her therapist. She then told police she suddenly remembered herself as a nine-year-old watching her father kill her friend. Later on Eileen changed her account of how she recalled the murder, at one point telling police that the details of the killing became clearer to her after she underwent therapy.

Professor Terr was an influential expert witness at this first criminal trial in the United States involving recovered memory. Professor Terr, who supports the idea of repressed memory, later wrote about Eileen's story in the book *Unchained Memories: True Stories of Traumatic Memories, Lost and Found* (BasicBooks, New York, NY, 1994).

Harry MacLean, who reported on the case in his book, *Once upon a Time: A True Story of Memory, Murder, and the Law* (HarperCollins, New York, NY, 1993), claimed that Professor Terr had repeatedly distorted the facts to suit her purpose. Professor Terr claimed to offer a dramatic proof of Eileen's truthful testimony when she described the "body memory" (a physical manifestation of trauma that the conscious mind has forgotten) of Eileen's repressed trauma. According to Professor Terr, Eileen had a habit of pulling her hair out, resulting in a balding spot on her scalp. Eileen had allegedly seen her father murder her friend with a blow to the head using a large rock.

According to MacLean, in his interviews with Eileen's mother, sisters, school friends, and teachers, no one could remember Eileen's pulling out her hair or having a bleeding spot on her scalp. Dr. Ofshe and Ethan Watters (*Making Monsters: False Memories, Psychotherapy, and Sexual Hysteria* Scribners, New York, NY, 1994) found more than 40 photos taken of Eileen during the rel-evant period that were wrongly withheld from the defense and which showed no trace of a bald spot.

In November 1995 a federal appeals court overturned George Franklin's murder conviction. By this time Franklin had served almost seven years of a life sentence. The court ruled that the trial had been tainted by the improper allegation that Franklin had confessed and by the exclusion of crucial evidence: Eileen had been hypnotized by her therapist, Kirk Barrett, prior to the first trial, making her testimony unreliable. The court ordered a retrial. On July 2, 1996, the prosecution dropped the charges, citing the problem of Eileen's hypnosis that, by California law, would probably prevent her from testifying. In addition, new DNA evidence showed that it was impossible for Franklin to have committed the second murder his daughter had accused him of, which she claimed happened when she was 15.

In June 1997 George Franklin filed a civil suit in federal court against his daughter, her therapist Barrett, and county officials, claiming violation of his civil rights. The suit alleged, among other things, that Eileen, Barrett, and county officials conspired to deny George Franklin the due process of law and violated his Fifth, Sixth, and Fourteenth Amendment rights to confront witnesses against him. He also sued Professor Terr for conspiring with Eileen to give false testimony.

In 2000 the court dismissed Franklin's suit against the county officials. The judge also threw out the claims against Professor Terr because "witnesses are absolutely immune from damages liability based on their testimony." The court dismissed the suit against Barrett because George Franklin failed to state the right claim that the therapist had conspired with a state official to deny him his constitutional rights. Franklin had sought a token $1 award from his daughter, but that too was thrown out.

Suing the Therapist

In what was one of the longest (13 weeks) malpractice trials in the American justice system, a jury awarded Elizabeth Carlson of Minnesota more than $2.5 million in 1996. Carlson had accused Dr. Diane Bay Humenansky of "negligent psychotherapy by using hypnosis, misinformation, coercion, threats, and suggestions to implant false memories of childhood abuse" (*Carlson v. Humenansky*, District Ct., Ramsey Co., Minnesota, Case No. CX 93-7260). The patient claimed that under Dr. Humenansky's treatment, she became convinced she had developed "alters," or multiple personalities, to help her cope with sexual abuses by her parents, relatives, and neighbors.

Carlson reported that during her more than two years of therapy, she felt worse and worse. Dr. Humenansky gave her books to read on incest, multiple personality disorder, and satanic abuse. Carlson also started believing that she was part of an intergenerational satanic cult. When Carlson and other patients met without the doctor, they were shocked to discover that they shared remarkably similar memories of abuse and had alternate personalities with the same names and traits. Since then eight other former patients have sued Dr. Humenansky.

Third-Party Suits

The courts now often hold therapists liable to a third party, usually the patient's accused parent, when they implant or reinforce false memories in their patients. Social worker Susan L. Jones, while treating Joel Hungerford's daughter Laura, convinced her that her anxiety attacks were the result of sexual abuse by her father. Jones not only advised Laura to cease contact with her father but also convinced the patient to file a complaint of aggravated felonious sexual assault against Joel. In addition Jones contacted the police regarding the alleged assault and aided the prosecution in indicting Joel Hungerford.

Hungerford sued Jones for the misdiagnosis and negligent treatment of his daughter's condition. Jones claimed that she owed Hungerford no duty of care, meaning that since she had treated Laura Hungerford, not Joel Hungerford, Joel Hungerford could not claim that her treatment had hurt him. On December 18, 1998, in *Joel Hungerford v. Susan L. Jones* (No. 97-657, 1998 N.H. LEXIS 94), the New Hampshire Supreme Court, in this case of "first impression" (with no existing precedent), ruled:

> [W]e hold that a therapist owes an accused parent a duty of care in the diagnosis and treatment of an adult patient for sexual abuse where the therapist or the patient, acting on the encouragement, recommendation, or instruction of the therapist, takes public action concerning the accusation. In such instances, the social utility of detecting and punishing sexual abusers and maintaining the breadth of treatment choices for patients is outweighed by the substantial risk of severe harm to falsely accused parents, the family unit, and society.

The Statute of Limitations

One of the legal issues contested in cases of repressed memory is how long the statute of limitations should run, since typically the victim has allegedly repressed the memories for many years. Most states have provisions extending the statute of limitation, either through state law or minority tolling doctrines. A minority tolling doctrine is a rule that says a statutory period is not counted until a certain date, for example, until the child reaches age 18.

COURT GRANTS EXCEPTION TO STATUTE OF LIMITATION. In 1991 Paula Hearndon sued her stepfather, Kenneth Graham, for sexually abusing her from 1968 to 1975 (when she was between the ages of 8 and 15). According to Hearndon, the traumatic amnesia she experienced because of the abuse lasted until 1988. Because of Florida's four-year statute of limitation, the lawsuit did not proceed.

In September 2000, however, the Florida Supreme Court, in a 5-2 decision, ruled that memory loss resulting from the trauma of childhood sexual abuse should be considered an exception to the statute of limitations (*Hearndon v. Graham,* No. SC92665, September 14, 2000, Supreme Court of Florida, 2000 Fla. LEXIS 1844).

The court, while observing that disagreements about recovered memory exist, stated:

> It is widely recognized that the shock and confusion resultant from childhood molestation, often coupled with authoritative adult demands and threats for secrecy, may lead a child to deny or suppress such abuse from his or her consciousness.

THE FALSE MEMORY SYNDROME FOUNDATION

As part of the backlash against the growing number of cases of repressed memory, an organization of parents claiming to have been falsely accused of child sexual abuse was formed in 1992. The False Memory Syndrome Foundation (FMSF) was founded by Pamela Freyd, whose daughter had accused her father of childhood abuse. (The daughter, Jennifer Freyd, is a psychologist at the University of Oregon who specializes in memory.) The FMSF publishes a newsletter six times a year and organizes conferences to support falsely accused parents. The foundation distributes information on what it sees as a dangerous movement in psychotherapy to encourage and accept all claims of childhood abuse without verification.

The FMSF and other experts who question the validity of repressed memory do not question whether sexual abuse occurs—it questions how often. Furthermore, they are concerned that false accusations will throw doubt on genuine cases of abuse.

Some mental health professionals have dismissed the FMSF as an extreme organization. The foundation has been accused of protecting child abusers and attempting to discredit the psychiatric profession. Opponents of the FMSF claim that rather than work toward improving therapy, the FMSF sided with those people considered extreme on its scientific board. (The board includes acknowledged experts such as Dr. Loftus, Dr. Ofshe, and Paul McHugh.) In their view, recovered-memory therapy is the practice of a very small group of therapists. Nevertheless, for the families torn apart by what they insist are false memories, the FMSF has been a lifeline to others suffering the same accusations.

IMPORTANT NAMES AND ADDRESSES

American Bar Association
Center on Children and the Law
740 15th St. NW
Washington, DC 20005
(202) 662-1720
FAX: (202) 662-1755
Toll-free: (800) 285-2221
E-mail: ctrchildlaw@abanet.org
URL: http://www.abanet.org/child

American Humane Association
Children's Division
63 Inverness Dr. East
Englewood, CO 80112-5117
(303) 792-9900
FAX: (303) 792-5333
Toll-free: (866) 242-1877
 http://www.americanhumane.org

Center for the Future of Children
David and Lucile Packard Foundation
300 Second St., #200
Los Altos, CA 94022
(650) 917-7110
FAX: (650) 941-2273
URL: http://www.futureofchildren.org

Child Welfare League of America
440 First St. NW, 3rd Fl.
Washington, DC 20001-2085
(202) 638-2952
FAX: (202) 638-4004
URL: http://www.cwla.org

Children's Defense Fund
25 E St. NW
Washington, DC 20001
(202) 628-8787
E-mail: cdfinfo@childrensdefense.org
URL: http://www.childrensdefense.org

Children's Healthcare Is a Legal Duty, Inc. (CHILD, Inc.)
P.O. Box 2604
Sioux City, IA 51106

(712) 948-3500
FAX: (712) 948-3704
E-mail: childinc@netins.net
URL: http://www.childrenshealthcare.org

Crimes Against Children Research Center
University of New Hampshire
20 College Rd.
126 Horton Social Science Center
Durham, NH 03824-3586
(603) 862-1888
FAX: (603) 862-1122
E-mail: kellyfoster@unh.edu
URL: http://www.unh.edu/ccrc

False Memory Syndrome Foundation
1955 Locust St.
Philadelphia, PA 19103-5766
(215) 940-1040
FAX: (215) 940-1042
E-mail: mail@fmsonline.org
URL: http://www.fmsonline.org

Family Research Laboratory
University of New Hampshire
126 Horton Social Science Center
Durham, NH 03824-3586
(603) 862-1888
FAX: (603) 862-1122
E-mail: mas2@cisunix.unh.edu
URL: http://www.unh.edu/frl

Family Violence and Sexual Assault Institute
6160 Cornerstone Ct. East
San Diego, CA 92121
(858) 623-2777
FAX: (858) 646-0761
E-mail: fvsai@alliant.edu
URL: http://www.fvsai.org

National CASA Association
100 W. Harrison St.
North Tower, #500
Seattle, WA 98119

FAX: (206) 270-0078
Toll-free: (800) 628-3233
E-mail: inquiry@nationalcasa.org
URL: http://www.nationalcasa.org

National Center for Missing & Exploited Children
Charles B. Wang International Children's Building
699 Prince St.
Alexandria, VA 22314-3175
(703) 274-3900
FAX: (703) 274-2220
National Child Pornography Tipline and CyberTipline. Toll-free: (800) 843-5678
URL: http://www.missingkids.org

National Center for Prosecution of Child Abuse
American Prosecutors Research Institute (APRI)
99 Canal Center Plaza, #510
Alexandria, VA 22314
(703) 549-9222
FAX: (703) 836-3195
E-mail: ncpca@ndaa-apri.org
URL: http://www.ndaa-apri.org/apri/
programs/ncpca/index.html

National Child Abuse Hotline
Toll-free: (800) 422-4453

National Clearinghouse on Child Abuse and Neglect Information
330 C St. SW
Washington, DC 20447
(703) 385-7565
FAX: (703) 385-3206
Toll-free: (800) 394-3366
E-mail: nccanch@calib.com
URL: http://www.calib.com/nccanch

National Council of Juvenile and Family Court Judges
Family Violence Department

P.O. Box 8970
Reno, NV 89507
(702) 784-6012
Toll-free: (800) 527-3223
E-mail: info@dvlawsearch.com
URL: http://www.dvlawsearch.com

National Council on Child Abuse and Family Violence
1025 Connecticut Ave. NW, #1012
Washington, DC 20036
(202) 429-6695
FAX: (831) 655-3930
E-mail: info@nccafv.org
URL: http://www.nccafv.org

National Criminal Justice Reference Service (NCJRS)
P.O. Box 6000
Rockville, MD 20849-6000
(301) 519-5500
FAX: (301) 519-5212
Toll-free: (800) 851-3420
E-mail: askncjrs@ncjrs.org
URL: http://www.ncjrs.org

National Domestic Violence Hotline
Toll-free: (800) 799-SAFE
URL: http://www.ndvh.org

National Resource Center on Child Maltreatment Organization
P.O. Box 441470
Aurora, IL 80044-1470
(303) 369-8008
FAX: (303) 369-3009
E-mail: nrccm@gocwi.org
URL: http://www.gocwi.org/nrccm

National Resource Center on Child Sexual Abuse
107 Lincoln St.
Huntsville, AL 35801
(205) 534-6868
FAX: (205) 534-6883
Toll-free: (800) 543-7006
URL: http://www.isurvive.org/resources/child.shtml

National Runaway Switchboard
3080 N. Lincoln Ave.
Chicago IL 60657
(773) 880-9860
FAX: (773) 929-5150
Toll-free: (800) 621-4000
E-mail: info@nrscrisisline.org
URL: http://www.nrscrisisline.org

Office on Child Abuse and Neglect (OCAN)
Children's Bureau
U.S. Department of Health and
Human Services
330 C. Street SW
Rm. 2422
Washington, DC 20201
(202) 205-8618
FAX: (202) 205-8221
URL: http://www.acf.dhhs.gov/programs/cb

Prevent Child Abuse America
200 S. Michigan Ave., 17th Fl.
Chicago, IL 60604-2404
(312) 663-3520
FAX: (312) 939-8962
E-mail: mailbox@preventchildabuse.org
URL: http://www.preventchildabuse.org

UNICEF
333 East 38th St.
New York, NY 10016
(212) 686-5522
FAX: (212) 888-7465
Toll-free: (800) FOR-KIDS
E-mail: information@unicefusa.org
URL: http://www.unicefusa.org

Violence Against Women Office
810 7th Street NW
Washington, DC 20531
(202) 307-6026
FAX: (202) 307-3911
URL: http://www.ojp.usdoj.gov/vawo

RESOURCES

The National Child Abuse and Neglect Data System (NCANDS) of the U.S. Department of Health and Human Services (HHS; Washington, DC) is the primary source of national information on child maltreatment known to state child protective services (CPS) agencies. The latest findings from NCANDS are published in *Child Maltreatment 2000* (2002). *The Third National Incidence Study of Child Abuse and Neglect* (NIS-3; 1996) is the single most comprehensive source of information about the incidence of child maltreatment in the United States. The NIS-3 findings are based on data collected not only from CPS but also from community institutions (such as day care centers, schools, and hospitals) and other investigating agencies (such as public health departments, police, and courts). The National Clearinghouse on Child Abuse and Neglect Information of the HHS provided an assortment of helpful publications used in the preparation of this book, including *Understanding the Effects of Maltreatment on Early Brain Development* (2001), *The Risk and Prevention of Maltreatment of Children with Disabilities* (2001), and *In Harm's Way: Domestic Violence and Child Maltreatment* (undated).

Other federal government publications used for this book include *Victims of Trafficking and Violence Protection Act 2000: Trafficking in Persons Report* (U.S. Department of State, Washington, DC, 2002); *Barriers to Employability among Women on TANF with a Substance Abuse Problem* (HHS, 2002); *Results from the 2001 National Household Survey on Drug Abuse: Volume I, Summary of National Findings* (Substance Abuse and Mental Health Administration, Rockville, MD, 2002); *Child Welfare Outcomes 1999: Annual Report* (HHS, 2002); *Sexual Assault Nurse Examiner (SANE) Programs: Improving the Community Response to Sexual Assault Victims* (Office for Victims of Crime, Washington, DC, 2001); *International Trafficking in Women to the United States: A Contemporary Manifestation of Slavery and Organized Crime* (Central Intelligence Agency, Washington, DC, 1999); *Blending Perspectives and Building Common Ground: A Report to Congress on Substance Abuse and Child Protection* (HHS, 1999); *Child Protective Services: Complex Challenges Require New Strategies* (U.S. Government Accounting Office, Washington, DC, 1997); and "Investigator's Guide to Allegations of 'Ritual' Child Abuse" (Federal Bureau of Investigation, 1992). The U.S. Advisory Board on Child Abuse and Neglect published *A Nation's Shame: Fatal Child Abuse and Neglect in the United States* (HHS, 1995). Gail S. Goodman et al. researched the *Characteristics and Sources of Allegations of Ritualistic Child Abuse* (1994) for the National Center on Child Abuse and Neglect, an agency replaced by the Office on Child Abuse and Neglect.

Different offices of the U.S. Department of Justice produce publications relating to child maltreatment. The Office of Juvenile Justice and Delinquency Prevention published *Prosecutors, Kids, and Domestic Violence Cases* (2002); *Nonfamily Abducted Children: National Estimates and Characteristics* (2002); *The Decline in Child Sexual Abuse* (2001); *Crimes against Children by Babysitters* (2001); *Child Abuse Reported to Police* (2001); *Offenders Incarcerated for Crimes against Juveniles* (2001); *Child Neglect and Munchausen Syndrome by Proxy* (1997); and *In the Wake of Childhood Maltreatment* (1997). The National Institute of Justice published *An Update on the "Cycle of Violence"* (2001); *Full Report of the Prevalence, Incidence, and Consequences of Violence against Women: Findings from the National Violence against Women Survey* (2000); and *Research on Women and Girls in the Justice System* (2000). The Bureau of Justice Statistics published *Summary of State Sex Offender Registries, 2001* (2002); *Prisoners 2001* (2002); *Sexual Assault of Young Children as Reported to Law Enforcement: Victim, Incident, and Offender Characteristics* (2000); *Prior Abuse Reported by Inmates and Probationers* (1999); and *Violence by Intimates: Analysis of Data on Crimes by Current or Former Spouses, Boyfriends, and Girlfriends* (1998).

Online Victimization: A Report on the Nation's Youth (Crimes Against Children Research Center, University of New Hampshire, NH, and National Center for Missing & Exploited Children, VA, 2000) discussed the findings of the first *Youth Internet Safety Survey. No Safe Haven: Children of Substance-Abusing Parents* (New York, 1999), by the National Center on Addiction and Substance Abuse at Columbia University, discussed the association between substance abuse or addiction and child maltreatment. Researchers from the National Center on Addiction and Substance Abuse at Columbia University, New Jersey Department of Human Services, Rutgers University, and the Mount Sinai School of Medicine examined the problems of substance-abusing women on welfare and the well-being of their children (*Barriers to Employability Among Women on TANF with a Substance Abuse Problem,* 2002). Prevent Child Abuse America published *Public Opinion and Behaviors Regarding Child Abuse Prevention: 1999 Survey* (Chicago, IL, 1999). The Gale Group thanks these organizations, universities, and government agencies for permission to use graphics from their publications.

The Family Research Laboratory (FRL) at the University of New Hampshire, Durham, is a major source of studies on domestic violence. Murray A. Straus, Linda Meyer Williams, David Finkelhor, Kathleen Kendall-Tackett, and many others associated with the laboratory have done some of the most scientifically rigorous researches in the field of abuse. Studies released by the FRL investigate all forms of domestic violence, many based on its two major surveys: the *National Family Violence Survey* (1975) and the *National Family Violence Resurvey* (1985). Much of the research from these two surveys has been gathered into *Physical Violence in American Families: Risk Factors and Adaptations to Violence in 8,145 Families* (Murray A. Straus and Richard J. Gelles; Christine Smith, editor, Transaction Publishers, Somerset, NJ, 1990).

Dr. Murray A. Straus is also widely known for his studies on corporal punishment, its effects on children's cognitive development, and its link to antisocial behavior among children and criminal violence. Dr. Straus and the Family Research Laboratory have kindly granted permission to use graphics from their publications.

Many journals published useful articles on child maltreatment that were used in the preparation of this book. They include the *National Institute of Justice Journal, Pediatrics, American Journal of Obstetrics and Gynecology, American Family Physician, Journal of Instructional Psychology, American Journal of Orthopsychiatry, Journal of Interpersonal Violence, Journal of Family Violence, Violence against Women, Psychoneuroendocrinology, Journal of the American Academy of Child Adolescent Psychiatry, Archives of Pediatrics and Adolescent Medi-*

cine, Journal of Child Sexual Abuse, Journal of the American Medical Association, Psychiatric Annals: The Journal of Continuing Psychiatric Education, Family Planning Perspectives, American Journal of Drug and Alcohol Abuse, Child Maltreatment, Lancet, Professional Psychology, Journal of Experimental Psychology: Applied, Neuron, American Journal of Psychiatry, Journal of Trauma and Dissociation, Journal of Consulting and Clinical Psychology, and the *Journal of Traumatic Stress.*

Washington Post articles by Pulitzer Prize winners and investigative reporters Sari Horwitz, Scott Higham, and Sarah Cohen describe the plight of foster care children who died as a result of government neglect (September 9–12, 2001). *Dallas Morning News* reporters Brooks Egerton and Reese Dunklin analyzed the record of the top leaders of the Roman Catholic church in light of the massive child-molestation allegations worldwide ("Two-Thirds of Bishops Let Accused Priests Work," July 12, 2002). The American Professional Society on the Abuse of Children (APSAC), in *The APSAC Handbook on Child Maltreatment* (Sage Publications, Inc., Thousand Oaks, CA, 2002), brought together a variety of child abuse experts to discuss ongoing controversies in their fields, as well as to challenge long-held assumptions and conclusions. The Center for the Future of Children of the David and Lucile Packard Foundation publishes information on major issues related to children's well-being. Information from *The Future of Children: Domestic Violence and Children* (1999), *The Future of Children: Protecting Children from Abuse and Neglect* (1998), and *The Future of Children: Sexual Abuse of Children* (1994) were used in this publication. The Center for the Future of Children graciously granted permission to use graphics from its publications.

Helpful books used for this publication include *Confronting Chronic Neglect: The Education and Training of Health Professionals on Family Violence* (National Academy Press, 2002); *The Epidemic of Rape and Child Sexual Abuse in the United States,* by Diana E. H. Russell and Rebecca M. Bolen (Sage Publications, Inc., Thousand Oaks, CA, 2000); *Neglected Children: Research, Practice, and Policy,* by Howard Dubowitz, editor (Sage Publications, Inc., Thousand Oaks, CA, 1999); *Understanding Family Violence: Treating and Preventing Partner, Child, Sibling, and Elder Abuse,* by Vernon R. Wiehe (Sage Publications, Inc., Thousand Oaks, CA, 1998); *The Book of David: How Preserving Families Can Cost Children's Lives,* by Richard J. Gelles (BasicBooks, New York, 1996); *Wounded Innocents: The Real Victims of the War against Child Abuse,* by Richard Wexler (Prometheus Books, New York, 1995); and *The Secret Trauma: Incest in the Lives of Girls and Women,* by Diana E. H. Russell (BasicBooks, New York, 1986).

Books used for information on recovered memory include *Resolving Childhood Trauma: A Long-Term Study* of Abuse Survivors, by Catherine Cameron (Sage Publications, Inc., Thousand Oaks, CA, 2000); Searching for Memory: The Brain, the Mind, and the Past, by Daniel Schacter (BasicBooks, New York, 1996); Betrayal Trauma: The Logic of Forgetting Childhood Abuse, by Jennifer J. Freyd (Harvard University Press, Cambridge, MA, 1996); The Myth of Repressed Memory: False Memories and Allegations of Sexual Abuse, by Elizabeth F. Loftus (St. Martin's Press, New York, 1994); Suggestions of Abuse: True and False Memories of Childhood Sexual Abuse, by Michael Yapko (Simon & Schuster, New York, 1994); Making Monsters: False Memories, Psychotherapy, and Sexual Hysteria, by Richard Ofshe and Ethan Watters (Scribners, New York, 1994); Unchained Memories: True Stories of Traumatic Memories, Lost and Found, by Lenore Terr (BasicBooks, New York, 1994); Once upon a Time: A True Story of Memory, Murder, and the Law, by Harry MacLean (HarperCollins, New York, 1993); and The Courage to Heal: A Guide for Women Survivors of Child Sexual Abuse, by Ellen Bass and Laura Davis (HarperCollins, New York, 1988).

The National Center for Prosecution of Child Abuse (NCPCA) of the American Prosecutors Research Institute in Virginia partnered with the National Clearinghouse on Child Abuse and Neglect Information in undertaking the State Statutes Project. Statutes at-a-Glance: Mandatory Reporters of Child Abuse and Neglect was part of this project. The Gale Group thanks the NCPCA for use of the statutes graphic. The Gale Group thanks the International Labour Office for graciously granting us permission to use graphics from Every Child Counts: New Global Estimates on Child Labour (Geneva, Switzerland, 2002).

Other international organizations publish literature relating to children. The United Nations Children's Fund (UNICEF, New York) published Profiting from Abuse: An Investigation into the Sexual Exploitation of Our Children (2001), while the Coalition to Stop the Use of Child Soldiers (United Kingdom) issued the Child Soldiers Global Report (2001). Child Maltreatment in the United Kingdom—A Study of the Prevalence of Child Abuse and Neglect, by the National Society for the Prevention of Cruelty to Children (London, UK, 2000), and Teenage Life Online: The Rise of the Instant-Message Generation and the Internet's Impact on Friendships and Family Relationships, by the Pew Internet & American Life Project (Washington, DC, 2001) were also used in the preparation of this book.

INDEX

Delinquency, 56–57, 57t, 58f
Department of Health and Human Services. *See* U.S. Department of Health and Human Services
Depositions, 88
Developmental problems, 55–56
Disabled children, 51
Disclosure of sexual abuse, 84–85
Disposition of reports, 34–36, 36(f4.1)
Dissociation, 56, 101–102
District of Columbia child protective services, 23
Dolls, anatomically detailed, 86–87
Domestic workers, 11
Drake, Brett, 30–31

E

Early childhood development, 55–56, 64–65, 65f
Education in family violence, 22–23, 22t
Educators and reporting, 21
"Effects of Partner Violence and Physical Child Abuse in Child Behavior: A Study of Abused and Comparison Children" (Salziner et al.), 54
Emotional abuse
    definition, 14
    reporting, 21
    verbal abuse, 52
    victim characteristics, 16
Endangerment standard
    defined, 41
    incidence, 41t, 42(t4.8), 43(f4.7), 44t, 45(t4.12), 50(f5.2)
    sexual abuse, 69
England, 2, 55
English, Diana J., 50
Enns, Carolyn Zerbe, 101
The Epidemic of Rape and Child Sexual Abuse in the United States (Russell and Bolen), 71
Europe, 1
Expert witnesses, 90–91
"Exploring the Multiplicity of Childhood Sexual Abuse with a Focus on Polyincestuous Contexts of Abuse" (Crowley and Seery), 71
"The Extent and Consequences of Child Maltreatment" (English), 50

F

Factors in child abuse
    disabled children, 51
    family structure, 49–50
    income, 50
    stress, 51
    toilet training, 51
    unemployment, 50
    verbal abuse, 52
    violent families, 51–55, 53f, 53(t5.2)
Failure to report, 19–21
False accusations, 91–92
False memories. *See* Repressed memories
False Memory Syndrome Foundation (FMSF), 101, 104, 105
"False Sexual Abuse Allegations by Children and Adolescents: Contextual Factors and

Clinical Subtypes" (Mikkelsen et al.), 91–92
Families
    factors in child abuse, 49–50
    fatalities and household composition, 66
    incidence by family structure, 43t, 44t, 50t
    income, 44, 45t
    preservation, 25
    risk factors, 17
    sibling abuse, 55
    size, 42, 44
    spousal violence, 51–55, 53f, 53(t5.2), 96
    verbal abuse, 52
"Family Patterns and Child Abuse" (Straus and Smith), 50, 52, 55
Family violence education, 22–23, 22t
Fatalities, 38–40, 39f, 39t, 66
Fathers
    neglect, 65–66
    sexual abuse perpetrators, 73
"Fathers and Child Neglect" (Dubowitz et al.), 65–66
Federal government
    child welfare service funding, 3
    data collection, 33–34
    definition of abuse and neglect, 13–14
    See also Legislation and international treaties
Fells Acres case, 97–98
Female circumcision, 11–12
Ferguson v. City of Charleston, 96
"The Final Report of the APA Working Group on the Investigation of Memories of Childhood Abuse," 103
Finkelhor, David, 30, 69, 70–71, 73
Flood et al., Landeros v., 19–20
FMSF (False Memory Syndrome Foundation), 101, 104, 105
Foster care programs, 3
"Four Commentaries: How We Can Better Protect Children from Abuse and Neglect" (Besharov), 29
Franklin, George, 104
Free Speech Coalition et al., Ashcroft v., 95
Freud, Sigmund, 67, 99
Freyd, Jennifer J., 102
Funding
    child welfare services, 3
    Title XX funds, 3

G

GAO (Government Accounting Office), 25
Gault, In re, 83
Gelles, Richard J., 25–26, 49
Gender
    criminality of victims, 59, 60(t5.5)
    mental health problems, 62
    online victimization, 75
    perpetrators, 44–45
    sexual abuse, 71–72, 73, 73(t6.4), 74, 75(f6.5)
    victims, 37t, 38, 41, 42t
Geoghan, John, 67, 78
Girls
    female circumcision, 11–12
    offenders, 57–58
    sexual abuse, 72, 78–79

Government Accounting Office (GAO), 25
Graham, Hearndon v., 105
Greenbrook Preschool case, 90

H

Hare Krishna, 5, 9
Harm standard, 40t, 42(t4.7), 43(f4.6), 43 t, 45(t4.11), 50(f5.1)
    defined, 41
    incidence, 40t
Harvard investigative model, 29
Health professionals and family violence education, 22t
Hearndon v. Graham, 105
Hearsay evidence, 89–90
Higham, Scott, 23
History
    ancient civilizations, 1
    apprenticeships, 1–2
    child labor, 2
    child welfare organizations, 3
    cleric abuse, 4–5, 9
    Colonial America, 1–2
    industrialization, 2
    Middle Ages, 1
Holmes, Lori, 87
Holmes, William C., 72, 74
Horwitz, Sari, 23
"Household Composition and Risk of Fatal Child Maltreatment" (Stiffman et al.), 66
Humenansky, Carlson v., 104–105
Hungerford v. Jones, 105
Hyperarousal, 56

I

Illinois, White v., 90
ILO (International Labour Office), 10–11
In re Gault, 83
Inappropriate reporting, 29–30
Incest. *See* Sexual abuse
Incidence defined, 33
Income, 44, 45t, 50
    See also Low-income families
Industrialization, 2
Ingram, Paul, 100
Inmates. *See* Criminality
Institute of Medicine, Committee on the Training Needs of Health Professionals to Respond to Family Violence, 22–23
International issues
    child labor, 10–11, 11t
    child soldiers, 9–10
    cleric abuse, 4–5, 9
    domestic workers, 11
    female circumcision, 11–12
    trafficking in children, 10, 10t
International Labour Office (ILO), 10–11
International Society for Krishna Consciousness (Iskcon), 5, 9
Internet victimization, 75–78, 76f, 77t
Iowa, Coy v., 89

J

Jacob Wetterling Act, 92–93
Jehovah's Witnesses, 5
Joel Hungerford v. Susan L. Jones, 105